Wellington and the Vitoria Campaign 1813

Wellington and the Vitoria Campaign 1813

Never a Finer Army

Carole Divall

Pen & Sword
MILITARY

First published in Great Britain in 2021 by
Pen & Sword History
An imprint of
Pen & Sword Books Ltd
Yorkshire – Philadelphia

Copyright © Carole Divall 2021

ISBN 978 1 52677 402 6

The right of Carole Divall to be identified as Author of this work has been asserted by her in accordance with the Copyright, Designs and Patents Act 1988.

A CIP catalogue record for this book is
available from the British Library.

All rights reserved. No part of this book may be reproduced or transmitted in any form or by any means, electronic or mechanical including photocopying, recording or by any information storage and retrieval system, without permission from the Publisher in writing.

Typeset by Mac Style
Printed and bound in Great Britain by
CPI Group (UK) Ltd, Croydon, CR0 4YY

Pen & Sword Books Limited incorporates the imprints of Atlas, Archaeology, Aviation, Discovery, Family History, Fiction, History, Maritime, Military, Military Classics, Politics, Select, Transport, True Crime, Air World, Frontline Publishing, Leo Cooper, Remember When, Seaforth Publishing, The Praetorian Press, Wharncliffe Local History, Wharncliffe Transport, Wharncliffe True Crime and White Owl.

For a complete list of Pen & Sword titles please contact

PEN & SWORD BOOKS LIMITED
47 Church Street, Barnsley, South Yorkshire, S70 2AS, England
E-mail: enquiries@pen-and-sword.co.uk
Website: www.pen-and-sword.co.uk

Or

PEN AND SWORD BOOKS
1950 Lawrence Rd, Havertown, PA 19083, USA
E-mail: Uspen-and-sword@casematepublishers.com
Website: www.penandswordbooks.com

Contents

List of Illustrations		vi
Preface		vii
Maps		x
Chapter 1	Preparations	1
Chapter 2	Farewell, Portugal!	25
Chapter 3	From the Esla to the Ebro	50
Chapter 4	The Road to Vitoria	75
Chapter 5	The Eve of Battle	90
Chapter 6	The Waterloo of the Peninsula: the Battle of Vitoria	110
Chapter 7	Consequences	184
Appendix 1:	Wellington's Army in the Vitoria Campaign Marching Strength 25 May 1813	193
Appendix 2:	Spanish Troops under Wellington's Command (as of 1 June)	197
Appendix 3:	The French Army under the Command of Joseph Bonaparte during the Vitoria Campaign (based on 1 May returns)	198
Appendix 4:	Allied Losses at the Battle of Vitoria	202
Appendix 5:	French Losses at the Battle of Vitoria	207
Appendix 6:	Wellington's Vitoria Dispatch	211
Notes		218
Select Bibliography		226
Index		231

List of Illustrations

1. The Marquis of Wellington. (*Royal Military Chronicle*)
2. Major General Sir Rowland Hill, commander of the Allied right column. (*Royal Military Chronicle*)
3. General Sir Thomas Graham, commander of the Allied left column. (*Royal Military Chronicle*)
4. Joseph Bonaparte, King of Spain. (*Author's collection*)
5. Marshal Jean-Baptiste Jourdan, French chief of staff. (*Author's collection*)
6. General Honoré Charles Reille, commander of the Army of Portugal. (*Author's collection*)
7. General Count Honoré Théodore Gazan, commander of the Army of the South. (*Author's collection*)
8. General Jean-Baptiste Drouet, Count d'Erlon, commander of the Army of the Centre. (*Author's collection*)
9. & 10. Two views of the battlefield of Vitoria from opposite sides of the valley. (*Private collection*)
11. The battlefield of Vitoria as depicted by Andrew Leith Hay. (*Author's collection*)
12. The bridge at Tres Puentes. (*Author's collection*)
13. The Battle of Vitoria (Heath and Sutherland). (*Private collection*)
14. The Death of Colonel Cadogan (J. Atkinson/Ackerman's Lithography). (*Courtesy of Colonel Henry Cadogan*)
15. The Fifth Division at Gamarra Mayor. (*Private collection*)
16. Allied artillery at Vitoria. (*Private collection*)
17. The Battle of Vitoria, final stages of the action (F.C. Lewis). (*Private collection*)
18. Memorial to the Allied victory at Vitoria. (*Author's collection*)

Preface

The Battle of Vitoria has been called the Waterloo of the Peninsular War, a battle that decided the fate of a nation, and of the man who had been made its king. The Iberian Peninsula had been among those lands whose destiny was decided by Napoleon Bonaparte, as he forced them into French hegemony. Portugal had already escaped the eagle's grip. 1813 would finally allow Spain to do the same. And the event that dealt the fatal blow to French interests was the action at Vitoria on 21 June.

Six months before, such a decisive dismantling of French power might have seemed unlikely, if not impossible. There had been great rejoicing in Britain as the victories of 1812 had followed fast upon each other: Ciudad Rodrigo, Badajoz, Salamanca, the triumphant entry into Madrid. But then came the failed attempt to take Burgos. The humiliation of defeat was exacerbated by a shameful retreat back to Portugal. Even at the start of 1813 the Marquis of Wellington, as he then was, commanded an army where demoralization was still rife, where sickness rates made campaigning impossible, and where in some battalions discipline had broken down completely. As he looked at them in their lice-ridden rags, still to be replaced by new uniforms, he must have realized that the first battle would be to turn these vagrants back into soldiers.

As for the French, they could celebrate the return of the king to his capital, even if few of them saw him as anything other than a hollow figurehead, and they could claim that the two Castiles and La Mancha were once again firmly in their grasp. Andalusia and much of Estremadura were lost, however, and unlikely to be regained, while Galicia and Navarre were infested with guerrillas who, mushroom-like, could be defeated here and then re-appear there. Yet, however wretched the state of his army, the enemy had lived to fight another day. And looking beyond Spain, the Russian disaster meant that Napoleon needed to fight back to stem the turning tide, and fighting back needed more troops, experienced men, to replace his disastrously heavy losses. King Joseph Bonaparte knew only too well how blind his brother was to the realities of the situation in Spain. No help would come from that direction, only a call to give up troops for the campaign in Central Europe. If they could have been sure of Wellington's intentions, it would have been possible to plan a counter-strategy. In 1811 Wellington had begun the pursuit that drove Masséna out of Portugal in February. In 1812 Ciudad Rodrigo had been taken in January. Yet in 1813, as the months passed, there was no movement from the enemy.

Indeed, Wellington was in no hurry. He knew that, whatever happened, the French were and would remain on the defensive. He needed time, and time was on his side. In those early months of 1813, his army was able to recover its strength, its spirit and its discipline. There were new supply lines to establish, reinforcements to integrate, new measures to make sure the losses to those natural causes, exhaustion, exposure and sickness, would not happen again. When he was ready, he would set in motion his Anglo-Portuguese army, with its notable German cohort, and the Spanish troops that were now his to command. He would lead them back to Spain and then, at his strategic best, use them to outmanoeuvre and harry the enemy until he had no choice but to turn and fight.

Wellington's strategy drives the narrative of the Vitoria campaign. His objectives and his means are clear, and his dispatches reveal process and progress. At the same time, many other voices, from that wealth of letters, journals and memoirs which the Napoleonic Wars engendered, add the personal dimension to the official account of events. They offer a range of experiences, perspectives and opinions which remind us that soldiers are not machines to be switched on and sent into action. They are human beings with all the strengths and weaknesses of humanity.

Taken together, even a small selection of these many eyewitness accounts creates the gamut of how men felt as they went to war; and, more to the point, how they felt as this campaign unfolded. Some are the heroes of their own story, whose accounts may need to be treated with caution. Others ask no questions and merely obey orders but can still write of the small but vivid moments that live in the memory. By blending the official and public with the individual and private we are able to judge the Vitoria campaign as both a historical event and as a deeply-felt personal experience, with all the idiosyncrasies that implies.

Their time is not our time. In a past world, that foreign country where they did things differently, they had attitudes and values that may now seem strange. But, whatever the writer's status, whatever the nature of his participation, these accounts help us to understand not just what happened but how it felt to be part of one of the most momentous campaigns of the Peninsular War.

As always, my thanks are due to all those who have assisted me in the preparation of this study, in particular Mick Crumplin, Andrew Bamford, John Downham and Rupert Harding for their unfailing support.

Author's note: place names have posed a particular problem. Although some can be identified despite the vagaries of spelling, others have to stand as they appear in the various contemporary works I have consulted. Quotations have also been reproduced exactly as they were originally written or printed.

Maps

1. The Iberian Peninsula.

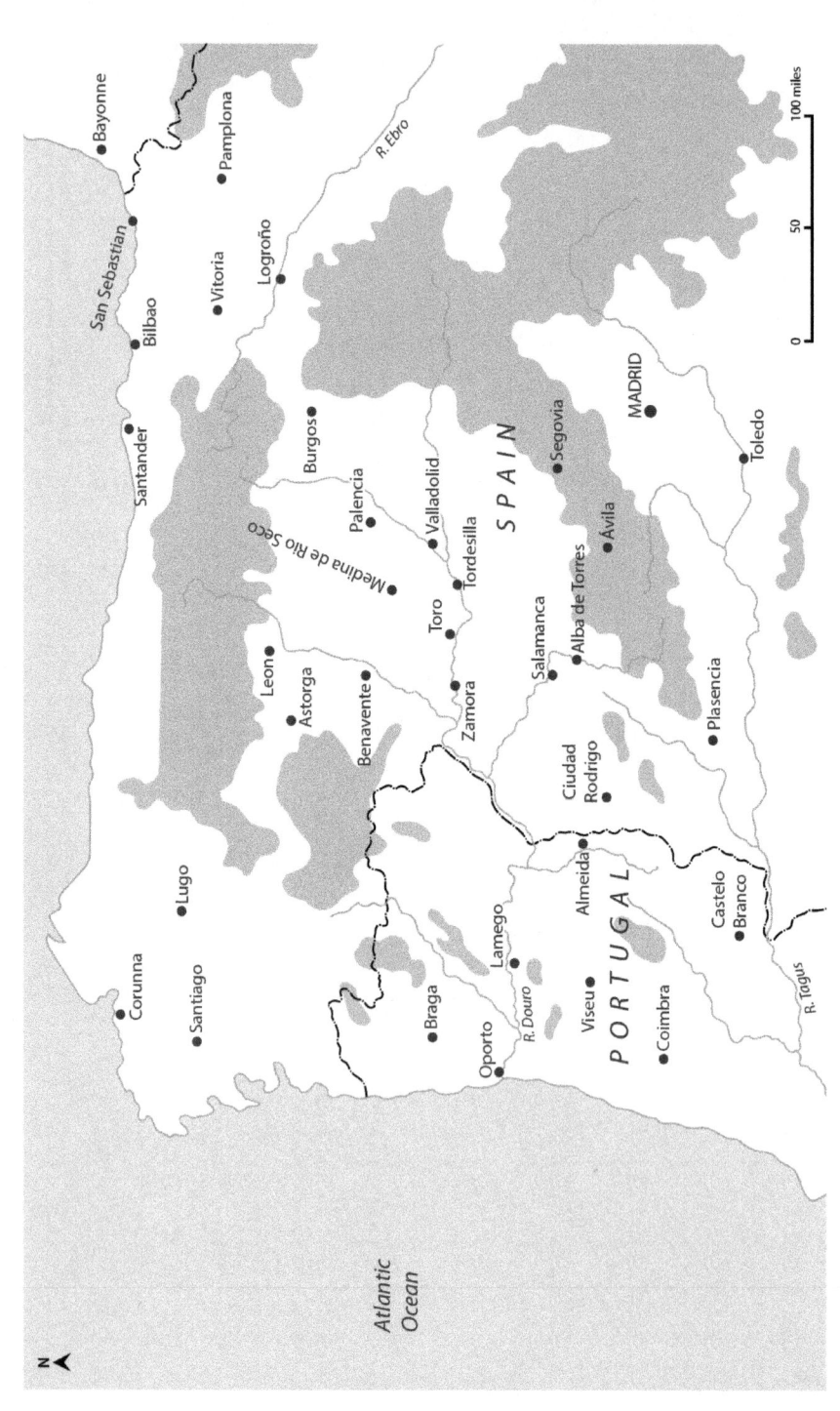

2. North-west Spain and Northern Portugal.

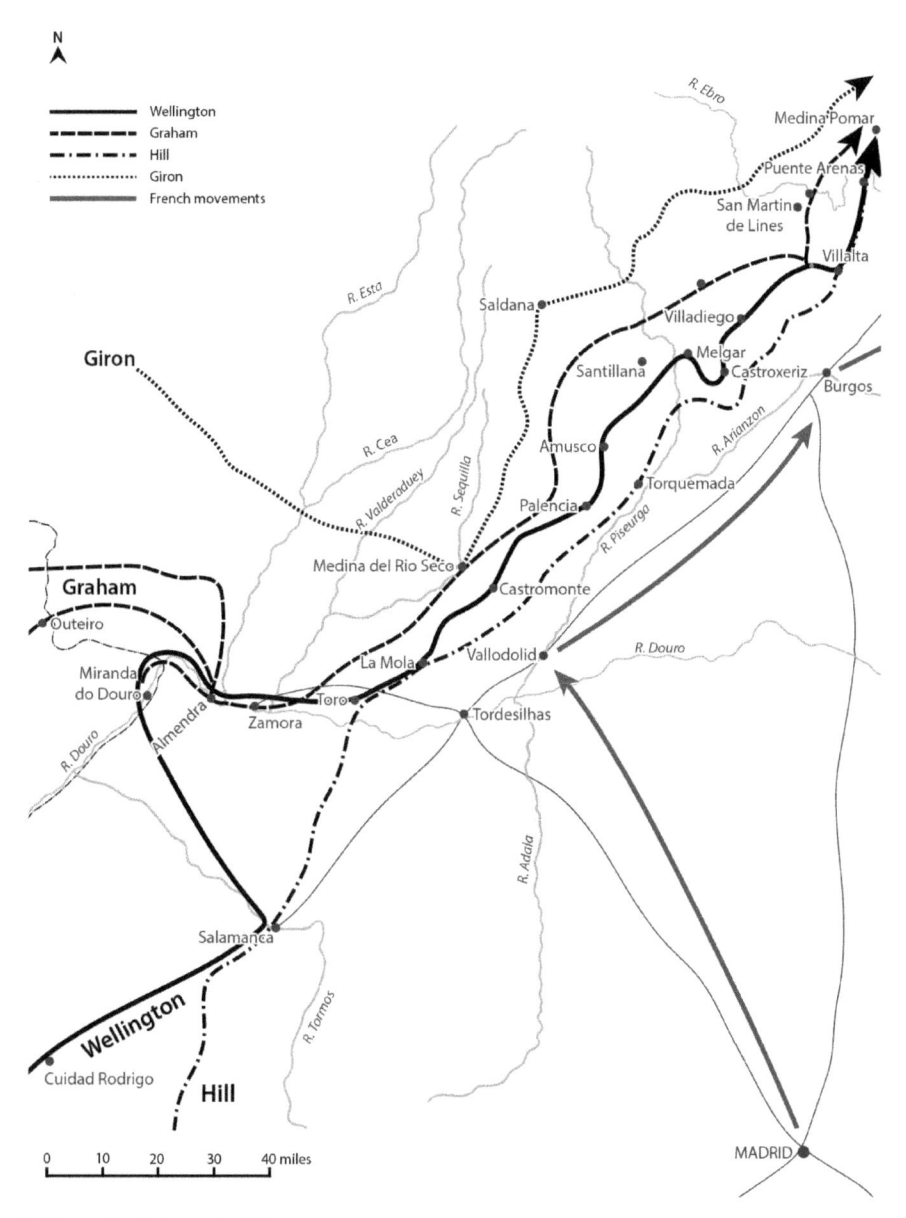

3. From the Esla to the Ebro.

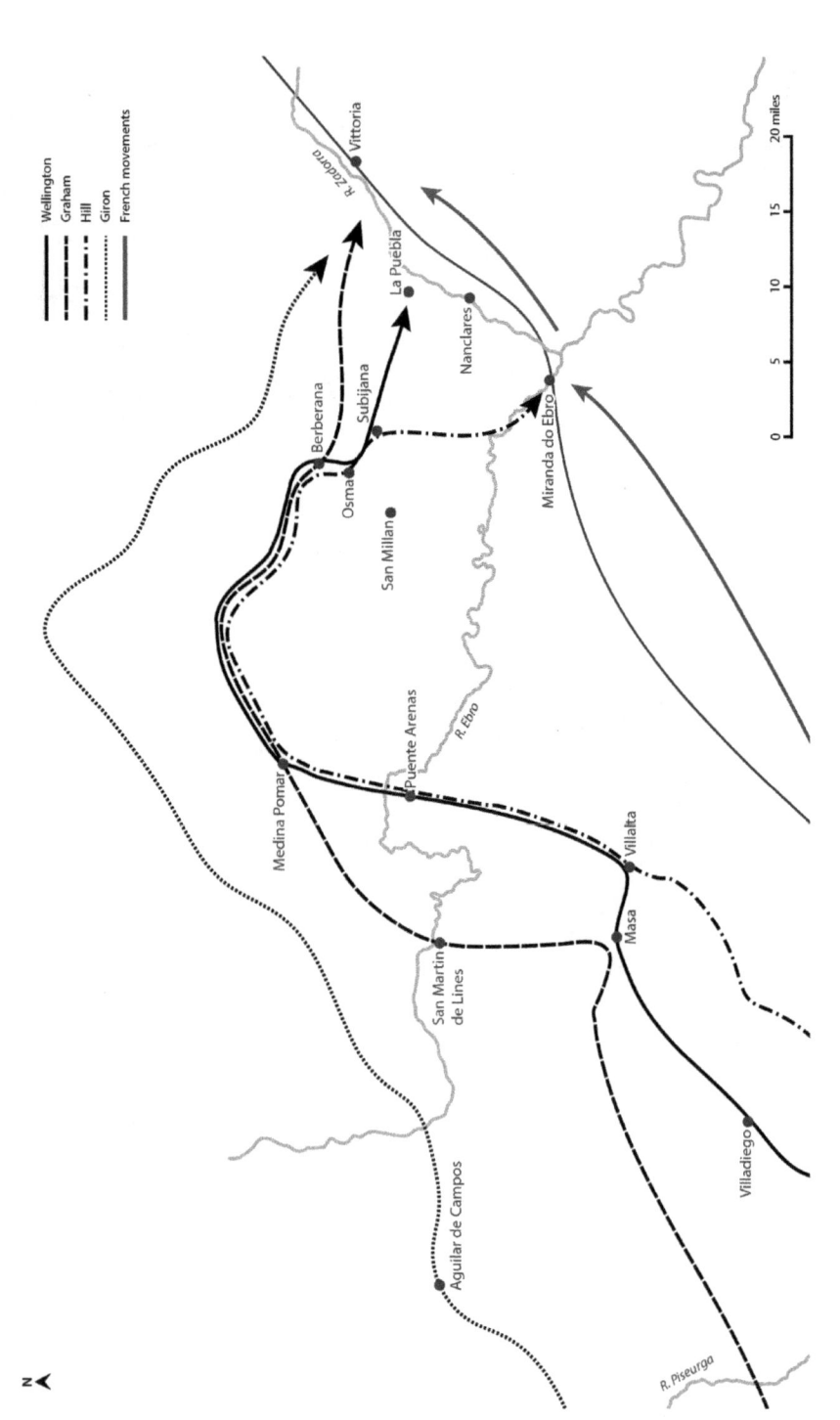

4. The Road to Vitoria.

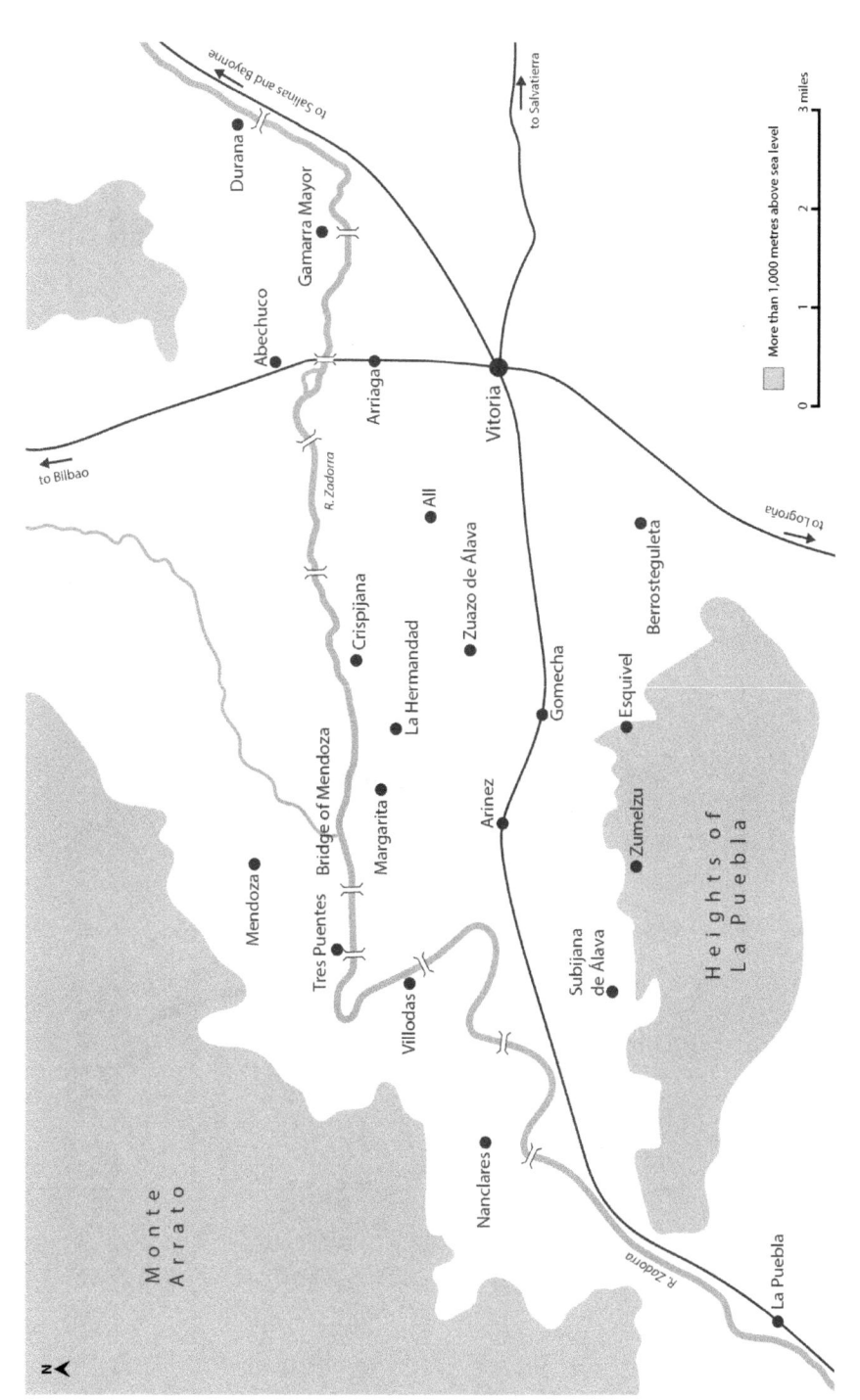

5. The Battlefield.

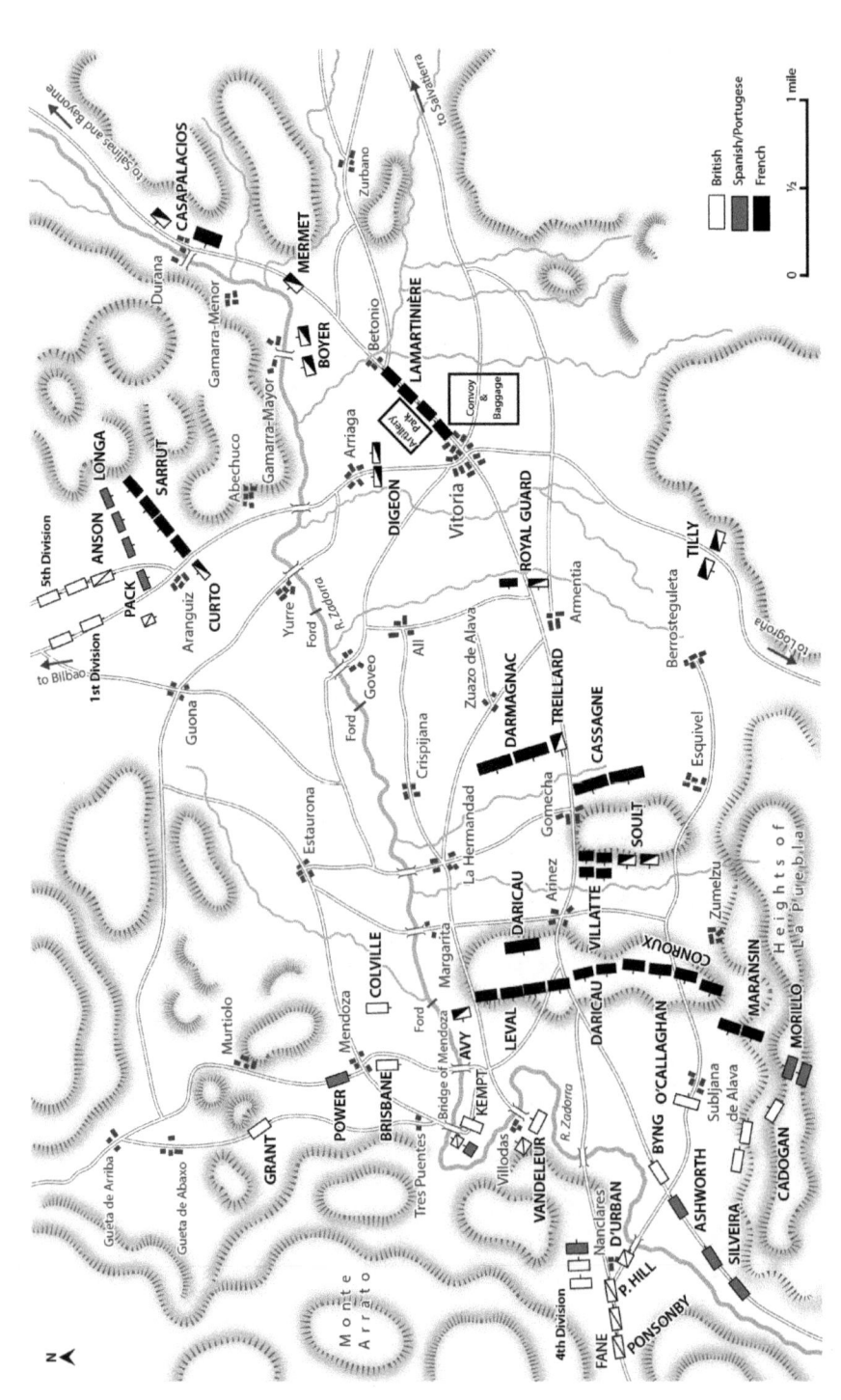

6. The Battle of Vitoria.

Chapter 1

Preparations

1812 had been a year of Allied victories: Ciudad Rodrigo, Badajoz and Salamanca, followed by a triumphant entry into Madrid. The French Army of Portugal, defeated at Salamanca, had retreated north in disarray. Marshal Soult, in command of the Army of the South, had been forced to abandon Andalusia. King Joseph Bonaparte had left his capital and fled eastwards to find refuge with Marshal Suchet. Yet when the Anglo-Portuguese returned to Portugal in November, they had all the appearance of troops who had suffered a crushing defeat. They had been deprived of supplies by the failure of the commissariat. The weather had punished them with persistent rain and low temperatures. Many of the men had lost their boots as they plodded through the mud. Their uniforms were little more than rags. Sickness was rife. Indeed, many did not make it back to Portugal, falling out to die or to become prisoners of the French. Even for those who had not been there, having remained with Hill in Madrid when Wellington matched north, Burgos had an ominous sound. What Wellington himself admitted was his worst scrape, the failed siege of Burgos, had brought the year to a demoralizing close.

Needless to say, the British public, as represented by the press, was less than impressed with this failure, although the blame was directed away from Wellington, who now enjoyed the status of hero. As Lieutenant John Aitchison of the 3rd Foot Guards wrote his father on 24 December:

> ... it is amusing to read in the London newspapers (which have come to the 4th inst) the opinions on the late campaign – so like our countrymen they are now as unreasonably *desponding* and abusive at our retreat as they were after our victory at Salamanca – unreasonable in their expectations of uninterrupted success!! I am glad however to notice that the blame is generally thrown upon the *Ministry*, not on the general and the army, although the latter

appears to me by no means exculpated from undertaking the siege of Burgos with so inadequate means, and it is upon this enterprise that the whole hinges.[1]

For the French, with Joseph restored to his throne, the Allies licking their wounds in Portugal and Suchet holding firm against Allied incursions on the east coast, the year could be said to have ended well or, at least, better than might have been expected. One general, however, realized that those earlier Allied triumphs had mortally wounded the French in Spain. As the Allies trudged back to Portugal, General Maximilian Foy wrote in his journal: 'The campaign is over. Lord Wellington retires undefeated, with the glory of the laurels of the Arapiles, subsequently having returned to the Spanish the country to the south of the Tagus, after we had to destroy our magazines, our materiel, our fortifications, in a word, everything which was a product of our conquest and could ensure its continuation.'[2]

Despite Foy's assessment, it was obvious that before there could be another foray into Spain, the state of the ragtag Allied troops would have to be addressed. At the most basic level, uniforms were in tatters. According to Lieutenant James Hope of the 1/92nd, 'When the regiment marched in here [Coria] on the 1st inst. [December] I really believe that there was not above one hundred shirts in the possession of the whole private soldiers. Their small-clothes were barely sufficient to cover their nakedness. Their jackets, which had once been scarlet, now possessed almost every colour that I could name.'[3]

As the new uniforms began to make their appearance, Thomas Howell of the 1/71st noted one particular problem of the discarded rags. 'We got here [Monte Moso] a new kit. Before this we were completely in rags; and it used to be our daily labour to pick the vermin off ourselves.'[4]

One of the measures insisted upon by the Surgeon-General, James McGrigor, was the production of regular returns from the general hospitals. These identified fevers of various kinds, typhus, dysentery and hospital gangrene as the most prevalent causes of death. McGrigor himself surmised, as the numbers of sick and dying rose inexorably, that the severe wet weather and other privations suffered by the soldiers led to fever, which would develop in too many cases into typhus and dysentery, assuming 'so malignant a character as to baffle the skill of the medical officer, the case frequently proving fatal within a few days sometimes after being committed to his care'.[5] Typhus was spread by lice which then laid their eggs on the skin of the men who wore the infested clothes.

The effects of these diseases on the exhausted battalions proved dramatic. Lieutenant George Wood of the 82nd recorded one of the most extreme cases.

> No sooner were we settled in our cantonments, than we experienced the fatal effects of the almost unparalleled sufferings we had undergone, and the sudden transition ... to comparative plenty brought on the most malignant complaints, especially fever, dysentery and rheumatism. The entire regiment was on the sick list, for a considerable time we had not a man on parade, not even convalescent men to attend to the sick.[6]

William Wheeler of the 51st likewise informed his family that: 'We had not long taken up our abode in this place [Moimento] when a fever of rather an alarming nature broke out amongst us, the natural consequence of the fatigues endured in the late campaign. About half our men are in hospital, and from the number of deaths our burying ground begins to have the appearance of a ploughed field.'[7]

Those who developed the sickness suffered severely. William Brown of the 1/45th, having spent three weeks working as an orderly, 'was then seized by the distemper. My head was immediately shaved and blistered, but being insensible, and in a high brain fever, I tore the plaster off, and threw it out of the window.' As a result his hands had to be tied down for several days. It was six weeks 'before any symptoms of recovery appeared, at which period I was so weak and emaciated I could hardly walk across the room'.[8]

Wellington would later enter into a debate with the Duke of York, Commander-in-Chief of the army, over the wisdom of sending weakened second battalions back to Britain, where they could perform their proper function of recruiting and training. Wellington argued that acclimatized weak battalions were of more use to him than stronger, unacclimatized battalions. There was evidence to prove his point in the fate of the 1st and 3rd Battalions of the 1st Foot Guards, who had only arrived in the Peninsula in October, joining Wellington's retreating force on the 25th. Aitchison observed as late as March that:

> The 1st Brigade of Guards has been, I believe, the most sickly in the army – they have lost upward of 600 dead – and they still have about 800 in hospital which is supposed to arise from both battalions having been in Walcheren – I never saw two finer-looking battalions than they were five months ago but they are not so strong as we are – they have just marched to Oporto to try the effect of a change of air.[9]

Aitchison was right that battalions which had been at Walcheren in 1809 suffered disproportionately from the effects of the fever which was the legacy of that campaign. (The 4th Foot was another example.) The other Walcheren battalions were well on the way to recovery, however, while the 1st Guards were still reporting disproportionately high casualties. As a result, they would not be able to take part in the Vitoria campaign.

Even with the recovery of health and the new uniforms, the Allied army was still in no condition to launch a new campaign. Wellington might write at the end of January to Lieutenant General Sir Thomas Graham, who was preparing to return to the Peninsula,

> I propose to take the field as early as I can, and, at least, to put myself in Fortune's way.
>
> Many of the regiments are already healthy; others, particularly the new comers, remarkably otherwise. We have, as usual, lost many men in the last two months of cold weather; but all the troops are well cantoned; and I hope that a rest for a month or two in the spring will set us up entirely.[10]

He was well aware, though, that 'early' was still some months away, and there was much to be undertaken in the interim. That the fruits of this preparation were soon evident becomes clear in a dispatch Wellington wrote on 28 March and sent to his brother Henry, who was in Cadiz as the British envoy to Spain. Yet, coupled with this satisfaction was his ongoing problem with the Spanish Junta. 'I wish, and propose, to open the campaign on the 1st of May ...' His intention was to strengthen his army with several Spanish corps, but the problem that threatened to thwart this plan was the failure of the Spanish government to produce the money that would enable these corps to prepare for a campaign.

> We shall be [ready], I hope completely; and if there was money, I should entertain no doubts of the result of the next campaign in respect to the Peninsula. But the Spanish government have so contrived their matters, that the arrangements concerted and agreed upon with me, have not yet produced a shilling, and as far as I can judge, are not likely to produce much. However, I cannot yet write decisively and officially upon this subject, as I have not the official reports; but I have certainly the most obstinate and worst tempered people to deal with (particularly General -----) that I have yet met in my life …

Having explained the financial problems, he continued,

> Depend upon it, that the result of the next campaign depends upon our financial resources. I shall be able in a month to take the field with a larger and more efficient British and Portuguese army than I have yet had; and there are more Spanish troops clothed, armed and disciplined, than have ever been known, and we are making a daily progress towards getting out of the chaos in which I found matters. But if we cannot realise the subsidy without falling on the resources of the British army, and can get nothing from the country, we shall end the next campaign as we did the last.[11]

One significant change in the general military situation, which should be noted at this point, was Wellington's appointment in November 1812 as commander-in-chief of the Spanish forces. Working with the Spanish government proved as difficult as with the Portuguese Regency, but there was one Spanish general whom he knew would prove co-operative. General Francisco Javier Castaños, the Captain General of Galicia, Castile and Estremadura, might not possess the greatest military skills but he would certainly act positively in support of the Allied campaign. As a result, Wellington would have at his disposal two Galician divisions, 21,000 strong, under the command of Castaños' nephew, General Pedro Augustín Girón. Other Spanish commanders whom Wellington knew well, Generals Pedro Morillo and Carlos d'España, and the guerrilla leader turned regular soldier Julian Sanchez, could also be called upon. A name to add to this list is that of Francisco de Longa, the gadfly guerrilla who was tormenting the French in the Biscay area, and who would eventually join the Allied forces.

6 Wellington and the Vitoria Campaign 1813

To return to the Anglo-Portuguese, 'During the winter cantonments the most unremitting attention was paid to restore the discipline and organization of the army, preparatory to renewed exertion. Various changes were made to its equipment and accompaniments, tending equally to convenience and efficiency ... It was now felt by England that the moment was arrived for putting forth her full strength.'[12]

Discipline was obviously a vital element of efficiency. Mr Francis Seymour Larpent, who had been appointed judge advocate general to Wellington's army, had arrived in the Peninsula the previous autumn, only to be swept up in the final stages of the retreat to Portugal. He had been sent specifically at Wellington's request to help clear the backlog of offences that now needed dealing with, and indeed dozens of new ones as troops, many of whom had lost all discipline under the severe conditions of the retreat, continued their iniquities. Mr Larpent's letters home make clear that he was a busy man during the early months of 1813.

Another aspect of efficiency rested with the quartermaster general's office. One of the most serious problems during the later stages of the 1812 campaign had been the malfunction of this department. The situation had become intolerable when Colonel James Willoughby Gordon, the Quartermaster General, who had already proved himself inefficient, if not downright ignorant of what was required of him, took it upon himself during the final stages of the retreat to direct the supply train to Ciudad Rodrigo via Felices, which was on a road that lay 20 miles away from the army's line of march. Nor did he see fit to inform Wellington of the decision he had made. Consequently, the troops suffered extremes of hunger, even as the cold and wet were weakening all but the strongest. Fortunately for the army, and for Wellington personally, Willoughby Gordon resigned at the end of the year on grounds of ill health. This was a welcome decision on his part because it was known that as well as being incompetent he was also suspected of sending back letters critical of the campaign which were finding their way into the main opposition newspaper.

Willoughby Gordon's departure opened the way for the return of a man with whom Wellington had previously worked well, Major General George Murray. He came back to Portugal in March and, with Wellington's support, immediately set about putting right all that had gone wrong during his absence. His powers almost equalled those of a chief of staff, which gave him some authority over other departments. Thus, if the Vitoria campaign is judged to have been effectively conducted, through the period of preparation and during the advance to the battle itself, then much of the credit must rest with Murray, a man who had first learnt his business in another thoroughly prepared campaign, that in Egypt in 1801.

A simple instance of his thoroughness and ability to come up with common-sense solutions was demonstrated when billhooks proved a problem. Every man was to be issued with a lighter billhook, which would enable the task of cutting furze, bracken and firewood to be completed more quickly, but, as he observed, 'As it will be impossible to complete the army with bill hooks we must find a substitute for them. I believe the best things to be had are the pruning knives used by the people of the country for pruning Vines.'[13] Murray consistently demonstrated the value of observation, common sense and an understanding of how an army best functioned.

Another matter that fell fully within Murray's remit lay in a decision that Wellington had taken at the beginning of March. The heavy iron camp kettles were to be replaced with lighter tin kettles so that the company mules could carry the tents that were now to be supplied for all non-commissioned officers and other ranks.

The advantages of these changes were quickly recognized.

> Previous to our advance, the greatcoats belonging to the soldiers were delivered into store. It was considered that the blanket was a sufficient covering for them at night, particularly as tents were served out for the use of the whole army, three to each company. These were to be carried by the mules that formerly conveyed the heavy iron camp kettles used for cooking, one mule being attached to each company. When near the enemy, and the baggage had been sent to the rear, these unwieldy and capacious kettles were not at all times to be had hold of. It had occupied the soldiers a considerable time to cook their rations … These iron kettles were substituted by a light tin kettle, one between every six men, to be strapped to their knapsacks and carried alternately on the march.[14]

Lieutenant John Cooke of the 1/43rd was definitely not alone in approving these measures. All those who had suffered the disastrous autumn retreat appreciated that exposure to the severe weather had occasioned not only the appalling sickness rates but also the exhaustion that had caused so many to fall out. Tents would provide shelter, both against inclement weather and the intense high-summer sun. And as Cooke pointed out, the new kettles would definitely speed up the preparation of food. Wellington's decisions also left Murray with another duty, planning the layout of the divisional camps once the army was on the march.

Two other senior officers made their return to the Peninsula in the spring of 1813. Lieutenant General Sir Thomas Graham, the victor of the Battle of Barrosa, has already been noted. He replaced Sir William Stewart in command of the First Division. Major General Thomas Picton, now recovered from the wounds he had received at Badajoz, assumed command of the Third Division. Both men would play a crucial part in the campaign as it reached its climax at Vitoria.

In order to make good the loss of manpower, many regiments received reinforcements.

> 'Johnnie Newcomes', of course, but [they] were soon drilled into a new form of discipline, which rather astonished some of their backs. They were men, chiefly volunteers from the Militia, who seemed to have had a leetle too much of their own way. But that was soon drilled out of them, and they were taught that the first duty of a soldier is 'to obey orders'.[15]

As Wellington had commented in his dispatch to the Duke of York, however, these newcomers pushed up the numbers of sick just as the acclimatized troops were recovering their health. The problem was even more severe in the new regiments that were sent out, as the experience of the 1st Foot Guards the previous autumn had demonstrated. The newness of these troops was immediately obvious. 'About this period the Life Guards and Horse Guards Blue, and the Hussar Brigade, joined the army from England and looked as fair and beautiful as lilies.'[16] Fair and beautiful they may have looked, but it soon became evident that even a well-disciplined regiment like the Blues, which had been praised three times when inspected in Lisbon, would have to learn what constituted acceptable behaviour.

Corporal Andrew Hartley, who was himself recovering from a severe attack of fever, recorded in his journal on 3 January: '... our men behave very badly to the Inhabitants of this Place [a village four miles from Belem], in return for which two was stabbed with Knives last Sunday night and now they have just brought into the Hospital two more one very badly wounded in several places but I think the cause originates in ourselves some unprincipled Men have provoked them to it.'[17]

It is doubtful if anyone regretted the departure of seasoned troops and the arrival of newcomers as much as August Schaumann, who served with the Commissary. In March he learnt that the 9th Dragoons, to whom he was attached, were to return to England, having first handed over their horses to the 13th Dragoons. He was to accompany them to Lisbon, where he would take charge of the newly-arrived 18th Hussars. 'As I had some experience of troops freshly landed from home, who were unfamiliar both with the country itself and with war conditions, and as I was also aware of the ridiculous pretensions of English cavalry regiments in general, and cordially detested them, my disgust may well be imagined.' To make matters worse, 'Mr Hodson, a clerk, who until my arrival had discharged the functions of commissary for the regiment, was beside himself with joy when I came to relieve him. The description he gave of the ludicrous pretensions of the officers of the 18th Hussars was not an edifying one, though it was nothing new to me.'

There was a further source of vexation for Schaumann. The new commander of the Hussar Brigade, Sir Colquhoun Grant, summoned the commissaries every day,

> to be reprimanded, and to listen to peremptory orders. Our protests and proposals, based upon the experience of many years, were good as useless. He imagined everything would be the same here as in England, and thought it exceedingly strange that we should dare to contradict so great a man as he thought himself to be. Was he not six foot high, and had he not a huge black moustache and black whiskers?[18]

As a corrective to Schaumann, it is worth noting the opinion of an anonymous officer of dragoons. He acknowledged that upon his arrival in the Peninsula the dragoon (light or heavy) would have had to learn the importance of caring for his horse without the arrangements of home and would also have to furnish forage for his horse and food for himself. The Hussar Brigade, however, along with the Household Brigade, 'reaped the fruit of long experience, and were treated in the most judicious manner'. Having spent two months at Belem, and then in quarters in the country near Lisbon, 'when they finally moved towards the army, it was by moderate marches, with occasional halts, by which means the hussar brigade arrived perfect as when it embarked at Portsmouth. It was a splendid brigade.'[19]

Grant was not the only new cavalry brigadier. Major General (as he became in April) Sir Henry Fane had commanded an infantry brigade under Wellington and Moore, and then a heavy cavalry brigade under Wellington. Ill-health had sent him home at the end of 1810. Two years later he was anxious to return but, as Wellington wrote to Lord Bathurst, the Secretary of State for War and the Colonies, 'I would be very glad to have the assistance of Henry Fane, but we have no vacancy at present.' At the end of the year, though, when Wellington was manoeuvring to remove one of his cavalry brigadiers, he made clear that Fane was the specific replacement he wanted. Thus Fane returned to command a heavy cavalry brigade comprising the 3rd Dragoon Guards and the 1st Dragoons, one of four brigades of heavy cavalry that Wellington could now call upon, as well as four brigades of light cavalry, Brigadier General Benjamin D'Urban's Portuguese Brigade and the 6th Portuguese Cavalry, in total over 8,000 troops. This was twice as many as he had had at Salamanca, a fact that would prove ironic.

It was now important to keep the troops of all three arms at their business so that they would be battle-ready by the commencement of the campaign, but also as a means of correcting the demoralization and lack of order which had characterized the final stages of the previous year's campaigning. As a result, life became a progression of 'parades and drills and field exercises', to say nothing of regular inspections, although, according to Lieutenant George Bell of the 2/34th, there was also time 'for some leetle horse racing'.[20] And the officers of the Light Division found time for a production of *She Stoops to Conquer* in the midst of all this activity.

The one arm where problems persisted, however, was the artillery. Their difficulties involved everything from the highest command to shortage of horses, forage and drivers. This last problem finally provoked Wellington to write to Bathurst on 2 April: 'We are greatly in want of drivers. I have written to Sir William Beresford to endeavour to borrow some from the Portuguese. If we cannot get them, I must take soldiers from the infantry, which it would be very desirable, if possible, to avoid.'[21]

Then there was the pontoon train, which had been lacking the previous year. Alexander Dickson, Lieutenant Colonel in the Portuguese artillery, was already concerned about the pontoons as early as the end of January. Initially, they were to be sent up the Tagus to Abrantes, but Dickson had struggled to find seamen to undertake the task, since the Portuguese Pontonier Company was not yet organized. When Portuguese seamen were eventually found, they demanded exorbitant terms of pay, rations and clothing.[22]

Another problem was the shortage of bullocks that would be required once the pontoons reached Abrantes, particularly as they would also be needed for the 18-pounder guns which arrived in February in preparation for an anticipated second siege of Burgos. And that was without considering the shortage of horses. Once the bullocks had been obtained, the slow progress of the pontoon train became a reiterated subject in the letters of both Dickson and Augustus Frazer, Royal Artillery (RA), who had arrived in Lisbon in December. The issue even attracted the attention of Mr Larpent, whose letters contained a running commentary on the progress of the pontoon train.

Aware that he could not commence the campaign in earnest until the pontoon train was in position for its assigned role, Wellington eventually lost patience and insisted that the bullocks should be replaced by horses. As a result, Second Captain Michael Cairnes RA, in command of the 10th Company during Dickson's absence, lost all his horses. In a letter to his stepfather of 12 May he made clear his feelings about Wellington's order.

> ... I have received a *Damper* which altho' perhaps considered by His Lordship unavoidable & essential to the service, has mortified & vexed me beyond all possible expression, that of having *all my Driver Establishment in toto* transferred to the Pontoon Train and my Brigade remounted by horses coming from Lisbon (which horses are to be tomorrow night within 2 leagues of this place). His Lordship was, I hear, pleased to express his regret at knocking up my brigade.[23]

Thus the pontoon train was able to trundle on its way, its destination the Esla, a river notably short of bridges, but the crossing of which was vital to Wellington's plans.

In other respects, matters were rather more satisfactory. Frazer inspected several troops, including Robert Bull's and William Webber's, and found them in excellent condition. Dickson had discovered the same about Cairnes'. Frazer was also impressed by the efforts of the commander of the Royal Horse Artillery (RHA), Colonel Thomas Downman, who was 'exerting himself to bring forward the Horse Artillery'.[24] Downman, however, was intending to leave the Peninsula for reasons of health, with the result that in April Frazer found himself in command of the horse artillery.

This promotion was less of a shock, since Downman obviously needed to be replaced, than Dickson's promotion in May to overall command of the Anglo-Portuguese artillery, even though he was only a captain in the British service. Once again, Wellington's lack of patience seems to have been the cause, coupled with doubts about the man who previously held the post. As so often with matters at headquarters, Mr Larpent knew how Dickson's promotion had come about. Having noted that Lord Wellington and Colonel Fischer, who had only been in the Peninsula for six months, did not agree, he explained: 'F---- is much of a gentleman, I think; draws, I hear, very well, &c, &c, but has a bad memory, is nervous, and raises difficulties, which I suspect Lord Wellington does not encourage, and expects things to be done, if possible.'[25]

Frazer looked at the situation from a professional perspective:

Colonel Fisher goes home, and I confess myself sorry for this, having had great reason to admire his arrangements. Dickson will be Fisher's successor ... Colonel Waller, being a senior officer, has been directed to remain at Lisbon; this Waller will probably not do. There is another senior Lieut-Colonel (Tulloch) in the Portuguese service, and several senior to Dickson in the British Artillery. All these perplexities will, I fear, lead to confusion at the moment we want the cordial co-operation of all. I fear we shall have a jumble, and that the public service may suffer. This would be a real evil; all other considerations are of little importance. I shall get on very well with Dickson: he was second to me in the South American Expedition, and then obeyed my orders with the implicit readiness which I shall now transfer to his. He is a man of great abilities and quickness, and without fear of anyone.[26]

That final sentence is the clue to Dickson's appointment. In order to have men whom he could rely upon, and Wellington knew he could rely upon Dickson, the feelings of other men could not be taken into consideration. Dickson himself, more aware of the possible embarrassments of his situation as junior to so many of the British artillery officers, chose to continue wearing the shabby uniform of his superior Portuguese rank.

So the months passed. Although Wellington's intention to start the new campaign on 1 May was frustrated by circumstances he could not control, particularly the lack of green forage, it was obvious by the end of April that the commencement of the campaign could not be too far off. Nor could it come too soon. First Lieutenant George Simmons of the 1/95th was able to write home on 30 April:

> The army is in high health and spirits. In a few days we shall take the field. I am heartily tired of this idle life. We have been five months in snug winter quarters without seeing the face of a Frenchman – a thing which has never happened before ... The campaign bids fair to be the most brilliant, as we shall have more than equal numbers to contend against. I hope to see the Pyrenees before September.[27]

John Kincaid, also of the Rifles, shared Simmons' optimism.

> In the early part of this month [May] our division was reviewed by Lord Wellington, preparatory to the commencement of another campaign and I certainly never saw a body of troops in more highly efficient state. It did one's heart good to look at our battalion that day, seeing each company standing a hundred strong, and the intelligence of several campaigns stamped on each daring bronzed countenance, which looked you boldly in the face, in the fullness of vigour and confidence, as if it cared for neither man nor devil.[28]

* * *

In the aftermath of the autumn retreat, there was an inevitable degree of pessimism in the Allied ranks as to whether it would be possible to eject the French from the Peninsula by military means alone. Even Wellington seemed touched by the general dejection. On 18 January 1813, however, he received news from the Prime Minister, Lord Liverpool, which completely changed his mood. Rumours of Napoleon's Russian debacle had been arriving for some time, but Liverpool's communication made clear the disastrous state of the Emperor's forces. One sure conclusion could be drawn. There would be no French troops to spare in the Peninsula. If evidence were needed that Wellington was now looking forward to the forthcoming campaign with a clear objective in mind, it came in a dispatch to Bathurst, written on 10 February.

> As it is possible that the events of the next campaign may render it necessary for the army to undertake one or more sieges in the north of Spain, and as all the heavy ordnance and stores attached to this army were sent round to Alicante in the month of June last, for the service of the troops expected from Sicily, I beg leave to recommend that the ordnance and stores contained in the enclosed lists should be embarked in transports and sent to Coruña, to be at my disposal as soon as may be convenient; and that twice the quantity of each article may be in a state of preparation in England, to be shipped when I shall report that they are necessary.[29]

From this it may be deduced that Burgos was not to be an impassable obstacle for a second time, and other French fortifications such as Pamplona and San Sebastian might also receive the Allies' attention. In other words, Wellington intended to push the French not just beyond the Ebro, but also beyond the Pyrenees.

About the same time, Joseph Bonaparte, *soi-disant* King of Spain, received a dispatch from the French Minister of War, General Henri Clarke, which made clear the problems Napoleon was about to create for his elder brother. Up to this point, Joseph had seen as his principal objective the restoration of his authority in those areas that the French still held. Andalusia, Murcia and Estremadura had to be considered lost, while guerrilla activity in Galicia and the Asturias meant that French possession of the north-west of the country was becoming merely nominal. He decided, therefore, to concentrate on the area of Spain from Leon to La Mancha, while also recognizing the importance of maintaining communications with France. And that meant dealing with the guerrillas in the Biscay area in order to keep open the all-important road to Bayonne. Unfortunately, these irregular forces were receiving aid delivered to them by Captain Sir Home Riggs Popham, and this support inevitably encouraged them to even greater activity. To make the situation worse, a vacuum had been created when 10,000 troops of the Army of the

North had been called down in order to force Wellington to relieve the siege of Burgos. These troops may have subsequently returned but their commander, General Louis-Marie-Joseph Caffarelli, was still struggling to contain the guerrillas who had taken advantage of their absence.

Joseph believed he would have time enough to strengthen his position before the commencement of any campaign because it was obvious Wellington would need even more time to prepare his own forces for any future activity. As Marshal Jean-Baptiste Jourdan, the King's Chief of Staff, noted in his memoirs, Joseph had a choice. He could focus on holding Old Castile by establishing his headquarters and centre of operations at Valladolid, while leaving only a *camp-volant* at Madrid, a small body of cavalry which would maintain a French presence in the capital while also being able to fly into action should the need arise. Alternatively, he could bring most of the troops to New Castile and return to Madrid. Joseph chose the second option on the basis that having his government in the capital, while obviously symbolic, would also help the Armies of the South and Centre to occupy the provinces of Madrid, Toledo and La Mancha, and the Army of Portugal, the provinces of Ávila, Salamanca and Valladolid. There was also a well-run effort, overseen by the general staff, to reorganize supply depots and hospitals and establish repair workshops for the artillery. In other words, 'nothing was neglected to put the armies in a full state to begin the campaign'.[30] Yet Jourdan also recognized that Joseph's situation was particularly difficult because while the king was persuaded that his seat of government should be in his capital, which enabled him to have a certain influence on the nation, the commander-in-chief should be in the theatre of war. Nor, in the popular view, did Joseph excel in either role.

George Bell, writing retrospectively, had some sympathy for Joseph, while recognizing his shortcomings.

> In war, nothing [is] so bad as failure or defeat; and this must have damped the King's courage a bit. His brother, the great Napoleon, they say, used to tell him that if he would command, he must give himself up entirely to business, labouring day and night: just the thing he was never cut out for, as will be found recorded in his history. Indeed, his cognomen was 'Roi de Bouteille'. He had a fine command, a great and brilliant army, an obedient army; but that soul of armies, the mind of a great commander, was wanting.[31]

Bell's judgement explains why Joseph was so dependent on his chief of staff, whom John Patterson was inclined to admire.

> Marshal Jourdan, as Major-General of the French army, was acting-manager of the whole concern; he, as well as Soult, was sadly intermeddled with by the King, which, in some measure, served to check his generalship ... Jourdan was a man of much ability, with a degree of military genius peculiar to many of the old French school of veterans, – men who contributed so largely to elevate the fame of France.[32]

It could be argued that the hero of Fleurus, which had been fought 19 years before, had lost something of his youthful talents, but it must also be conceded that he, no less than Joseph, was hamstrung by the orders emanating from Paris and then, when Napoleon began his campaign against Prussia, Russia and Austria, from Central Europe via Paris.

Evidence of this was quick in coming. Whatever Joseph may have intended was frustrated by the Bulletin for 3 December 1812 and then by Clarke's dispatch. The Bulletin reached him early in January, and was then followed by a private letter. Between them, they made absolutely clear the scale of the catastrophe that had befallen Napoleon in Russia. The implications for the Peninsula soon became clear, as Wellington had been quick to appreciate. Firstly, it needed no message from Napoleon to establish that there would be no reinforcements. There then arrived a stream of couriers from Paris. The most recent of these dispatches from Clarke was dated 4 January although it did not reach Joseph until the second week of February. The instructions it contained required the king to bring his headquarters to Valladolid. The Armies of the Centre and the South were to move into Old Castile, with a division of the latter occupying Madrid. The Army of Portugal was obliged to send as many troops to the Army of the North as Caffarelli demanded. Clarke, very much Napoleon's mouthpiece of course, also explained that General Honoré, Count Reille, in command of the Army of Portugal, had already been ordered to direct one of his divisions to the Ebro, to make it available for Caffarelli. There were further orders relative to specific regiments, most of them in the Army of Portugal. To keep the Allies in check, Napoleon also required the guns that had defended Burgos to be brought south in order to threaten Ciudad Rodrigo, a move designed to convince the enemy that an invasion of Portugal was a possibility. A separate order concerned Marshal Nicolas-Jean de Dieu Soult, Duke of Dalmatia, who was to return to France. Whatever Joseph's response to the other orders, this last must have gratified him, since his relationship with Soult had long since broken down and he had been urging his brother for some time to recall the marshal from Spain. In sharp contrast, he had established an excellent working relationship with Marshal Jourdan, who never seemed to forget that Joseph was King of Spain.

With Soult's departure, General Honoré, Count Gazan now took command of the Army of the South. News also arrived that General Bertrand Clausel would command the Army of the North, since Caffarelli (another of Joseph's *bêtes noires*) had also been summoned back to France.

After receiving these instructions from Paris, Joseph ordered Gazan to leave General Jean François Leval's division, General Jean-Pierre Maransin's infantry brigade and General Pierre Soult's light cavalry brigade in Madrid. He was then to move his other three divisions expeditiously to the provinces of Ávila, Salamanca, Toro and Zamora, to fill the gap that the orders to the Army of Portugal had created. Before these movements could be fully implemented, however, yet another communication arrived from Paris, notionally from Clarke but yet again conveying Napoleon's orders. Dated 12 February, it reached Joseph on 13 March. Because it so clearly reveals Napoleon's misconceptions, and the subsequent problems Joseph would have to contend with, it is worth quoting in some detail.

> His Majesty is most anxious to know what has been done in Madrid in pursuance of his instructions; and his constant disappointment leads him to dread that the precious period of two months, during which the English [i.e. the Allies] have been inactive, has been lost. He trusts that, at latest, the 29th Bulletin has shown to your Majesty the necessity of opening and securing by every possible means your communication with France. This can be done only by throwing the forces in your Majesty's hands on the line of communication between Bayonne and France, and by sending into Navarre and Aragon troops sufficient to destroy the bands which lay waste these provinces.
>
> The Army of Portugal, acting with that of the North, is sufficient for these purposes, and the Armies of the Centre and the South can hold in check the English until circumstances change. The Emperor

commands me to reiterate to your Majesty that the use of Valladolid as a residence and as headquarters is an indispensible preliminary.

Having decreed that the troops should be distributed between Valladolid and Salamanca in order to go on the offensive against the Allies, the letter then suggested that to frustrate the enemy's plans 'we must always be ready to move forward, and to threaten a march on Lisbon, or the conquest of Portugal. At the same time the communication with France must be easy and safe, which, as I have already stated to your Majesty, can be effected only by employing the time while the English are inactive, to pacify Biscay and Navarre.'[33]

This makes clear that Joseph was to conduct what was essentially a holding operation in Spain. He had been given three distinct tasks: defeat the guerrillas, keep the Allies penned in Portugal and maintain safe communications with France. Unfortunately, Napoleon never seems to have appreciated the constant threat that the bands of irregulars posed. Defeated in one place, they could re-form and then threaten elsewhere. Nor did he properly evaluate the strength of the Allied armies, which he put at 50,000, when the true number was more like 75,000. Perhaps most seriously, he seems to have assumed that Wellington would follow his previous practice when he finally decided to invade Spain, while choosing to believe that Joseph had men in plenty to conduct a defensive campaign.

The implementation of the movements Napoleon required his brother to make would take until early April. Reille had already sent Barbot's division to join the Army of the North, as separately instructed. He now sent a further three divisions, those of Foy, Taupin and Sarrut, to join Clausel. He then established his headquarters in Toro and occupied the province of Palencia and part of Leon with his two remaining divisions, Generals Antoine Maucune's and Thomas Lamartinière's. His cavalry and a division that had been transferred to him from the Army of the Centre were watching the approaches from Galicia, where General Girón and the Army of Galicia were posted. The headquarters of the Army of the Centre, acting as a reserve, were at Segovia, to cover Leval in Madrid and separated from the rest of the French army by a chain of mountains. The Army of the South was holding a position from Zamora, on the Douro and close to the Portuguese border, to Toledo on the Tagus, in response to Lieutenant General Rowland Hill's position at Alcantara.

By the end of March Joseph had established his headquarters at Valladolid, as instructed. His departure from the capital, which was greeted with indifference by the citizens of Madrid, was the signal for a general departure: government functionaries, courtiers, servants, wives, other women, children, anyone who had openly identified with the French cause. They brought with them everything of value that they could lay their hands on: paintings and other objets d'art, books, jewels, money, even furniture, in effect the fruits of five years' plundering. Jourdan suggested it would be prudent to send this convoy on to Bayonne but Joseph was reluctant to dismiss such loyal subjects. It proved to be a misjudgement, as there were reckoned to be as many as 3,000 wheeled vehicles of various kinds trundling behind the French armies as it moved north. And yet, strangely enough, this convoy would prove both disastrous and unexpectedly fortuitous to the French in the aftermath of the Battle of Vitoria.

Once all the movements had been completed, Joseph and Jourdan were able to concentrate on defending the line of the Douro between Toro and Tordesillas, on the assumption that Wellington, as before and as Napoleon obviously expected, would advance into Spain along the Salamanca to Valladolid route, although there was some concern that Hill's position might imply an attack from the Tagus. They also believed that holding the Douro position in strength would deter an Allied advance long enough for Clausel to deal with the guerrillas and then bring the Army of the North to join them; or, at the least, to release those divisions that properly belonged to the Army of Portugal.

Although all this might seem satisfactory, there had been yet another instruction from Paris which further demonstrated where French priorities now lay.

> Napoleon had to recall troops from Spain to fill the gaps that the unfortunate campaign [in Russia] had caused in the ranks of the army, and it was too often the best officers and the most experienced soldiers who went first. As for Wellington, he had profited from the five months' pause in hostilities to continue to strengthen his army: by the end of winter there were some two hundred thousand men ready to begin the campaign. Their motivation and resolution contrasted with the confusion and uncertainty that overwhelmed the French and Spanish who remained loyal to King Joseph Bonaparte.[34]

While the size of the Allied force is an exaggeration, this comment by a French historian is definitely pertinent.

The implications for Joseph's forces soon became clear. Captain Hippolyte d'Espinchal of the 2eme Hussars had been on detached duties, dealing with the guerrillas who were operating to the south of Madrid. When he returned to the capital, he found, when reporting to the colonel, that 'many officers and non-commissioned officers destined for France; some because of their rank for the Imperial Guard, others for the depot to look for conscripts. It was the third time that we had separated from our brave comrades in four months; also, the regiment found itself reduced to 17 officers instead of the 40 when I arrived there and, to increase the inconvenience, it was on the brink of losing its colonel.'[35] One may be sure that, however many conscripts were found at the depot, they would not compensate for the experience of the men lost to the 2eme Hussars and all the other regiments similarly affected.

* * *

By the beginning of April, as already noted, the French were in the positions indicated by the orders from Paris. According to Larpent, in February the Allied dispositions were in the following areas: the First Division was on the Upper Mondego; the Second Division in Estremadura, around Coria; the Third Division at Moimento de Beira; the Fourth Division on the Douro; the Fifth Division on the same river, around Lamego; the Sixth Division on the northern slopes of the Estrella mountains; the Seventh Division at Moimento de Serra; and the Light Division holding a line on the border between the Coa and the Agueda, along with Alten's cavalry. The cavalry was dispersed towards the coast. Significantly, when the later movements of the Allies are considered, the two independent Portuguese infantry brigades, Pack's and Bradford's, were posted at Penafiel and Villa Real, to the north of the British divisions, the whole of D'Urban's Portuguese cavalry was even further north, beyond Braganza and close to the Spanish frontier. Wellington's headquarters were at Freneda. These positions, allowing for some changes of divisional headquarters, would remain the same until April. As the map indicates, they fall into two groups, one clearly indicative of an advance towards Salamanca but the other, suggesting a different approach. Before the month was out, there would be the first manifestations of what that approach might be, for

Wellington intended to pursue a strategy that would force the French to move at his bidding. He was, in fact, about to bamboozle them.

On the French side, Joseph saw a need for some minor adjustments to his position. He was becoming increasingly concerned that Medina del Rio Seco, a central point in the dispositions of his armies, was vulnerable to an Allied attack. Towards the end of the month he ordered Reille to use his two divisions specifically to guard communications between Miranda and Palencia, and Palencia and Burgos, since these key points were on the Great Road which led from Madrid to Bayonne. This was crucial because communications were still being disrupted, so that it was taking as long as 25 days for dispatches to reach Valladolid from Paris. As a result, by the beginning of May Lamartinière's division and attached cavalry were at Briviesca to protect communications between the Ebro and Burgos, while one of Maucune's divisions, also with attached cavalry, guarded the Valladolid to Burgos road. The rest of Reille's cavalry continued to watch Girón's Galicians who were also within striking distance of Spain, in the Benevente area.

Two problems continued to trouble the French command. The most immediate was their total ignorance of Wellington's dispositions, which, if they had known them, might have given them some idea of his intentions, and why he had so delayed the start of the campaign. Jourdan lamented that:

> Despite the care that the chief of staff gave to the secret informers, despite the extravagant amount of money paid to them, we were always unable to procure even the least exact information about the Anglo-Portuguese army. The reports we received were so contradictory that instead of giving clarity they only increased concern. The commander of the Allies, much more fortunate, was exactly informed of the strength and dispositions of the armies that opposed him and received timely advance of their movements.[36]

Furthermore, what limited information the French did receive from their spies was not merely contradictory but often inaccurate. The other vexation, which hindered their choices when it came to campaigning, was the strict instructions to deal with the guerrillas in Galicia and Biscay before all else. As a result, Joseph could not concentrate his forces by calling in the detached divisions of the Army of Portugal, however desperate his need of them, or command that the Army of the North join the main force. The activities of the guerrillas, particularly Francisco Espoz y Mina and Francisco de Longa (the latter's successes being carefully recorded by Wellington in his dispatches), were, in fact, a running sore.

Up to this point, there had been only one encounter between the Allies and the French, at Bejar on 20 February. General Foy, who had hitherto devoted his energy to dealing with guerrillas, brought a small force of about 2,000 troops to the town in order to test Hill's defences. Bejar was held by the 50th Foot and the 3rd Portuguese Caçadores and Foy initially came up against some of the 50th on outpost duty. When other battalions from the first brigade of the Second Division were sent in support the situation changed. As James Hope wrote to his friend:

> ... at every one of the gates, there were parties of the 50th regiment stationed, over whose lifeless trunks it behoved the foe to march, before he could obtain his objective. The attack was made with great spirit, but the enemy was repulsed with the undaunted bravery so peculiar to that excellent corps. Again and again they attempted to force a passage; but these reiterated attempts only served to heighten their disgrace; for, after a severe conflict, of an hour's duration. Foy was compelled to withdraw his troops from the gates of Bejer, with the loss of his aide-de-camp, who was killed, several other officers, and about 100 killed and wounded.[37]

One of the developments in April that suggested the start of the campaign would not be too far in the future concerned Lieutenant Colonel William Gomm, on the staff of the Fifth Division. On the 11th he was about to start a letter to his sister when he received an order from headquarters 'to proceed immediately to the Tras-os-Montes, to reconnoitre a district of country through which it is probably intended part of the army should advance into Spain'. He had expected his reconnaissance to last two weeks, but it was three weeks before he was back in Lamego and again writing to his sister.

> I am talking about a new campaign ... The army is fully equipped, and its losses repaired, and I think it is fully equal to its purpose. We shall probably have enough to do, but go some distance to seek it. Part of the army, including this division, will perhaps cross the

Douro here, and march through the mountains upon Zamora and Valladolid. I shall like it, for the beaten path is rather a tedious one.[38]

On 28 April Wellington sent a dispatch to Bathurst in which, having remarked on the enemy's lack of any significant movement, he added the information that his own troops 'have moved however, and the cantonments are closing up with a view to the movements which I propose to commence in the first days of May'.[39] He had known for some time that his initial plan to start the campaign on 1 May would not be realised because of the problems with the pontoon train and a shortage of forage. On 11 May, however, another dispatch to Bathurst finally revealed just what he was planning for the French.

> I propose on this side [of the Peninsula] to commence our operations by turning the enemy's position on the Douro, by passing the left of our army over that river within the Portuguese frontier. I should cross the right in the same manner, only that I have been obliged to throw the right very forward during the winter, in order to cover and connect our cantonments; and I could not well draw them back for this movement without exposing a good deal of country and incurring the risk of a counter movement on the part of the enemy. I therefore propose to strengthen our right and to move with it myself across the Tormes, and establish a bridge on the Douro below Zamora. The two wings of the army will thus be connected, and the enemy's position on the Douro will be turned.
>
> The Spanish army of Galicia will be on the Esla on the left of our army at the same time that our army will be on that river.
>
> Having turned the enemy's position on the Douro, and established our communication across it, our next operation must depend upon circumstances. I do not know whether I am stronger than the enemy, even including the army of Galicia; but of this I am very certain, that I shall not be stronger throughout the campaign, or more efficient, than I now am; and the enemy will not be weaker. I cannot have a better opportunity for trying the fate of battle, which, if the enemy should be unsuccessful, must oblige him to withdraw entirely.[40]

Wellington's reference to 'this side' of the Peninsula relates to what was happening on the east coast. As in the latter half of 1812, the strategic importance of the Anglo-Sicilian and Spanish forces that were operating in what might be considered Marshal Louis-Gabriel Suchet, Duke of Albufera's territory, was to keep that marshal so occupied that he would be unable to join Joseph with the Army of Aragon. In the dispatch quoted above, Wellington included the instructions he had sent to the Allied commanders.

> Sir John Murray, and Generals Copons, Elio, and the Duque del Parque. Sir John Murray has informed me that he proposes to carry into execution the plan recommended in the first instance, viz., the attack upon Tarragona; and, by a letter from him of the 30th, I understand that he is well satisfied with what is proposed for him and the troops on that side. I likewise enclose an extract of a letter form him of the 24th, which shows the nature of Suchet's position, and how impracticable it would be to make any thing of it in any other manner.[41]

The Allies had already held off a strong French attack on 13 April at Castella, although Murray's failure to take advantage of Suchet's setback, thus enabling the French to escape virtually unmolested, was a possible warning of his future conduct.

As for the Allied force on the western side of the Peninsula, they were now ready to march. Indeed, the left under Graham was already on its way to the challenging wastes of the Tras-os-Montes, with Braganza as its objective. On 22 May Wellington left Freneda to follow the familiar road to Salamanca. The 1813 campaign was underway.

Chapter 2

Farewell, Portugal!

Wellington's strategy may be said to have depended upon a simple assumption, that the French would see what they expected to see. They would interpret the Allied movements as Wellington intended that they should; essentially, they would conclude that he had chosen once again to advance along the route to Salamanca and then to the left bank of the Douro. Lieutenant General Sir Rowland Hill's command comprised the Second Division, General Pablo Morillo's Spanish division, Brigadier Charles Ashworth's Portuguese brigade and Lieutenant General Francisco da Silveira, Count of Amarante's Portuguese division. These troops, as already noted, were posted in Estremadura, more specifically in the region of Bejar and Baños. Thanks to the misinformation that spies were carrying to the French, they were seen as a possible threat to Madrid, or even as the spearhead for a foray into Old Castile. Consequently, Joseph had already urged his army commanders, particularly Reille and Gazan, to remain watchful. As a result, once Hill called in his troops, there was every chance that Joseph would believe his fears were justified.

Hill was soon to be joined by the Light Division, the light cavalry of Major General Viktor Alten and Major General Henry Fane's and Lieutenant Colonel Robert Hill's heavy cavalry, Julian Sanchez's lancers and Lieutenant General Carlos d'España's Castilians. He would then have 25,000 men under his command, with a particularly strong cavalry presence. This was no accident. The cavalry would effectively screen the infantry, thus helping to convince the French that Hill's was the main Allied force. Hill was now ordered to draw in his forces towards Tamames, while the Light Division and the various cavalry units would soon begin their advance towards San Muñoz.

Graham had more than twice as many men as Hill, about 52,000. His command was made up of the remaining six infantry divisions, Major General Dennis Pack's and Lieutenant General Thomas Bradford's

Portuguese, the heavy cavalry of Major General the Honourable William Ponsonby and Major General Eberhard von Bock, Colonel Sir Colquhoun Grant's Hussar Brigade and Brigadier General William Anson's light cavalry. Ahead of them lay a march 'across a country which, from its wildness, and the extreme badness of the roads had hitherto been avoided in military operations' but this flanking movement of Graham's would 'render null the formidable line of the Douro'.[1] By crossing the river to the right bank in Portugal, a movement of which the French remained unaware, they had already made irrelevant the defensive works which the enemy had been strengthening against an attack towards the left bank.

If all went to plan, Graham's troops would be in the region of Braganza via the route Murray had prepared for them and at the time Wellington required. (Murray would be busy preparing routes for the next five weeks and beyond.) The intention was that Denis Pack's Portuguese, William Anson's and the Honourable William Ponsonby's cavalry brigades and the First Division should reach Braganza between 21 and 24 May. Bock's cavalry, the Fifth Division and Henry Bradford's Portuguese would reach Outeiro between the same dates and would be joined there by Benjamin D'Urban's Portuguese cavalry. The Third Division were to be at Vimioso by the 20th and the Fourth, Sixth and Seventh Divisions, the Hussar Brigade and the 18th Portuguese Brigade were to reach Malhadas and Miranda de Doura between the 21st and the 27th. Further routes would then bring the troops to Tabara, Losilla and Carvajales between the 28th and the 30th. Finally, the pontoon train was expected to have laid a bridge at Barca de Villa Campo, about a mile below the junction of the Esla and the Douro, where it should arrive on the 30th, despite its persistently slow progress. At the same time, General Pedro Augustín Girón, in command of the 4th Spanish Army, would arrive with at Benevente with his two Galician divisions, this being the site of the nearest bridge.[2]

One man who had good reason to doubt whether this timetable would be met by all the troops was William Gomm, doubts he shared with his sister in a letter written on 13 May, although at the same time there is a clear note of optimism.

> It is pleasant to find one's labours turned to some account; and I believe this will be the case with my late reconnaissance, for I believe there will be no part of it that will not be acted upon. We shall border upon the impossible on several occasions before we reach the

frontier, and I am in hopes I shall make my guns carry their point against the opinions of all the wise men of the province ... The weather is favouring us. The rains have ceased for several days, and I am in hopes I shall find my mountain torrents dwindling fast into murmuring streams.

It would seem that others had even more doubts. 'I have just been interrupted by an officer, an artilleryman by trade, who tells me, looking very significantly, that he is told the roads are very bad on the other side of the water. These people are as nervous about their guns as the people they fire at are about their shot.'[3]

A further concern was the commander of the column himself. Second Captain Charles Dansey RA, attached to the First Division, wrote to his mother that he was delighted to hear that 'our old commander has again joined the army, don't have any anxieties about the Ist Division, for I'm sure no bad fortune will ever attend so good an officer & so good a man'.[4] Mr Larpent, a more detached observer, having dined with Graham, although ready to concede that he was 'a very fine old man' also commented that 'he does not indeed look fit for this country work; every one seems to think and say the same, and also that he is broken since he was here. It is quite a pity to see such a fine old man exposed as he must be.'[5] Graham would continue to provoke such mixed opinions as the campaign progressed.

Both the difficult terrain and the distances that needed to be covered necessitated an earlier start for Graham's troops than Hill's. As routes were received and the first marches made, there was inevitably considerable speculation about the operation they were to undertake. John Aitchison, writing to his father on 9 May, knew that the First Division was to move the following day but

> at present we know nothing, as the route has yet to be given to us, but a few hours more will let us know in what direction we are to march. It has been reported for some time that the enemy were concentrating on the Douro. And it is now said that to enable us the better to drive them from it we shall at once cross that river at Lamego (Portugal) and then moving north enter Spain and form our conjunction with the Galician army at Benevente. Toro is reported the central point of the enemy, so that it is most probable that some part of the British

army will move by the north of Portugal – I hope it will not be our division, as the roads there are very bad and mountainous and that by Salamanca is in the country flat and good.[6]

Aitchison always tended to take a rather pessimistic view. Others, like George Wood, were much more positive. 'At length the long looked for route arrived; a march from Santa Marinha, about the middle of this month, as fresh and in as good spirits as if we had never suffered by the incidents consequent on this exposed and active life.'[7] There can be little doubt that after the long period of inaction and the late start of the actual campaign, most inclined to Wood's optimism. If nothing else, there was a sense that this time they were equipped with everything necessary to their efficiency and comfort, despite the promise of an arduous campaign.

The first step was to bring all the troops across the Douro to the right bank. Most of the cavalry was already north of the river and those that were still to the south were easily able to cross by a bridge of boats at Oporto. From there they would advance towards Braga, and then across the more hostile territory to Braganza and Miranda de Douro. Yet even in this safe country there could still be problems, as Lieutenant John Vandeleur of the 12th Light Dragoons experienced. On the 17th the dragoons reached the village of Boticas, a day's march from Chaves, where:

> The people, seeing us in our new dress, took us for French Dragoons, and the greater part of them fled to the neighbouring mountains, of which there was no *scarcity*. We were ordered to halt in this village. On the 18th, unfortunately, some of the inhabitants left their winehouses open, which was soon found out by the 12th, who lost no time in conveying it away in camp kettles, canteens, earthen pots, etc., they all got rather intoxicated in the course of the evening.[8]

But there were few British soldiers who could resist the lure of free alcohol.

The infantry began to move on 14 May when the Fourth, Sixth and Seventh Divisions left their cantonments. The Third and Fifth Divisions, who were closer to the intended crossing points of the Douro, moved on the 16th. Finally, the First Division, without the sickly Guards Brigade which remained at Oporto, left Viseu on 18 May. Barges and other boats had already been assembled at Peso de Regua, São João de Pesqueira and the Barca de Pocailio to prevent congestion on the approaches to the river.

The Third Division used the ferry at São João de Pesqueira. Having been encamped in a wood the previous night, 'At a very early hour this morning [the 18th] the troops began to pass the river Douro in boats: some little confusion unavoidably occurred, and a part of the baggage was not got over that night. We were all the afternoon climbing the rocky heights beyond the river, which rendered it late at night before we encamped.'[9]

Captain John Edgecumbe Daniell of the Commissariat, attached to the Third Division, might have noted 'some little confusion'. Lieutenant William Swabey RHA took a rather more jaundiced view, as he often did. 'At 4 o'clock we marched down to the passage of the Douro, the descent is adorned by various beauties of prospect and fertility. On getting to the passage, my long formed ideas of the campaign were quite confirmed. Instead of building a bridge for which there was every material at hand, we were passed over in a wretched ferry-boat, which operation took three hours ...' Nor was that the worst of the experience.

> The ascent from the river is a frightful undertaking for artillery, being long and steep; our men gave infinite satisfaction by the active way in which they embarked and disembarked their carriages and horses; but we met with an unfortunate accident with a gun and ammunition waggon, which after being pulled by hand a great way up the wharf, broke away from the men and were considerably injured. Six wheels, thirty-six felloes [the outer rim of a wheel] and spokes had to be replaced; fortunately, we halted at Torre de Moncorvo, and the damage was repaired. The ascent from the Douro is the most tremendous ever encountered by artillery.[10]

Meanwhile, the First and Fifth Divisions crossed at Peso de Ragua and the remaining three divisions at Poncinho. By mid-May the whole of Graham's command was over the Douro and on the march to Spain.

* * *

While Graham's troops were advancing towards the unknown wastes of the Tras-os-Montes and Hill's command was beginning to draw together, Joseph and Jourdan were still concerned about their own dispositions. The Army of the South, of course, had been totally displaced by the loss of Andalusia the previous year, and was now as misnamed as the Army of

Portugal. Its commander, General Honoré, Count Gazan's headquarters, which had been at Toledo, were now at Arevalo, some 50 miles south of Valladolid, with General Jacques Tilly's cavalry. General Augustín Darricau's infantry brigade and General Alexandre Digeon's cavalry were on the Douro between Zamora and Toro. General Eugène-Casimir Villatte's division was at Salamanca and General Nicolas Conroux's at Ávila, watching Hill. Jean François Leval's division still maintained a presence in Madrid, according to Napoleon's instructions, while General Jean-Pierre Maransin's independent brigade and General Pierre Soult's cavalry were south of the capital, still trying to extirpate the guerrillas.

Obviously, the absence of a large part of General Reille's force in the north-west created a deficiency in the strength of the Army of Portugal that Joseph and Jourdan had to live with. Joseph had written to his brother, requesting the power to summon these troops south should the need arise, but Napoleon was now in Central Europe and Clarke merely iterated the order that the struggle against the guerrillas must take precedence over everything else. As a result, although one brigade of General Antoine Maucune's division was at Palencia, near enough to be called in, and the other was at Burgos, General Thomas Lamartinière's division was now further north on the Ebro, his task being to maintain communications with Clausel. General Jacques Sarrut's division was even further north, on the Miranda del Ebro to Bilbao road, to maintain contact with Foy, who was operating in the Bay of Biscay area. The rest of the detached troops were in the mountains of Navarre, where they were co-ordinating with two of Clausel's divisions against Francisco Mina. Consequently, they were impossible to locate.

Reille had gained Jean-Baptiste Darmagnac's division from the Army of the Centre and had positioned it at Medina del Rio Seco. His cavalry lay nearer the Esla, to keep watch against any threatening movement by Girón's Galicians. Only the Army of the Centre, under the command of Jean-Baptiste Drouet, Count d'Erlon, which had received General Louis Cassagne's division from the Army of the South to compensate for the loss of Darmagnac's, was sufficiently concentrated, around Segovia, to react rapidly and in force to any Allied advance.

From their headquarters at Valladolid, where the King's Guard, 2,500 strong, was stationed, both Joseph and Jourdan were only too well aware of how long it would take to bring all their troops into close contact. Nor could they prepare with any certainty until Wellington made a movement which should give them some indication of his further intentions. Yet they were not even sure of the dispositions of the nearest Allied troops, Hill's Second Division and his various auxiliaries.

Only on 18 May, according to Jourdan, did the French gain some vague notion of Wellington's next move in the campaign. Joseph ordered Gazan to increase his reconnaissance of the Portuguese frontier. At the first signs of definite Allied movement, he was to order Leval to evacuate Madrid and also send his cavalry to protect Villatte's withdrawal from Salamanca. Then he was to concentrate his forces on the Rio Trabancos, except for Darricau's troops, who were to remain at Toro. Reille would bring Darmagnac's division closer to his cavalry on the Esla, call in Maucune and reconnoitre towards Benevente to verify the recently-received information that some Allied troops were advancing in that direction. Thus Joseph intended to concentrate all his troops on the Douro, in order to respond effectively to either of two possibilities, that the Allies would advance directly from Salamanca or swing towards the Esla.[11]

It is significant that in his memoirs Jourdan further commented that Joseph should have ignored Napoleon's orders and summoned Clausel to join him with the detached divisions of the Army of Portugal and whatever troops he could spare from the Army of the North. The king's failure to do so, in obedience to the emperor's conviction that the loss of Galicia and Navarre was the biggest threat to the French position in Spain, proved a fatal mistake. Without these troops the French could only call on 45,000 infantry and 10,000 cavalry. This might be sufficient to conduct a defensive campaign but it was certainly not enough to take the offensive against an Allied army that was potentially 75,000 strong. As a result, the initiative would consistently remain with Wellington.

To stay with the French, on 24 May Gazan reported that the enemy had crossed the Agueda and was advancing on Salamanca. This clearly proved that more troops than just Hill's were on the move. It was also the moment for Leval to start evacuating Madrid as soon as Allied intentions became clear, an order which Gazan now sought Joseph's permission to implement. Yet instead of obeying, Leval chose to come to Valladolid and question whether the order was genuine. Not surprisingly, this disobedience was a serious setback because none of the planned realignment of the other French units was possible until Madrid had been abandoned. Even a day's delay might prove critical and it would take several days for the evacuation to be completed.

Further reports of Allied movements now began to arrive. Reille confirmed that there was some Allied cavalry on the Esla, along with a suggestion that there were other Allied troops at Braganza. The former, however, were subsequently misidentified as the Commissariat looking for supplies and the latter as an expedition from Ciudad Rodrigo to buy barley, thus causing the French to concentrate on the advance to Salamanca.

Darricau at Zamora claimed there were 2,000 cavalry at Alcañices, about 25 miles from Braganza. This was even more disturbing because French spies were suggesting this was where the Allies would cross the Douro. These same spies suggested that 30,000 infantry were approaching, more misinformation which had Darricau preparing to retire from his present position, despite its importance to any defence of the more likely crossing points. Gazan approved this decision, first instructing Darricau to blow up the bridge. Once Zamora had been abandoned and Madrid evacuated, Gazan would obey Joseph's orders and establish his headquarters at Trabancos, with Leval's, Conroux's and, once he arrived, Villatte's divisions in close proximity. Joseph, however, when he issued the orders, had instructed that Gazan should leave his cavalry to cover Villatte's withdrawal from Salamanca, which he neglected to do. And Villatte, having learnt that the Allied columns were at Tamames and San Muñoz, intended to hold his position until he could judge the situation for himself. As for Reille, he was waiting for Leval to cross the Guadarrama mountains so that he could focus on his own orders, to stop the Galicians on the Esla. He was already sending urgent messages to Maucune to join him so that the defence of that river could be strengthened.

Jourdan's comment in his memoirs on the French situation at this point was distinctly rueful. He conceded that the advantage lay with the Allies because 'the imperial armies were dispersed across the whole surface of Spain',[12] a judgement with which it is difficult to argue. He might have added that Wellington's strategy was also drawing them away from where they would have concentrated most of their force, had they been better informed.

On 19 May, a day after the French had first suspected that the start of the Allied campaign was imminent, Hill commenced a march that seemed to be heading for Ávila. Jourdan, however, had immediately appreciated that Salamanca was his objective, a view that was justified three days later when Gazan confirmed the direction of the Second Division's advance. Since Hill was not following the easier route from Ciudad Rodrigo to Salamanca, there were challenges from the start, particularly for the artillery as they approached the Sierra de Francia. This confirmed the truism that an army could only march as fast as its guns. Webber noted in his journal that even on the first day, as they marched for Jarmilla, they encountered a road that was impassable for artillery and had no choice but to leave the guns at the bottom of a steep incline, which meant they would have to return the second day to deal with them. The next day, marching towards Baños, they again had to abandon their guns until the following day. Only on the 22nd were they able to clear the Puerto de Baños without damaging the gun carriages.[13] And this would not be the only time that the passage of the artillery caused problems.

Meanwhile, the Light Division was also on the move, fording the Agueda on the 20th. By the 22nd they were camped near San Muñoz on the Huebra. Cooke remembered an attractive scene. 'Many of the forest trees were covered with beautiful blossoms, and the plumaged tribe hopped from branch to bough.' There were potent reminders of darker days, though, to spoil this idyll. 'Here and there a solitary skeleton lay bleached, reminding us of those starved, drenched, and wounded victims, whose cries for help as we marched past them on our retreat from Burgos and Madrid the previous winter, still rang in our ears.'[14] Not that a soldier could afford to live in the past, and Cooke also commented on the animated voices of the troops as they made their way through the woods at the start of a new campaign.

Captain Jonathan Leach of the 95th shared similar thoughts as he remembered bivouacking without fires, soaked by rain and sleet, 'cold, wet, half-famished, and nearly in rags'. Now, however, ' the weather, the country, and every face, looked smiling and gay' for they now had 'the cheering prospect before them of driving the imperial legions nearer to their own country'.[15]

As the two divisions, the Allied cavalry and Hill's auxiliary troops came together, there was some interesting evaluation of the different units, all of which are a further reflection of the positive state of the army. For example, Frazer encountered the recently-arrived Spanish regiments of Hibernia and Mallorca at Ciudad Rodrigo and described them as particularly fine-looking troops, while Thomas Playford of the 2nd Life Guards was so impressed with some of the Portuguese that he paid them the ultimate compliment: they were nearly as good as English regiments. Of particular interest, as they had been since their arrival, was the Household Brigade, who had seen no action since the early days of the French Revolutionary Wars. The cavalrymen had to tolerate some good-natured ribbing, though. A typical response was that of Edward Costello of the 1/95th. 'On the third day's march, our battalion encamped in a wood near Salamanca, where we were joined by the Life Guards and the Oxford Blues [Horse Guards] that had just come out from England. We beheld them drawn up at the side of the road, and their fresh, well-fed appearance gave rise to many jests at the "householders" expense.' Yet the seasoned troops were also a novelty to the newcomers. 'I learnt that because of our dark clothing and embrowned visages, they took us for a foreign regiment.'[16]

Although not with Hill's command, Lieutenant John Rous of the Coldstream Guards was also thinking about some foreign troops, in his case the Spanish. Having dismissed the lower classes as 'lazy wretches' and the higher classes as 'profound vain cowards', he did concede that it was unfair

> to find much fault with the character of the Spanish soldier. He wants nothing except to be well-drilled and commanded by a Spanish officer who has the spirit and energy of a British, German or French officer; the Spanish peasantry are perhaps the finest looking men in Europe, they have too much pride to be commanded by foreigners and no confidence in their own noblemen.

As for using them in action, he could only hope that they would 'occupy a space in the line', after which they could be used 'to butcher the unfortunate wounded which just suits their character and is in fact only a retaliation for what the French did when they entered Spain'.[17] It would have been interesting to know what he thought when Spanish troops joined Graham's column, particularly troops that until recently had been irregulars, but his letters make no mention of them.

On the 22nd Wellington left Frenada for Ciudad Rodrigo. There are various versions of the story of how he marked his departure from

Portugal. One such has it that as he crossed the frontier he 'turned round his horse, took off his hat and said, "Farewell Portugal! I shall never see you again."'[18] Glover, who cites it, adds the comment that it seems an uncharacteristically histrionic gesture for Wellington. If taken merely as a suggestion of his mood at the beginning of the campaign, it does adequately convey the confidence of the Allied army from the highest rank to the lowest foot soldier.

By the 24th the two columns had become one and the Allies now advanced along the familiar route to Salamanca. Wellington had been informed that Villatte had only his own infantry division and the 12th Dragoons, while the nearest French force of any size was Darricau's at Zamora. Also on the 24th further information was received that Villatte had summoned a detachment from Ledesma to Salamanca. This effectively isolated him because it broke his communication with Darricau. The following day Allied headquarters were at Matilla, less than 20 miles from Salamanca, while some of the cavalry were on the Tormes. Early on the 26th the first troops, the cavalry of Alten and Fane, crossed the river, the former by the bridge, the latter by fords. Villatte had already realized that the Allies were closing in on Salamanca and now knew that the time had come to abandon the place, although not as early as might have been considered prudent. As a result he was forced into a fighting withdrawal.

Frazer was with Wellington and his staff, which gave him an excellent spectator's view of the subsequent action. His account was written the next day in a letter to his wife.

> The scene was very fine; below us our own vedettes, beyond them those of the enemy: each side supported by picquets of their own. To our right and rather behind us as we looked towards the city, were the village of Arapiles, and the two hills bearing the same name, on which was fought the battle of Salamanca. Still more behind us we observed on two roads nearly parallel, the heads of the two columns forming Hill's division. It began to be very hot. We looked through our glasses, and observed the enemy drawn up; a couple of battalions and a squadron to the right of the city near a ruined convent; two squadrons on one side of the Tormes near the bridge, a half squadron guarding the ford about a mile above the town, near

the village of Santa Marta, and a battalion in reserve behind the city. In the plain intervening between our hills and the town, the 1st German Hussars inclined by degrees towards the ford of Santa Marta, favoured by the inequalities of the ground, which concealed them from the view of the enemy. The 14th Light Dragoons edged along the right bank of the Tormes, keeping beyond the reach of the enemy's fire. The enemy appeared in some confusion, though they remained stationary, as if waiting for something. Looking beyond the city in the direction of Miranda de Douro and Zamora, we could see their pickets withdrawing and their mules and baggage joining them from all sides. In this way we remained till ten o'clock, by which time the head of Hill's right column, which consisted of cavalry, and Bean's troops of horse artillery, under General Fane, were within two miles of the village of Santa Marta, and evidently marching for the ford. The enemy a little before this began to move, at first in the direction of Toro, but very soon, as if wavering, bent to their right, and kept close to the Tormes in the direction of Arevalo and Madrid. Hitherto Lord Wellington, with his staff of about forty persons, had remained stationary. We now descended, and passing the head of the Portuguese columns of Hill's corps, galloped to the ford of Santa Marta. We had for some time seen that the enemy would be much pressed if our cavalry, already jaded by a long march, could be thrown across the Tormes in time to hang on their rear. On reaching the ford we found that General Fane, whose movements had been concealed by the undulations of the ground, had crossed the river, and we saw his six squadrons gaining the rising ground beyond. It became now necessary to leave head-quarters, and to gallop on, which Harding and I did. On gaining the rising ground, we found the enemy retiring rapidly, but in good order. Owing to ravines and intricacies of ground near the river, which obliged the horse artillery to make a detour, it was not possible to bring the guns into play for some time, during which the enemy had gained a league and a half from the city. At that distance, however, from Salamanca, the guns opened with effect; every shot going through the ranks of the unfortunate enemy, who retired with great rapidity, but in great order. In this manner, our guns pursuing them with as much quickness as very deep country, occasionally intersected with hollow roads, would allow, the enemy gained the village of Aldea Lengua. There was at this moment an opportunity of attacking them with every probability of forcing them to lay down their arms, but strict orders having been given not to pass a ravine close by the village of Aldea Lengua, the moment (never to be regained in war) escaped. When it was just gone, we were allowed to go over, and passing the village with some difficulty, continued our pursuit for a league and a half further, pouring our fire on the enemy. By this time we had overtaken many, unable from fatigue to march further. At Aldea Lengua the enemy abandoned the caissons of a gun and howitzer which, after firing two or three rounds, escaped: the coach of General Villatte, the French commander, had previously been taken. About three quarters of a league beyond the village we came upon them, and after some firing, there seemed a favourable moment for a charge, which two squadrons of ours attempted, but without success; the enemy forming in squares, and repulsing them by a volley, which did, however, little execution.

At this point Frazer was hit by a spent ball, but this did not prevent him from giving his wife a sympathetic view of the defeated French. He assessed their losses as about a hundred men, almost all of them killed by the fire of the horse artillery.

> The poor Frenchmen threw down their knapsacks to march with greater rapidity: throwing away two sacks of excellent biscuit and much corn … [the] troops afterwards when in motion marched with great celerity, and bore our fire with great gallantry. I saw more than one instance of a desperate refusal to surrender; one poor fellow was at length cut down by three dragoons, who in vain required him to surrender; another, severely wounded, tried to destroy himself.

Much affected by these earlier events, Frazer did not join in the evening's celebrations in Salamanca. Instead, he went to bed early, 'though not without some sorrowful ideas at the sight I had witnessed. There was not even the false emotion of honour where there was no danger, and to slaughter flying enemies, though duty requires it, is nevertheless shocking.'[19]

When the news reached him of what had happened, Jourdan's response was scathing. 'Villatte should have withdrawn as soon as he realised he was outnumbered. Instead, he chose to defend the passage of the Tormes and entered into a combat that was certain to result to his disadvantage. As a result he lost some hundred men and some guns.'[20]

On the Allied side there were some compliments for the French which echoed Frazer's. Captain John Blakiston of the 17th Portuguese Line, for example, commented: 'This retreat was highly creditable to our enemies, and proves, not so much the power of discipline, (for of that the French have not much,) as the conviction that every experienced soldier possesses, that in such circumstances there is no safety but in discipline.'[21]

Others, however, were less complimentary. Captain Thomas Browne of the 23rd, then attached to the adjutant general's office, noted in his journal that 300 prisoners were taken, many of whom were drunk, and that a complete rout of Villatte's division took place.[22] Since Browne was also with headquarters, his very different judgement serves as a reminder that even eyewitness accounts need treating with caution. Others also commented upon drunkenness. Webber further suggested that the men had been carousing all morning.[23] It may be, of course, that those who were drunk fell out and were taken prisoner; but it could have been that they suffering from sunstroke, which would explain those who were found rolling on the ground, foaming at the mouth as if suffering a fit.[24]

As for the reason why Villatte delayed his departure from Salamanca, whereas Jourdan implies a certain vaingloriousness, Allied rumours suggested that either he had been determined to eat his breakfast or he had been strolling through the streets with his mistress when the alarm was given that the enemy were approaching. Although Villatte made his escape and was able to retire on Medina del Campo and join Conroux's division, his mistress was not so fortunate, being in Villatte's carriage when it was taken by the Allies.

Wellington remained in Salamanca for just two days, during which he heard a *Te Deum* in the cathedral, received the plaudits of the people, and reviewed Hill's command.

> Early in the morning of the 27th, commanding-officers were requested to have their battalions in as high order as they possibly could, in order to pass the Marquis of Wellington in review on the march. At seven o'clock the head of the column moved from the encampment towards Salamanca, the walls of which we kept on our

left hand, till we arrived at the northern gate, when, touching the road leading to Toro, we made a quarter-wheel to the right, and proceeded towards the latter.

On a height, about four or five miles from Salamanca, the marquis took post with his numerous staff. Every battalion, as it approached the reviewing-general, halted a few moments to dress the companies, and then moved past in ordinary time. The morning, being extremely beautiful, – not a cloud to be seen, – the appearance of the troops was truly magnificent. As each corps passed, the marquis paid them some flattering compliment; and as the last company saluted, he turned round and said, 'Sir Rowland, I will take the gloss off your corps this campaign.' How far the marquis kept his promise the sequel will shew.[25]

Having satisfied himself that all was well with Hill's command, Wellington then made a secret departure to join Graham and the rest of the Allied forces. Hill remained in Salamanca for six days, a period during which many of the officers took the opportunity to socialize. There was a serious purpose to Hill remaining there and Wellington making a furtive departure, however. The French were to be convinced by this subterfuge that the Allied attack would take place somewhere between Salamanca and the Douro, thus distracting their attention from Graham's movements.

* * *

On 27 May, Villatte continued his retreat towards Nava del Rey, while on the same day Gazan decided to withdraw from Arevalo to Rueda, and then establish his headquarters on the Zapardiel in order to be closer to Villatte, of whose movements he was now aware. He was also expecting Conroux to leave Ávila and move in the same direction. Conroux then established himself at Medina del Campo, where Villatte joined him, as did Tilly's dragoons. On the 31st d'Erlon reached Olmeda, bringing with him Cassagne's division and its cavalry. At the same time Leval should have crossed the Guadarrama mountains, but there was still no certain news of him.

Nevertheless, the other French forces were now more concentrated, and positioned behind the Zapardiel in order to meet the Allied threat.

Yet any further movement was impossible until Leval and his nearly 5,000 troops arrived.

Meanwhile, General Julien Mermet, with Reille's 1st Cavalry Division, was still reconnoitring from a position north of Benevente. The information he was sending to headquarters, however, was consistently inaccurate. Both the claim that there were two Allied divisions at Alcañices and Caravajales and the supposition that 3,000–4,000 enemy cavalry had arrived in the area were false. He even named Julian Sanchez and Luis, Count Penne Villemur as in command of Spanish cavalry units when both men were with Wellington.

As for Leval, he had finally left Madrid on 27 May, having spent several days organizing the evacuation. His troops were dispersed throughout the city, a situation that had been forced on him by the need to contain the population, which had become increasingly hostile after Joseph's departure. D'Espinchal, with 120 of his hussars, was involved in supervising a safe withdrawal in the face of the dangers posed by the now turbulent citizens. The French, however, behaved with calm courage under considerable provocation, according to d'Espinchal. At the same time, there were still a large number of officials and their families who also needed to be evacuated, as well as the lengthy column of carriages and waggons that accompanied them. For d'Espinchal there was also a personal regret. He had to say farewell to the marquise with whom he had been conducting an affair for some months.

A rather different impression of the French departure is created by the recollections of Captain Andrew Leith Hay, whose duties as an exploring officer had taken him to Toledo. There he had posted information concerning events in Central Europe, which at the time were not going well for Napoleon. As a result, he had been taken prisoner and, refusing to give his parole, had been sent to Madrid, where Leval had imprisoned him in excessively harsh conditions. On the 27th, he found himself part of the departing column, being forced to march with the 88eme de la ligne.

> Madrid, on this morning, presented one of those remarkable scenes incident to the war; the bustle attending a march of troops being accompanied by the confused departure of part of the population, whose political opinions during the struggle now rendered it unsafe to remain behind. Persons of rank, forced from their hitherto

comfortable homes, were intermixed with all orders of the community, and alike contemptuously treated by the French troops. Quantities of carriages, cars, waggons, or laden mules, were urged onward to join the cavalcade, while numerous groups of the remaining population witnessed these departures with silent but expressive contempt.[26]

The departing troops and the fleeing civilians now took the route over the Guadarrama mountains, heading for Segovia, which they reached on 31 May.

* * *

At the same time, Graham's column was now drawing together as the troops approached their destinations according to Wellington's dispatch of 18 May. On the 24th Gomm was able to report from Outeiro that his guns

> behaved very well, but their officers required more driving than their horses; and had I not been more interested than they in the success of the enterprise, there was, on more than one occasion, opposition enough to have turned an obstinate man from his opinion. The weather fought against us at the beginning, but it is now settled summer, and we shall fry for the next five months. We halt here to-day and tomorrow, and then make four days' march to Losilla, a place about a league on this side of the Esla, and five from Zamorra.[27]

Artillery was always going to be a problem on a march across terrain which could not be less suitable for it, and it is understandable that the officers tended to be precious about their guns. One aspect of the preparations for the campaign was proving successful, however. Private William Wheeler of the 51st wrote home:

> On the 24th, we encamped on the plains of Miranda and find a great difference already in having tents. The Spaniards are lost in admiration at the sight. I know of nothing more surprizing to the eyes of a stranger than to see our canvas towns rise in a moment. Indeed I was not aware myself of the effect it has on the mind until one day I was at some distance from our camp talking to some Spaniards that inhabited a small village near us. We were in full view of our division but the tents were not pitched. I heard the bugle sound to stand by the tents. I managed to draw the people's attention into an

opposite direction from the camp till the bugle sounded again, this was in about a minute. I then pointed to the camp, how were they surprized. A minute before nothing was to be seen but the soldiers, now the whole camp was studded with several hundred bell tents as white as snow and as regularly placed as if it had been the work of much labour and time.[28]

As the Allies marched further up country, reconnaissance became increasingly important. On the 24th, Swabey was sent to explore the front to gain as much information as possible, and also to locate the Spanish cavalry. Making an early start at 5 am, he rode ten leagues and established that there were no French on this side of the Esla, that they had left Benevente, and there were only 800 cavalry and infantry at Zamora. Some of Girón's Spanish cavalry, he was told, was approaching Astorga to cover the advance of the Galician army. He also learnt the names and positions of the various fords on the Esla from helpful locals, although he came to the conclusion that none of them would prove of much use, particularly as the river had been swollen by intermittent heavy rain since early spring.[29]

Two days later, he was out again, this time with Graham himself as well as with Colonel de Lancey and Lieutenant Pitts of the Royal Engineers. Those who had reservations about Graham's age might have been surprised by the course of the expedition, the purpose of which was to find somewhere to throw a bridge across the Douro in order to facilitate communication with Hill's column.

> It was 5 o'clock when we started at a full gallop, as is the custom of Sir Thomas Graham. As he had fresh horses, three at different points, I only one, Colonel De Lancey two, and Pitts being only moderately mounted, we were soon left in the lurch; whether the General is mad or blind I have not decided; it required one of those imperfections to carry him in cold blood over the rocks and precipices. I should as soon have thought of riding from Dover to Calais; nevertheless I followed him ...[30]

Swabey was again sent to inspect the fords, and decided that only two were practicable. At much the same time, Vandeleur was sent on patrol with two of his dragoons to feel where the French were.

I found them to the amount of near 250 with 4 guns on picquet at the north side of the bridge at Benevente. When I got within two miles of them I halted my two men and went on myself, relying on Ratler until I got close up to their vedettes, and saw all that I wished to know. Two of them being rather dubious as to who I was, rode after me at full speed. I turned about and went back at a canter, letting those fellows keep pretty close. I allured them away about half a mile, but they got too cunning. If I could have got them as far as my two men, we certainly should have taken them. I was extremely fortunate, for on my way home I met a Spaniard going towards the French, to sell them some fine fresh trout which I did not scruple to take from him (but mind ye I paid him, not what he asked, but what I considered enough).[31]

By 26 May, Graham's troops were sufficiently concentrated to make a concerted advance in three columns, never more than 12 miles apart. On the left were the First Division, Pack's Portuguese and Anson's and Ponsonby's cavalry. They were marching for Tabara along country roads. In the centre, making for Losilla, five miles south of Tabara, were the Third and Fifth Divisions. Bradford's Portuguese and Bock's heavy dragoons. They were later joined by D'Urban's Portuguese cavalry who, of course, had been operating in the border area for some months in the role of scouts. Finally, the right column, comprising the Fourth, Sixth and Seventh Divisions and Grant's hussars, was marching towards Caravajales. The left column was also required to establish contact with Girón, who should have left Astorga on the 26th. The Galicians would then march to Benevente and cross the Esla there using the damaged bridge.

By the 29th all the units, infantry and cavalry, had reached their destinations. This was also the day when the pontoons were known to be close. The following day Graham rode to Caravajales, where he was joined by Wellington and his staff. Then, at daybreak on the 31st the left column assembled on the banks of the Esla, ready to cross by the Alhendra ford. Wellington had already ordered the nineteen pontoons to be taken to the village of Alhendra, which was on the Spanish side of the river, but French vedettes could be seen on that side, in position to prevent the movement of the pontoons, so it became necessary to force a crossing. Wheeler, who was involved in this dangerous attempt, described what happened.

> In the night we [the 51st and the Brunswick Light Infantry] moved to the ford in company with the Huzzar Brigade. When we came to the river we halted, took off our pouches and placed them on our knapsacks, the belt hanging down in our front, then marched into the river in columns of subdivisions.
>
> It was soon evident that we had either missed the ford or that the water was risen by the rain. Which ever was the cause, we soon found the water was too deep and the stream so rapid that in a very short time the whole of the infantry was upset. Some sank to the bottom borne down by the weight of the firelock and knapsack, to say nothing of the pouch containing sixty rounds of ball cartridges. This proved to be the awkwardest companion of the whole for as soon as we were upset the pouch would slip off the knapsack and hang suspended round the neck, thus placing us in a very critical situation and was of itself sufficient to drown a man without the other encumbrances. But for the Hussars I should not be alive to tell the tale, they flew to our assistance and picked up as many as they could. It will be much easier for you to conceive the confusion we were in when I tell you the river is divided at the ford into three parts by two islands, each part is about the breadth of the Avon [at Bath]. There were three regiments of Cavalry and two of Infantry plunging about in it and so dark we could scarcely see each other, besides expecting every moment to receive a volley from the enemy.
>
> The manner in which we crossed after order was in some measure restored is as follows. The Hussars each took a firelock the infantry soldier having hold of the stirrup. A Sergeant of the 15th Hussars conveyed two of us across in the following manner. I held hold of the stirrup, the other man held fast by the horses tail, the Sergeant carrying each of our firelocks.[32]

Then, once the leading troop of hussars had crossed, it

> proceeded up the hill by a tolerably broad road. On the top of the hill a French picket of about forty dragoons was discovered, the Frenchmen fired a few shots, and took to their heels, – away they went, the hussars after them. The officer and about thirty of his

men were captured, and the few remaining reached the supporting body, which had turned out in considerable force, when the hussars retired.[33]

Having now dealt with the French threat, the next task was to manoeuvre the pontoons into place so that they formed a usable bridge, an operation that was completed in two and a half hours. The infantry were now able to cross safely, and most of them had passed over by the end of the day. The cavalry still used the fords, though, with the result that the German Heavy Brigade and the Portuguese cavalry lost seven or eight horses and three or four men drowned. Some of the cavalry actually spent over 20 hours in the saddle that day.

William Swabey certainly believed he had never experienced anything as dangerous as fording the Esla. Taking great care, though, the troops managed to get across without mishap, except for a baggage mule belonging to Lieutenant Newland 'which was carried off its legs down the stream and shamefully abandoned by his servant. At last it was brought up against an island, and seeing nobody would start I swam my horse there, and landing was enabled to hold the animal till some of the men took courage, came and fully rescued his things.'[34]

On 1 June, while the last of the infantry were still crossing the Esla, the Allied cavalry rode on to Zamora, only to find that it had been abandoned by the French, although not before they destroyed the bridge across the Douro. Darricau had actually left Zamora as soon as he realised that Graham's troops were on Spanish soil and joined Digeon near Toro. Headquarters now arrived at the town, and Mr Larpent was delighted with the reception they were given.

> The people received us very cordially, scattered roses over our heads, cried *viva* &c., &c., and hung all their counterpanes and the hangings of their rooms out of the windows. The lady at my quarters embraced me, and was very kind, but – she was old. There was another like a plump English woman, to whom I passed on the compliment.
>
> The people entertained Lord Wellington and the staff with a concert, lemonade and ices, &c. The former did not admire this time lost in singing psalms to him, as he said. I met him in the evening riding down to the bridge to direct, in his Spanish uniform. In the

morning he was on one side of the pontoon bridge, and Marshal Beresford on the other. I almost knocked myself up running about to see Zamora, as we were to march again the next morning. I could not attend a little dance given by Lord Wellington in the evening, and except for the iced lemonade, I believe I should have been in a fever.[35]

The next day, Digeon had formed his brigade of dragoons on the plain near the village of Morales de Toro where they were discovered by the Hussar Brigade, 1,500 sabres strong, who were on the march to Toro. Grant promptly decided to attack and gave orders that while the 18th Hussars should turn the French left, the 10th should make a direct attack and the 15th were to form column, to act as a reserve. At the same time, the horse artillery under Major Gardiner, who had joined the hussars just that morning, opened fire, whereupon

> the 10th, under the immediate direction of Colonel (now Sir Colquhoun Grant) advanced to the charge. The leading squadron upset the advance of the French, who went about. Colonel Grant did not allow the Frenchmen any time for consideration, but, continually pressing forward with the 10th, the enemy was never enabled to recover from the disorder which had been caused by the first impetuous charge of the 10th, who closely pursued him, while the 15th were retained in column ready to deploy, had Dejean [Digeon] been able to bring up any reserve. As this was not done, the whole honour of the day fell to the 10th, who certainly performed their duty in a most admirable manner. The pursuit was continued to a bridge, which passes a little rivulet, after which the road winds a little in ascending a hill. Had Colonel Grant now brought up the 15th, which was formed in column of troops, and perfectly fresh, he might have succeeded in nearly destroying the French division, as after ascending the hill, which was an obstacle of no moment, the road passes through a plain of about half a league, and the French dragoons were not in any state to make any effectual resistance, but as it was impossible to see any part of the country beyond the crest of the hill, and as a body of infantry might have been in attendance, which would have enabled the dragoons to form, as well as forming an obstacle to our progress, there can be no doubt that the colonel acted most judiciously in calling a halt.

Later reconnoitring revealed the presence of a sizeable column of infantry, although it was questionable whether it was actually in position to intervene at the time of the skirmish. Nevertheless, acting only on what he could see, Grant 'acted in the most gallant manner, as he felt confident that the squadrons he saw would be an easy prey for his brigade, and having defeated the foe, and secured about two hundred prisoners, he completed his day's work creditably, and in not risking a check, he showed himself most worthy of the desirable situation he had been placed in.'[36]

The anonymous writer of this account could not recall the exact number of casualties taken by the hussars but thought it was about twenty killed or wounded. The French had two officers and 208 men taken prisoner, and their total losses were probably well over 300. Whatever the exact figures, the writer was justified in his comment that 'This was a most auspicious debut for the hussar brigade'. It was also mentioned as a notable event in many of the letters and journals; even Aitchison referred to it approvingly. For once the cavalry had been kept in check and not galloped off in the hell-for-leather fashion that Wellington so deplored. Furthermore, the action at Morales was certainly a factor in the French departure from Toro, but again only after they had destroyed the bridge. Yet Grant and the hussars were not alone in taking prisoners. James Hope had seen French prisoners on their way to the rear and had learnt that twenty-five of them 'were the lawful prize of that enterprising partisan chief, Don Julian Sanchez'.[37] Sanchez would continue to harass the French throughout the campaign.

Wellington had summoned Hill from Salamanca as soon as Graham's position on the Esla was secure. On the same day as the hussars triumphed at Morales, the head of Hill's column was approaching Toro. His troops had undertaken a forced march from Salamanca

> across bare country. We halted to cook during the heat of the day then resumed our movements and reached the vicinity of Toro in the evening. There we encamped on the left bank of the Douro among some luxuriant, well-watered vegetable gardens, the sight of which proved very refreshing after a long, sultry, and weary march. It was most gratifying to observe with what relish the officers and soldiers devoured the raw cabbages, onions and melons.[38]

Before Hill's troops could join Graham's on the right bank of the Douro they needed to cross the river, and before they could do that, the bridge needed to be repaired, the central arch and, according to some accounts, another of the arches having been blown up. 'Lieutenant Pringle of the Engineers effected this by dropping ladders on each side [of the breach] and laying planks from one to the other, a little above the water.'[39] The soldiers were then able to descend the ladders, cross the planks and ascend the ladders on the opposite side, all of which could be done with little difficulty. It was potentially dangerous, however, as Hope discovered:

> The boards were so elastic that but for General Stewart who remained on the north side of the broken arches until all the infantry had passed, I would inevitably have fallen into the river and been drowned. On perceiving me reeling to the left side, and quite close to the edge of the temporary erection, the general sprang forward and caught my hand just as I found myself on the eve of tumbling head foremost into the river.

Such a temporary arrangement was obviously unsuitable for wheeled vehicles, so the guns and the baggage carts 'found their way to the right bank by a ford a little above the bridge; some of the smallest kinds were swimming'.[40]

In Toro itself, the consequences of the action at Morales the previous day were clearly visible in the form of prisoners, wounded men and captured horses. These last were raw-boned animals 'huddled together in a courtyard and bore evident marks of bad provender, escort duties, marches, and counter-marches. Nearly all had the most horrible sore backs, almost frying in the sun. Innumerable flies settled on and irritated the poor animals.' As for the prisoners, who were about to be escorted on their way to England, Cooke was must struck by their hairy countenances, including one man 'with a long red beard which reached to his middle'. Their officer 'who looked angry and highly indignant, maintained a profound silence'. As for the wounded, Grant had expressly commanded that they should be given every attention, so 'a number of English medical officers were busily employed dressing [their] wounds, some of which were of a most shocking description from sabre cuts on their heads and faces.'[41] Such, indeed, were the typical wounds received during an encounter with the light cavalry.

By 4 June, all the Allied infantry was in and around Toro, where Wellington had established his headquarters. Some of the cavalry was further forward, with patrols being sent to make contact with Girón, who had now passed through Benevente. Thus Wellington had concentrated his army, having only d'España's Spaniards as a detached force further south on the border and Sanchez on scouting duties, which, as already noted, included harassment of any French he came across. What lay ahead was an advance 'over a sun-burnt, parched, brown, uninteresting country, affording scarcely any wood or water, and still less provisions, with a terrific sun over our heads'.[42] But it is fair to say that morale was high and success was confidently anticipated.

The French, though, were now under considerable pressure. Although the Madrid contingent had finally reached Segovia on 31 May, and had subsequently drawn closer to the rest of the Army of the South, the last troops did not come in until 2 June. At this point, the Army of the South was posted between Tordesillas and Torrelobaton, the depleted Army of Portugal at Medina del Rio Seco, and the Army of the Centre at Valladolid. Headquarters were at Cigales, and only Maucune, at Palencia, remained detached. Also on 2 June, Joseph issued orders that everything and everyone, except the troops and whatever was immediately necessary to them, was to move north, guarded by Spanish troops. The following day, with Hill's arrival confirmed (so that any French offensive action was rendered impossible), and Wellington in Toro, the troops joined the civilians and their paraphernalia in retreat. Yet they were firmly in control of the Great Road to France, there were still some defensive positions they could take up, several small supply depots had already been established and Burgos Castle, recently strengthened, was an obvious place to make a stand. The campaign was far from over, and Wellington's next objective was to force the French to abandon the Great Road.[43]

Chapter 3

From the Esla to the Ebro

As the last of Hill's troops crossed the Douro by the improvised bridge, the French, having abandoned Valladolid as well as Toro and Zamora, marched to take up a position on the Pisuerga. Their right was at Palencia, where Reille had his headquarters and where Maucune was reunited with the Army of Portugal, except that it consisted of only its cavalry and one borrowed division. D'Erlon was at Magaz and Gazan at Dueñas. By 5 June this line had been extended for the simple reason that there was not enough food for an army of the size of Joseph's, forced to live off the land. The king now transferred his headquarters to Torquemada. This was just a temporary measure, however. There was no indication that the Allies were preparing for an immediate advance, and such information as had reached Joseph suggested that Wellington intended to bring his army to the upper Carrion and upper Pisuerga in order to reach the Ebro before the French.

Joseph now found himself in a quandary. Jourdan had already suggested that they should cross the Douro and threaten Portugal, thus frustrating whatever the Allied commander was planning. He pointed out that if they were to suffer a setback, they could withdraw to Aranda de Douro, and then retreat to Burgos or Zaragoza. Clausel would be able to join them in either place. Yet, if this plan were adopted, Joseph would have failed to obey his brother's order that he must at all costs maintain communications with France. His hope was that Clarke would authorize Clausel to join the main army. The dispatch that reached him on 5 June, although written three weeks before, dashed this hope. Based on a claim that Wellington had detached 15,000 men for some unstated purpose, Joseph was instructed to take advantage of this weakening of the Allied strength by both threatening Portugal and sending more of his troops to support Clausel or even to Aragon. All this dispatch proved was that the war in Spain could not be directed from Paris, and even less so from Central Europe, but for Joseph it was nothing short of disastrous.

Joseph's response was that of a desperate man.

> I know nothing about Aragon. I have never received a report from any of the commanders there. I don't even know their names. Clausel has already all the infantry of the Army of Portugal but one division. I have by all accounts eighty thousand men against me, and only forty thousand to oppose them. Am I to order the Army of Portugal to join me? I have asked you this already. If it be the Emperor's wish, I beg you to give Clausel the necessary orders, for I suppose that you receive reports from him. I receive none. I am telling him of our situation; but I cannot say if he will think it right to join me in the plain of Burgos. As a good Frenchman and servant of the Emperor I repeat to you once more, Let us beat the English: that is the best way to make the Spaniards our friends.[1]

Reconnaissance to establish the Allied position now revealed that enemy cavalry was probing the French outposts, and that the Allies appeared to be on the move. There was the possibility of making a stand on the Carrion but Joseph's senior officers pointed out that having the Torquemada defile behind them meant it was not a good position for a battle, should it come to that. Yet any further movement would have to be governed by the enemy's line of advance. A simple and surer device than spies was now used to discover more about Wellington's movements. It took the form of a letter from Gazan to the Allied commander, suggesting an exchange of prisoners. Leith Hay was the French trump card, since they could assume Wellington would be anxious for the return of his exploring officer. The man chosen to carry the letter was the hussar captain Hippolyte d'Espinchal.

Gazan summoned d'Espichal at 6 am on 6 June to carry what d'Espinchal himself described as an unimportant dispatch to Wellington. At the same time he was to observe the movements and the direction of the Allied troops. (D'Espinchal, of course, referred to them as the English troops.) This mission, which did not offer any real danger, was still a delicate affair because it was obviously vital not to reveal that the envoy's principal purpose was to spy on the enemy and commit to memory everything that was seen and heard.

Accompanied by a trumpeter and six hussars from the elite company, d'Espinchal set off and soon met up with the Allied advance guard, about

4,000 strong. He could also see other troops marching towards the French left flank with the obvious intention of turning it in order to disrupt the retreat. Summoned by the trumpeter, a hussar officer conducted d'Espinchal to the commander of the advance guard, by whom he was received politely, but was not allowed to see Wellington who, he was told, was five leagues in the rear. Instead, a staff officer took the letter and the advance guard then continued their march. D'Espinchal, according to his own account, now felt that he had seen enough to discern the enemy's intentions and needed to make his escape before his own intentions were suspected. He also recognized that the advance guard was moving in the direction of Dueñas and Gazan's troops, who needed to be warned. He requested permission to join his hussars and once with them went off at a gallop, outpacing the pursuit.[2]

Much of this may be exaggeration, but the crucial fact that d'Espinchal returned within four hours made clear that the retreat must continue. The French now drew back to a position on the high ground beyond the Pisuerga, with their right at Castroxeriz and the rest of the army in position around Torquemada. Joseph believed that they could remain here for several days, but his senior generals pointed out that the position was still constrained by the Torquemada defile to their rear, and that the shortage of bread was becoming critical. In these circumstances, Burgos, with its strengthened defences and a well-stocked supply depot, was felt to be a more secure option.

On 7 June the retrograde movement continued. By the 9th Reille, with Darmagnac's and Maucune's divisions, acting as the advance guard, took position behind the Hormaza. The Army of the South was posted behind Arcos and the Urbel, with the cavalry on the Alanzon. The Army of the Centre, still with Cassagne's borrowed division, was in reserve in and around Burgos, where Joseph had established his headquarters. Here he learnt that Girón's Galician army was marching in concert with Wellington's movement and since he believed it to be 25,000 strong, this only deepened his despair.

The convoy of refugees and officials with their carriages and baggage carts had reached Burgos some time before, having been sent ahead in order not to hinder the march of the army. Unfortunately, they had then consumed a large part of the supplies held there before continuing towards Vitoria escorted by General Lamartinière. This meant that Burgos could no longer be regarded as a refuge for an extended stay. It also indicated that sooner or later the French would have to stand and offer battle. To do so, though, they needed Clausel and part of the Army of the North, or at the very least Reille's detached divisions. Although Joseph had written to Clausel some time before, explaining the situation in which the main army found itself, he had received no reply. Nor had there been any response to his dispatch to Clarke. On 9 June, therefore, he took the decision that Jourdan believed he should have taken much earlier and summoned Clausel to join him. To make sure the dispatch reached the general, he sent it with an escort of 1,500 men.

* * *

On 3 June, working on the assumption that Hill's troops would quickly complete their crossing of the Douro, Wellington had issued his general arrangements for the following day. The Allies would now advance in three columns, with Girón's Galicians as an outlying force. Graham, on the left with the First and Fifth Divisions, the two independent Portuguese brigades of Pack and Bradford and Anson's and Bock's cavalry, would have his troops ready to march at daybreak, taking the road to Medina del Rio Seco. The centre column, which would be the headquarters column, comprising the Third, Fourth and Light Divisions, D'Urban's and Ponsonby's cavalry brigades and the reserve artillery, were to march to La Mota, where they would receive further orders. The Household Brigade, having forded the Douro, would then march for Casasola. On the right, Hill's pre-campaign command, plus the Sixth and Seventh Divisions, the Hussar Brigade and Alten's, Fane's and Long's cavalry brigades, would proceed to the area between Morales and Torrelobaton, where Hill would establish his headquarters. Further right, Sanchez was to operate in communication with Fane and Alten.[3] It would have been advantageous to call in Girón at this point to put further pressure on the French right, but the Galicians were dangerously ill-supplied with ammunition and Wellington had none to spare. All he could do was send an angry dispatch to the Spanish war minister, Don Juan O'Donoju, reminding him and the Junta of the promises they had made about supplying their troops.

Webber was one of the last to ford the Douro on the 4th, only to discover that it was more that chest high for the horses. They also had a struggle to get the guns and ammunition waggons across against the strong current. Not surprisingly, they reached the other side with soaked baggage. As the rest of the brigade marched on to Morales, Webber made a detour into Toro to buy wine. Here he witnessed the arrival of General Castaños, who was 'so beloved by the Spaniards, everyone crowded near the gates to see him arrive. Bells were ringing and at last he appeared, escorted by his Cavalry. He was received by all ranks with the loudest acclamations – ladies cheering him from their windows and waving their handkerchiefs to him as he passed.'[4] Nor was the welcome accorded to Morillo, when he arrived soon afterwards, any less fulsome. Indeed, Webber believed the *vivas* must have nearly deafened the poor man. But the Spanish needed their heroes as much as any other nation, and these two men had not only been constant in their opposition to the French occupation of their country, they had also worked willingly with the British.

The people of Toro were not the only ones with reason to celebrate. Daniell recorded in his journal that

> the [Third] division made a long and tedious march, being occasionally interrupted and impeded by other divisions from the roads often crossing each other, which at length brought us all near La Mota, and the whole army encamped upon an extensive plain in view of the town, where Lord Wellington, in commemoration of the old King's birthday, gave a dinner to the General Officers of the army, to which the Generals of the 3d division went from the camp.[5]

Since Webber started his journal entry for the 4th with the words 'God Save the King', it is probable the significance of the day explains his visit to Toro to buy wine. Nor is it likely that the senior officers and the Royal Artillery were the only ones to drink the king's health. Significantly in this context, Frazer had written to his wife on the 3rd that the men looked well and would remain in good health if they could be kept from excess. This, he felt, was the advantage of encampments, 'inasmuch as the men being out of town, will be more out of the way of temptation'.[6]

A long march on a hot day, though, might put particular pressure on a company commander. According to John Blakiston,

> on such occasions the situation of an officer commanding a company is worse than that of a slave-driver. To have to urge the men beyond their strength, and to be obliged to turn a deaf ear to their entreaties

to be allowed to fall out, until the poor wretches sink from exhaustion, or are pronounced incapable of proceeding by the surgeon, was by far the most disagreeable duty that fell to my lot.

Not only would the poor captain be blamed for the number of men left behind, but for the officer 'who comes in immediate contact with the soldiers whose sufferings he witnesses, it is really heart-rending. I boast not very nice feelings, yet I have frequently, in a long march, dismounted and loaded my horse with the packs of such poor fellows as I thought the least capable of keeping up.'[7]

While the infantry of the centre column at La Mota, and the other two columns not far away, pitched camp for the night, some of the cavalry rode into Valladolid, which had been passed on the march. Here they found ammunition and other stores which the French had left behind in the haste of their departure. Sanchez was similarly lucky at Arevalo, where he found a store of grain. As the pace of the advance increased, and the Commissariat came under increasing pressure to keep up, any such finds were to be welcomed.

During the next couple of days, headquarters advanced to Castromonte and Ampudia, which was Wellington's location when d'Espinchal brought Gazan's letter. Hill on the right was on his way to Dueñas and Palencia, hence d'Espinchal's encounter with his advance guard, and Graham had passed beyond Medina de Rio Seco. Girón, with or without ammunition, was also on the move on the left, in parallel with Graham, who was under orders to maintain contact with him. The cavalry continued to be thrown forward, with the result that some of them witnessed the departure of the last of the Army of the Centre from Palencia on the morning of the 7th.

There were also signs of skirmishing between Allied and French cavalry as the troops advanced. John Green of the 68th, in the Seventh Division, noted that they passed dead men and horses, killed in an encounter with the enemy's rearguard, in which affray about twenty rations of bread fell into Allied hands. Green also described the welcome they received from the local population.

> Early on the following morning we marched through a village, and were very much delighted with some of the Spaniards, who danced the fandango, and others of them shouted 'Long live the English!' This day we marched through several villages: the bells rang, the

peasants shouted, and there was nothing but joy and gladness, and the best of feelings manifested towards us by the Spanish peasantry.[8]

The weather, however, failed to live up to the warmth of the reception Green experienced. On 6 June Lieutenant William Swabey RHA wrote in his journal that they had 'Marched to a terrible cold and bleak bivouac with continued rain. We all looked very darkly at each other, not only because we trembled at the idea of our horses losing their condition, but also lest the march by road should be impeded, and Lord Wellington's rapid movements be at a standstill.'[9] The bad weather continued until the 11th, when Swabey was finally able to report that everyone was in high spirits because the rain had cleared. Nor had it impeded the pace of the Allies' advance.

John Vandeleur had a different thought in his mind when he wrote a letter home on the 6th. 'We are now on the direct road to Burgos. The 4th division have lots of new scaling ladders, there is a train of 24 guns, twenty-four pounders, on the road from Corunna. Thank God the cavalry don't storm forts.' In all other respects the campaign was going well. 'We are now in the thick of the business, horses saddled every night at dusk, and remain so all night, but we are all as happy as possible. We have got a month's pay, plenty to eat and drink, horses in good condition, and an enemy flying before us. What can we desire better.'[10]

There was indeed good reason for feeling that all was well for the Allies, when everywhere they went the were greeted as friends. John Cooke remembered passing through Palencia, where the whole town was *en parade*.

> The sun shone brilliantly, the sky was an heavenly blue. Clouds of dust marked the line of march of glittering columns. The joyous peasantry hailed our approach and came dancing towards us, singing and beating time on their tambourines. When we were passing through the principal streets of Palencia, from the upper windows of a convent the nuns showered down leaves on our dusty heads, and the inhabitants declared, by way of compliment, that the Oxford Blues were nearly as fine as the Spanish Royal Horse Guards.[11]

Larpent agreed that

> the Life-Guards and Blues looked well on their entrance into Palencia, and on their march yesterday: the former, however, seem

dull and out of spirits, and have some sore backs among their horses. The Blues seem much more up to the thing, but they are neither of these very fit for general service here. Lord Wellington saves them up for some grand coup, houses them when he can, and takes care of them.[12]

It should be noticed in passing that Wellington had recently been appointed Colonel of the Blues.

One of those Oxford Blues, Corporal Andrew Hartley, instead of describing the architecture of Palencia, as was his wont when arriving somewhere new, was entertained by quite a different thought. 'Joseph Bonaparte marched out of this place yesterday and some of His Army marched this morning He is represented as being more fit for a Ladies Toilette Companion than calculated to endure the fatigue of a Camp.'[13] Some of the French generals would probably have agreed with him.

The weather, which had started to deteriorate on the previous day, or on the 7th according to Swabey, continued wet and cold on the 9th, with some heavy rain during the night. This caused particular suffering for the Portuguese because, as James Hope told the recipient of his letters: 'Our men being provided with tents, did not feel it, but the poor Portuguese soldiers I pitied from the bottom of my heart, they having nothing but their blankets to shelter them from the inclemency of the weather.'[14] Yet these discomforts did not seem to disheraten the Portuguese who, according to Larpent were 'in the highest order, their men really look at least equal to ours, better than some ... The whole army marches very fresh hitherto, but the Portuguese in particular, and arrive (the last mile even) singing along the road.'[15]

Nevertheless, for both British and Portuguese the weather was a trial, for which grog provided some remedy. 'Lieutenant-General the Honourable William Stewart being now in command of the [second] division, ordered an extra allowance of grog to be issued to the soldiers on the morning of the 9th; but this order not having been attended to by the Commissary of Colonel Ashworth's brigade, the said Commissary received a severe reprimand in division orders.'[16]

Another problem, caused by the landscape rather than the weather, was how to prepare food. According to William Surtees of the 95th,

> in all these late movements we had experienced a great deficiency of fuel for cooking and drying our clothes when wet, neither forest

nor bush-wood to be seen for days together, and indeed scarcely one solitary tree to be met with – nothing but corn; so that we were occasionally compelled to resort to the cruel and unchristianlike expedient of pulling down houses to obtain the timber with which they were built for the purpose of cooking, or we must have eaten our food raw. This, however, was done in a regular and systematic order, the Alcalde of the village pointing out such houses as were to be doomed to the fire, and the troops taking no more than was absolutely necessary.[17]

John Green no doubt faced the same problem but more immediate were the conditions in which they had to camp and the increasingly frequent food shortages. On the 10th the 68th 'encamped in a kind of swamp and we were obliged to gather sticks to lay at the bottom of our tents, to raise us out of the water. In the streets betwixt the tents it was ankle deep with mire and water.' Having mentioned in passing that Wellington and his staff were quartered in a nearby small town, this led onto the other grievance. A comrade had actually ventured into the town, and now returned with about 6lbs of flour, taken from a peasant: 'this was a valuable prize to us, who were nearly famished for want of bread: it was of more value to us at this time than gold or silver'. Green claimed that he experienced a 12-day period when he received in total no more than 3lbs of bread or biscuit. As a result the men were driven to eat herbs and bean-tops, and boil the blood of the slaughtered bullocks. Nor were the men in the ranks the only sufferers. While on commissary guard, sentinel over some mouldy bread, he came upon an officer stealing a loaf.[18]

Obviously, the food shortage must be ascribed to a failure of the Commissariat, but in their defence, they in turn were struggling to cope with the speed of Wellington's advance, a problem that would get worse as the terrain became more challenging. Despite the weather and the other difficulties the troops were encountering, they were marching across easy terrain, even if those marches started early and covered many miles. They were crossing a fertile plain where wheat and barley were the main crops. As a result, the horses 'fed on green barley the whole march, and got fat. The army has trampled down twenty yards of corn on each side of the road (forty in all) by which the several columns have passed. In many places much more, from the baggage going to the side of the columns, and so spreading further into wheat.' Yet Captain William Tomkinson of the 16th Light Dragoons felt that the Spanish 'must not mind their corn if we get the enemy out of the country'.[19]

By the 11th the headquarters and right columns were advancing on Burgos, while Graham's column was well to the left of the Great Road and seemingly heading for the upper waters of the Ebro. Rumours were now circulating that the French were dismantling the castle before abandoning the town. Captain Cairnes wrote optimistically to his stepfather:

> Lord W. rode off this morning to Burgos & has, they say, been fortunate enough to see the Enemy's whole force. It is reported to consist, scraping everything together, of not more than 67,000 men. We have of English & Portuguese (entirely exclusive of all Spanish corps) 70,000. In these numbers I do not include either our own or the French force to the eastward. Sir John Murray's Corps has embarked to be relanded on the Coast of Catalonia. The Enemy will be hard driven we think.
>
> How completely & brilliantly Lord W's movement so low down across the Douro, has succeeded in turning the Enemy's Right Flank from the Esla, Zamora, Toro & all these places in detail. They say that till the arrival of Gen. Graham's force on the Esla, the Enemy thought Lord W. was conducting his whole army on Salamanca & Valladolid.
>
> All this was done without firing a shot beyond some trifling Cavalry affairs, which of course shews how masterly & unexpected it has been.
>
> His Lordship by the direction we are taking appears to pursue his plan of moving well to the Left. He seems to intend passing by Burgos, which I think indicates his conviction that the Enemy mean to get as quick as possible over the Ebro.[20]

Cairns also mentioned in this letter that his new horses were working extremely well, and his old drivers, whom he had been promised would return to him, were in the neighbourhood, so that he could anticipate their arrival before long. He had also been posted to the Seventh Division. These developments probably explain his improved attitude to Wellington.

Wellington himself had now taken the decision to attack the most exposed of the French forces, the Army of Portugal, which was positioned on the high ground of the Espejar Heights rising up from the village of Hormaza. He entrusted the task to Hill's column, although Graham's column was not so far away that it could not come up in support if the French sent in reinforcements to strengthen Reille. On the 12th the Second Division, Silveira's Portuguese and Morillo's Spaniards advanced directly against Reille, while the Light Division, with the Hussar Brigade and Ponsonby's heavy cavalry in support, prepared to put pressure on Reille's right flank.

Lieutenant Moyle Scherer of the 2/34th, in O'Callaghan's brigade of the Second Division, was involved in the advance on the heights, noting that they broke camp and began to move at about 5 am. Before the Allies began their advance, though:

> The enemy skirmished very prettily with our cavalry at Hormasa, a small village, on a river of that name, and made a short stand to favour the retreat of the main body of their rear guard; they then retired slowly up the heights, above Hornillo, whither we followed them. They had at Hormasa about four squadrons and three battalions. Their infantry formed line on these heights, and, as we ascended on their flank, threw it back, changing its direction, but still presenting us a front. At last, perceiving that we were in great strength, and had large bodies of cavalry up, they threw themselves into squares, and retiring over the river Arlanzon, joined the remainder of the French corps under Count Reille, and the whole took the road to Burgos. These troops manœuvred very rapidly and steadily; and effected their retreat in most beautiful order, in the face of our cavalry, and under the fire of some of our artillery, which, however, did very little execution.[21]

Captain Charles Cadell of the 1/28th was also in O'Callaghan's brigade. He described events which ended in frustration for the brigade.

> We advanced rapidly under the gallant Colonel O'Callaghan; and just as we had mounted the hill, we found, to our disappointment, an immense ravine separated us from the enemy. Their right being turned, they retired so rapidly, that we could not come up with them; but were obliged to look on while the cavalry and Major Gardiner's horse artillery attacked them most gallantly. A squadron of the 14th Dragoons, under Captain Miles, took a gun and some prisoners

before they could pass the Arlanza. In the evening the brigade returned to the village, leaving a strong picquet of the 28th on the heights.[22]

William Webber recorded a different aspect of the action which he ascribed to Wellington's wider intentions. He had already noted in his journal that there were 'about 6,000 British Cavalry formed in column' in the field. He then described the scene:

> On this high plain while the weather was fine and clear, all our force and that of the enemy seemed displayed as at a review. In the distance and very clear to the eye were seen the walls and castle of Burgos, with the grand spires of the cathedral and several large Churches. The setting sun added very much to the grandeur of the scene, but all became suddenly darkened and the most tremendous thunder storm damped the pleasures of the day. It seems lord Wellington showed this large force of Cavalry to give the enemy an idea that the greatest part of the army was marching on Burgos, as they would naturally conclude that we had Infantry in proportion and during the affair he seemed anxious they should see the whole of the Cavalry, as they were formed in Brigade, after the enemy retired across the river, and took up ground on the riverside brow of the hill.[23]

Not surprisingly, on the French side d'Espinchal was full of praise for the rearguard's 'brilliant combat', particularly the light cavalry, and suggested that the French guns had severely punished the Allied infantry, which is certainly not born out by the casualty figures.

In fact, Reille had initially waited until he could assess the strength of the Allied advance, but once he became aware of the second force that was swinging round behind his right flank he knew the time had come to withdraw. He pulled his troops back behind the Urbel, which brought him closer to Gazan, before crossing the Arlanzon and taking position south of Burgos. This was not a good move, however, as Jourdan realized. It made the Army of Portugal vulnerable to a second Allied attack, particularly as the Arlanzon cut off some of the troops from the rest of the French forces.

There were now three options open to Joseph. First, the whole army could be repositioned on the Urbel, or second, it could be sent across the Arlanzon in order to take up a better position beyond that river. Yet to adopt either of these options, particularly the latter, would not only draw them away from their critical line of communication with France, it would also pose the same problem as fighting on the Douro, in that it would allow the Allies to pass to the right and then attack with the expectation of inflicting a defeat which might prove fatal to the French position in Spain. The third option was to close up on the Ebro, which would enable a quicker concentration of all the French forces, including those which should be coming from Galicia and Biscay. Not surprisingly, this was the option Joseph chose.

According to his memoirs, Jourdan now suggested that before they continued the retreat, they should send a corps well to the left, towards Villacayo and Medina del Pomar, which would weaken the advantage Wellington had over them, and would also allow them to observe his movements. This corps would not be compromised because retreat was possible by any of the routes to Bilbao, depending on circumstances. Other people (Jourdan does not name them) claimed that the tracks which led to the upper Ebro were impassable for artillery. Nor did they believe it would be possible for Wellington to engage the army at this point. Furthermore, they assumed he would follow the Great Road, and that the only troops on his left would be Girón's Galicians. Joseph accepted these objections and ordered that the whole army should follow the direction of the main road towards Medina del Ebro, where headquarters would be established on the 16th.[24]

There was also one positive development at this point. At last, a dispatch had arrived from Clausel. Admittedly, it had been written on 4 May, but it was enough to convince Joseph that communications had finally been restored with the Army of the North, and he now confidently anticipated Clausel's obedience to his recent order that he should join the main army. Separate summons had also been sent by General Thouvenot, the governor of Vitoria, and to Generals Sarrut and Foy, both detached from the Army of Portugal. Sarrut was ordered to march to Briviesca, and was already known to be approaching that town, while Foy was to come to Medina del Ebro. Once all these troops arrived, the French would be able to adopt a sensible, indeed the wisest, course and make a stand on ground of their own choosing. This, of course, was the one thing they had been unable to do ever since they began their retreat, as Wellington harried them from one position to another.

In preparation for the withdrawal, it was necessary to disperse the troops since the main route to Medina del Ebro would not allow for a tightly concentrated advance. Joseph's headquarters, at Quintanavides, transferred to Briviesca on the 14th and Pancorbo on the 15th. Reille had already been rejoined by Lamartinière and would soon have Sarrut back under his command, so he now sent Darmagnac back to the Army of the Centre. The Army of Portugal was to take position at Espejo, with orders to keep his right flank clear. An advance guard of the Army of the South would be posted before Pancorbo, with the rest of Gazan's troops on the left of the Ebro, behind Medina. The Army of the Centre was directed to Haro, the only place where the French were likely to find supplies.

Even before the French started their retrograde movements, the decision had been taken to blow up Burgos Castle, which was neither well provisioned nor in a fit state to withstand an attack despite the recent repairs. There were still mines in Burgos Castle from Wellington's siege the previous year. According to Jourdan, General d'Aboville, in command of the artillery park, was afraid that should the enemy get to France, he would use them against Bayonne. He proposed, therefore, that the mines should be filled with a little powder and then placed a short distance apart so that they would explode when the first was fired. Based on his experience, he was confident that there would be no damage to the town. Furthermore, the mines would only explode once the troops had left Burgos. As a result of this misplaced confidence, on the morning of the 13th the explosion took place while a brigade of dragoons was marching out. The splinters covered the town and killed or wounded a hundred men, many horses and a certain number of inhabitants.[25]

D'Espinchal was with the cavalry left behind to oversee the final evacuation of Burgos. He blamed d'Aboville's imprudence for the devastation.

> In five minutes, we had three officers, 20 hussars and 30 horses killed by pieces of shrapnel; the impossibility of avoiding this dreadful disaster created disorder and confusion everywhere; a battalion of the 13th light infantry, on the left of the regiment, was almost entirely wiped out. A number of officials, still in the town, perished along with a great quantity of inhabitants. This horrible explosion, which did not last more than an instant, offered a spectacle the more

terrible with the cries of the wounded, the dead, the destruction of a large number of houses.[26]

For the Allies, the explosion came as a complete shock, but a welcome one. Moyle Scherer, having lamented the fact that the previous evening there had been nothing to eat and no wood for fires, continued:

> The morning, however, brought with it consolation; for, at early dawn, while gazing with my glass at the distant castle of Burgos, I had the satisfaction to see it suddenly enveloped in thick white smoke, and the sound of a tremendous explosion announced to me that the enemy had blown [it] up, and would of course abandon it. In ten minutes a second explosion followed, and, in about a quarter of an hour, I could distinctly see the yawning ruins.[27]

While John Kincaid later reported that 'the explosion shook the ground like an earthquake and made every man jump upon his legs',[28] George Simmons wrote in his journal that it 'afforded us great delight. I, speaking for myself, would much sooner have a fair field to fight on, rather than storm a town.'[29] William Swabey agreed. He 'was with everyone else surprised and delighted at hearing at 7 o'clock this morning a heavy explosion which soon turned out to be Burgos, ill-fated Burgos, flying in the air. Here ended the curse of the English army, the obstacle to all our designs.'[30]

As a final word on the destruction of Burgos Castle, d'Espinchal was full of praise for the commander of the Allied advance guard who, when informed of the disaster, sent an envoy to General Soult, granting safe passage for an hour to the remaining French troops and to care for the wounded. This noble conduct and generosity was greatly appreciated by the army and by the king, who took the trouble to send an aide to the Allied camp to testify his acknowledgement.[31] Unfortunately, d'Espinchal identified the Allied general as Erskine, which is obviously an error.

With Burgos no longer an obstruction to the Allied advance and the French once more retreating, Wellington was able to send Bathurst an updated resumé of the current situation. First he informed him of the action at Hormanza. Then he continued:

> The enemy took post on the left of the Arlanzon and Urbel rivers which were much swollen with rain, and in the course of the night

retired their whole army through Burgos, having abandoned and destroyed as far as they were able, in the short space of time during which they were there, the works of the castle which they had constructed and improved at so large an expense; and they are now on their retreat towards the Ebro by the high road of Briviesca and Miranda. In the meantime the whole of the army of the allies has made a movement to the left this day; the Spanish corps of Galicia under General Girón, and the left of the British and Portuguese army under Lieut. General Sir Thomas Graham, will, I hope, pass the Ebro tomorrow at the bridges of Rocamunde and San Martin.[32]

Later on the 13th, Wellington wrote again to Bathurst from his headquarters at Villadiego: 'We keep up our strength, and the army are very healthy, and in better order than I have ever known them. God knows how long this will last. It depends entirely upon the officers.'[33] This, of course, was a familiar theme. After the catastrophe of the retreat from Burgos he had blamed the junior officers for not keeping order.

Wellington had actually slowed his advance as the shortage of supplies became ever more critical. In Graham's column, for example, the Fifth Division had been without bread since 8 June and the First Division was on half rations. Tomkinson noted on the 12th:

> The whole army halts this day. All commissaries are ordered to have four days' bread in hand by 7 a.m. on the 13th. From the rapid advance of the army, no supplies can come from the rear. The country gives bread and corn, as hitherto these have not failed, and this in a country that has been plundered and destroyed by the enemy for the last five years. It was said before our march, that until the harvest came in not a pound of bread, by way of supply to the army, could be procured.[34]

Despite the problem of bread and the attendant hunger, there was a feeling in Graham's column of progress made and that they would soon be upon the French as both armies neared the Ebro. William Gomm, for example, wrote home: 'I am anxious to cross the Ebro, and to know something more than we do at present of the French position. They seem to be quite unprepared to meet the force Lord Wellington has collected, and to meet it in the way in which he has disposed of it.' He also had another piece of information. 'The guerrilla force, under Mina and Longa, will join us immediately, and I think Lord Wellington will have a disposable force little short of 150,000 men on the Ebro.'[35] This was an exaggeration, but that the Allies would well outnumber the French in any forthcoming action was a fact. In the event, only Longa, now a brigadier in the regular Spanish army, with his force of over 3,000 brigands turned regular soldiers, would join Graham's column and play a particular part when the French were finally brought to battle.

Even more optimistic than Gomm was James Hope, who wrote to his friend:

> A very little time will now decide where the grand struggle for Spanish liberty is to take place; much further we cannot advance, without coming on French territory. Whenever the mighty conflict shall take place, and whatever may be the issue of the important struggle, you may rely on every thing being done by this army that man can achieve, for a finer army never took the field. Never did an army answer the dread call with greater cheerfulness, nor express more unbounded confidence in their officers.[36]

On the 14th, Wellington and some of his staff, including Frazer, rode early to Burgos to establish that the French had indeed abandoned both town and castle. Richard Fletcher, the chief engineer, was sent ahead to reconnoitre. The others went on,

> looking about us a little, as we saw the enemy's vedettes and had no troops with us. As we advanced the vedettes retired, and we learnt from the country-people that they were preparing to leave Burgos. After fording the Alanzon, the bridge over which was blocked up, and jumping over half a dozen ditches, the little bridges of which were broken down, we reached the hills above the town, and about a mile from it we could distinctly observe the castle in ruins and straggling people in several parts of the town; some, scrambling over the timbers and ruined remains of a church and of the castle. Still no one ventured out of the town to us, and we were apprehensive of being taken if we went in … We had already crossed the road to Valladolid, and pursuing our route a little further, we could clearly perceive, on the plain beyond the town, the enemy in full, and

apparently confused march of cavalry and infantry, preceded by a multitude of mules and beasts of burden. Some Spaniards (peasants), also, about this time assured us that the enemy had quitted the town, leaving at the gate a picquet of fifty dragoons.[37]

Certain now that he could march on without leaving a French-held citadel in his rear, Wellington continued his advance to the Ebro. This would lead to a series of marches through country, the beauty of which provoked raptures of delight in both officers and men, these in themselves a reminder that the influence of Romanticism was widespread at this time. John Blakiston found himself one day in the beautiful valley of the Hormaza river, rich in woods and romantically situated villages, and the next, crossing 'a mountainous country, occasionally intersected by pretty valleys' which brought them to 'a pleasant wood'. Arriving here at about 4 pm, they pitched their tents with considerable relief, 'the day having been very hot, the troops much fatigued'.[38]

For the gunners, though, however beautiful the scenery, there was always the problem of protecting the guns from the ravages of bad roads. On this occasion,

> the roads were so bad as to prevent more than three men going abreast – and sometimes even they were obliged to file through parts covered with large pieces of rock – yet we kept up with those in front. The General Officers and others gave us great credit for the attention we paid.
>
> Three or four of our wheels suffered and the wheel horses were much shaken, but we met with no accident. We found that by coming this way we had turned the position of Pancorvo on the Ebro, which the enemy had expected us to attack, from necessity (as they thought) through marching on the road. The peasantry told us they had never seen artillery travel through the pass as we did this day and we supposed the enemy were not aware of its being practicable, especially as the heavy rain had made it so much worse.

Webber was also able to take heart from his belief that 'Our army was never more healthy, indeed I should think troops in England cannot be in better shape. Marching to a certain degree agrees with most men if the weather is favourable and they are well supplied.'[39]

It would seem that the artillery were better supplied than some other parts of the army, particularly as Webber, when comparing this advance with the previous year's retreat, while acknowledging the general failure of the Commissariat, believed that his brigade had been the best supplied in the whole army.

William Tomkinson, on the left with Graham's column, received an order at 9 am to march on San Martin. When he arrived there he discovered that all the troops of the column had now crossed the Ebro. This led him to contemplate the French situation. He already knew from local reports that they were on their way to Vitoria by a road that passed through Miranda del Ebro. He came to the conclusion, therefore, that they must be unaware of Graham's position 'as a division might have stopped the whole column at the bridge of San Martin, as well as the other at Bocamonde, where some of the column likewise crossed'. He also commented on Wellington, who had looked at his brigade and been well pleased, 'He is in high spirits, and says to-morrow the whole of the army shall be across the Ebro. They must either fight or retire out of Spain.'[40]

Whether he remained in such high spirits later in the day is questionable. Larpent reported how, having passed through country that reminded him of Wiltshire,

> we then entered a rough, wild country, with rocks &c. All lost our way nearly, including General Murray, the Quarter-Master-general, with whom I was riding, Lord Wellington himself, and nearly all the baggage. We were nigh to a place called Brulla, should have passed Cuirculo, and near Urbel de Castro, whereas we got through a rugged pass in the rock, and came down to a pretty, picturesque village, called La Piedra (from the rocks around it I conclude); there we fell in with the fifth division. We at last, after passing another little space called Fresnoy, and leaving Urbal de Castro, down in a valley on our right, with a curious small castle on a pointed hill close to it (from whence the name), we arrived at this wretched place [Massa]; the houses here would not in any way hold half of us.[41]

A letter from Alexander Dickson to Major General McLeod, written on 19 June, summed up the situation five days earlier:

Head Quarters move on the 14th to Masa and Nidaguila, a village adjoining. It now became evident that it was the intention to turn the position of the Ebro by passing it high up, Sir Thomas Graham, with the 1st and 5th Divisions moving upon San Martin de Elines where there is a bridge over the Ebro, followed by the 3rd Division, and the 4th and Light Divisions with three brigades of Cavalry marching upon Puentearénas, followed by Sir R. Hills Corps. The 6th and 7th Divisions I know not the routes of.[42]

The following day the Allied centre and right advanced through even more dramatic scenery until they reached the Ebro itself. William Surtees almost let his pen run away with him as he described the effect the valley of Veras had had on him.

This is one of the most picturesque and beautiful vales in Europe, I dare say. When you arrive at the brow of the high ground over the Ebro, a sight breaks upon you all at once that is indescribably grand and beautiful; – a large river rolling under you, beyond which a rich and fertile valley, laden with the fruits of a hundred orchards, with charming villas and farm houses dispersed through all the lawn; a stupendous bridge, of which I know not how many arches, leading you across this magnificent river; the whole closed by high and beetling rocks jutting out of the high woody bank on the opposite side. It really appeared like enchantment when we first arrived in sight of it, from the long dreary plain we had been so long traversing.[43]

Surtees was not alone in his response to this natural beauty. Richard Heneghan, Assistant Commissary with the Field Train, particularly noted how Wellington and the headquarters staff dismounted and led their horses down the rocky path to the Ebro.

On the left were to be seen, sometimes emerging from the morning mist, that still hung upon the mountains, and sometimes from behind the jutting rocks, the columns of the several brigades of Hills' corps, winding down the zig-zag roads below us; smiling plains, thickly studded with villages and vineyards, lay stretched along the valley. The heat was intolerable, and those who have suffered from the darting rays of a southern sun, can alone understand the avidity with which we sought the shelter of some cherry trees that lay by our sloping route.[44]

They eventually reached the river and headquarters was established at Qintana, where they could watch the troops crossing the bridge to ascend the opposite bank, which was, as Browne recalled in his journal,

> of the most singular character. It almost resembles a winding staircase, overhung with immense rocks – The clattering of the horses hoofs, & rolling of the Artillery over the surface of this rock – the long irregular lines of glittering Bayonets – the different uniform of British, Portuguese & Spaniards, with here & there an Officer on horseback mingled with the ranks – the singularly storm-like appearance of the sky, as the sun was setting, when this passage took place, rendered the scene more beautifully impressive than anything I can remember.[45]

At the river soldiers and officers alike of the Light Division came upon something they had not tasted for many a long day. After they had crossed the bridge at Puente Arenas, they saw 'a number of sturdy, thick-legged women from the mountains of the Asturias. They were loaded with fresh butter.' Not having tasted that commodity for more than two years, Cooke quickly made a purchase. 'I carried the treasure in the front of my saddle until we encamped but, as ill luck would have it, there was no biscuit served out on that day.' The following day the Light Division marched on to Espejo. They passed through several villages and Cooke, determined to acquire bread for his butter, asked the villagers to sell him some. All shook their heads in response. Finally, he saw a priest who, in return for a peseta, gave him bread. 'On taking up our ground for the day, the baggage made its appearance, and ample justice was done to the bread and butter by myself and my companion.'[46] Such were the small treats that eased the pressure of hard campaigning.

There was also no small sense of achievement that they had outflanked the French to cross the Ebro unopposed. For Simmons it was instanced by the way the band of the 95th struck up the 'Downfall of Paris', followed by some national tunes as a reminder of 'Old England'.[47] For Samuel Broughton, surgeon with the 2nd Life Guards, who crossed the Ebro on the 15th, it was the thought that they had 'entered what Buonaparte's aggrandizing system chose to hold as annexed for ever to France, thus rendering this river, instead of the Pyrenees, the boundary between the two countries'.[48] It had been a hard day's march for the Household Brigade, though, and 'A Spectator would hardly conceive it possible that Cavalry could descend these precipices into the Valley in many places almost perpendicular but we decended safely without accident the Cannon being let down with Ropes by the Infantry – the River Ebro is very narrow there being near its source.'[49] For the artillery, the descent to the river was indeed a challenging experience, with even Wellington wondering whether the guns could pass because 'the descent was very sudden and steep, the road very roughly paved, not very wide, and in places with frightful precipices at the sides'. Swabey claimed 'It was the most nervous thing I ever did; we had the good fortune to get down without injury though a slip would have been fatal.'[50]

It is interesting to note that even as Wellington's strategy of turning the French right was taking shape, senior officers were still enjoying the finer things of life. Frazer wrote to his wife on the 15th that the previous day he had dined with Marshal Beresford. 'We had an excellent dinner, served up on very superb plate. The Marshal's table is allowed to be the best in the army; it is furnished, as we are told, by the Regency of Portugal.' Frazer also had a comment to make on the descent to the Ebro: 'one horse fell over the precipice and was killed. There was such a scramble of guns, dragoons, infantry, and baggage that chaos seemed to have come again. We were much amused by the men getting into the cherry trees, at which we met all at once with great number.'[51]

By the 16th all the Allied troops were across the Ebro, with the exception of one British division. On the 15th Wellington had sent orders to his brother-in-law, Major General Edward Packenham, to halt the Sixth Division, which he commanded. Ostensibly, they were to cover the magazines and stores but Oman questioned this, since it seemed unnecessary to detach about 7,000 men for the purpose. He suggested instead that Packenham might be required to support the Galicians, whom Wellington had ordered to advance rapidly towards Bilbao in order to disturb the French garrisons along the Biscay coast.

The last of the Allied troops to cross the Ebro were Hill's right column. Scherer was as struck as others had been by the magnificence of the scenery and he reflected that 'In a scene so lovely, soldiers seemed quite misplaced, and the glittering of arms, the trampling of horses, and the loud voices of the men, appeared to insult its peacefulness.' Its effect, which lasted for several days, was 'to make us cheerful and contented'.[52] Webber's journal breaks off just after he had reported the words of General Stewart, who commanded the Second Division. He 'said he had travelled through most parts of Europe celebrated for their natural beauties, and on the banks of the Rhyne in particular, but he never saw anything to surpass the grandeur of this'.[53]

As already noted, though, this kind of grandeur was also the most difficult for the artillery and the baggage train in particular to pass through. It certainly explains why the French had made no effort to defend the upper Ebro; it simply had not occurred to them that an army would attempt to advance over such terrain.

A surprise for Kincaid, and an indication of how detached Graham's column had been during the advance, was suddenly to come across the Fifth Division,

> lying encamped. They were still asleep, and the rising sun, and a beautiful morning, gave additional sublimity to the scene; for there was nothing but the tops of the white tents peeping above the fruit trees and an occasional sentinel pacing his post that gave any indication of what a nest of hornets the blast of a bugle could bring out of the apparently peaceful solitude.[54]

The Light Division continued towards Medina de Pomar, where they camped beside a river, and where there was an unfortunate contretemps with the local people. The rapidity of the Allied advance had outpaced the Commissariat and rations were now in desperately short supply (except for a field marshal in the Portuguese service, of course). Edward Costello of the 95th and a couple of his comrades decided to find some sustenance. They went into the village and offered money for bread. The suspicious villagers, however, demanded an extortionate price, whereupon the soldiers brazenly helped themselves and then made a dash for safety – but not fast enough. 'We were overtaken by some of the swift-footed peasantry, who came up to us with knives and clubs. The dearly-obtained bread put our lives in jeopardy because we were all totally unarmed. Being without even our side-arms, our party had recourse to stones for defence.' With the Spaniards threatening to kill them, death was staring the British soldiers in the face. Fortunately, 'several men of the 43rd and 52nd, which belonged to our Division and who were foraging like ourselves, came running up. It was now the turn of the Spaniards to retreat, which they did in a hurry.'

Nor did the problems for Costello and his comrades end there. At this point General Sir Lowry Cole, in command of the Fourth Division, appeared on the scene with some of the staff corps. He called upon them to halt, whereupon the 'plundering rascals ... plunged into the river – which at that part was very deep – and started to swim across, holding the bread in our teeth. Sir Lowry, in an agitated tone that did honour to his kind heart, called out, "Come back, men, for God's sake. You'll be drowned. Come back, and I'll not punish you."'[55]

The Seventh Division were also short of rations but found safer ways to deal with the problem. For William Brown of the 45th, the solution was growing in the bean fields. Although the plants were still immature, they were torn up by the roots and the leaves, hulls and tender tops were boiled 'and then devoured with the greatest avidity. Such was the battalions sustenance for five days.'[56] Wheeler and the men of the 51st were also allowed to take the beans from the fields, but they were given wheat or rye in place of bread. Halting where there were water mills, they were able to grind the corn, whereupon Wheeler would assist his comrade, Jack, in making dough balls.

Despite the hunger and sometimes desperate measures of his men, Wellington had good reason to feel quietly confident about the development of the campaign. On the 17th, he informed his brother Henry in Cadiz that

> the whole army have crossed the Ebro, and we are in march towards Vitoria and the high road to France, of which I hope that we shall be in possession in a day or two.
>
> It is reported that the King is in march by Haro and Longroño towards Pamplona. We have not yet heard of any very large force on this side of the Ebro. The last large corps I heard of was encamped at Briviesca on the night of the 14th. We saw the lights of a small corps last night at Frias.[57]

For once Wellington's information was wrong. Joseph was now making for Vitoria by the shortest route. Whether he would be able to stay in Vitoria was another matter. As Frazer told his wife in a letter of the 16th, we know little of the enemy at this moment, nor, strange as it may seem, are we sure who commands his army: whether Marshal Jourdan or General Gazan; Joseph Bonaparte is of course nominal, and merely nominal commander. The enemy is irresolute, his plans seem disconcerted by our sudden advance. We know that he is distressed for provisions. All the dry corn of the little valley we left to-day has been carried off to Briviesca. The adjacent country has probably been equally drained. We believe that Miranda [del Ebro] and Vitoria will both be abandoned from want of provisions, and it is possible, if we can advance rapidly, that Pampeluna may not receive a garrison from want of supplies.[58]

There could be no doubt that the momentum of the campaign was running more strongly than ever in favour of the Allies.

Chapter 4

The Road to Vitoria

The French withdrawal was a slow affair; although they were not following the most difficult routes to the Ebro in military terms, the artillery and the numerous equipages conveying the baggage and plunder of the officers frequently obstructed the progress of the troops. This alone was enough to depress the usually optimistic d'Espinchal, who had come to the conclusion that the unhappy Army of Spain had fallen out of the emperor's favour, with the result that it was neither being properly reinforced, despite the number of troops taken from it, nor efficiently supplied. There was no chance of advancement or reward. Discontent was general. Even the retreat was blamed on Napoleon for removing Marshal Soult from command.[1]

Marshal Jourdan was well aware that the French were in a very vulnerable position. Although they had gained Lamartinière's division and would soon have Sarrut's, they desperately needed the other detached divisions of the Army of Portugal, as well as Clausel with the Army of the North. There was no guarantee that Joseph's orders would be obeyed, when any recalcitrant general could argue that they contradicted the primacy of the emperor's commands. Yet these reinforcements, if they did arrive, would enable the main army to stand and take the offensive against the Allies on something closer to equal terms, and that despite Wellington's skilful manoeuvring.

Andrew Leith Hay had by this time been given into the custody of General Lamartinière, the chef d'état major of the Army of Portugal, with instructions from General Gazan to detain him at Briviesca until the Army of the South arrived. Once in Briviesca, the general seemed to believe the prisoner's detention should be of the most severe kind. Leith Hay was rescued from this imprisonment by Baron d'Orsay, colonel of the 122me de la ligne, who agreed to release him upon receiving his parole and to find him quarters in the town. Unfortunately, these were opposite Lamartinière's own. D'Orsay was definitely a gentleman (in the contemporaneous meaning of that word) and Count Gazan would prove the same. Lamartinière was something quite different. Not only did he consider the presence of a British officer offensive, he also extended his antagonism to the whole nation, an attitude Leith Hay had earlier experienced from General Leval in Madrid.

> I have seldom seen hatred more strongly depicted than in the occasional glances of his bloated countenance, as, turning towards the window from whence I surveyed him, he seemed to regret that inflicting summary punishment was not within his jurisdiction. In the French army it was noticeable the marked dislike to the English manifested on all occasions by this officer, upon whom beating appeared not to have produced the usual effect, that of creating respect.[2]

In contrast, when General Gazan arrived at Breviesca on the 14th, although he initially took Leith Hay to task for putting up the proclamations at Toledo that had so annoyed the French, 'His lecture appeared to be one more of necessity than inclination; it was couched in very different terms from those of General Leval, and a kindliness of manner bespoke no personally hostile feeling.' The reason Gazan wanted to see Leith Hay was to inform him that he had received a communication from Wellington, presumably in response to the letter d'Espinchal had carried to him. He agreed with Gazan's suggested prisoner exchange and requested Gazan to send him the name of an officer currently being held in England as an exchange for Leith Hay. Gazan even invited Leith Hay to write a letter in support of his own. Should Wellington agree, Leith Hay would immediately be sent to the Allied command post.[3]

From this point onwards Leith Hay was able to socialize with French senior officers. He noted, in particular, that they were puzzled by the non-appearance of the Allies, except for Sanchez's lancers, who haunted their rearmost troops as if to hurry them on their way. This absence, of course, was permitting the French to pursue their leisurely retreat undisturbed, or so they reasoned. They were even optimistic that Wellington was allowing enough time for Clausel to join them. Consequently, it came as a surprise to Gazan to learn that the whole Allied army was now concentrated on the left bank of the Ebro. This certainly shattered French complacency that Wellington must have been following their line of march because there was no other practical route.

The French now moved on to Miranda del Ebro and Leith Hay, having given his parole, was at liberty to ride with any part of the column that he chose, although always with two gens d'armes in attendance. As a result he was able to take a good look at both the civilians accompanying the Army of the South, many of them ladies dressed *en militaire*, and the troops. He was particularly impressed by the gunners, who were notably well-equipped and well-disciplined. In his opinion, 'Of the different corps of the French army, none appeared more efficient than the artillery. The brigades accompanying the three armies, I had, on this occasion, an opportunity of observing, were invariably well appointed – horses, carriages, accoutrements, all seemed in perfect order.'

He was not so impressed by the general discipline of the other troops, noticing among other things that there was less observance of the distinction between officers and men that one would find in a British army. This he ascribed to conscription, which could bring men of good family into the ranks. He had to concede, however, that despite 'all this apparent laxity, it was impossible to see the French armies without being impressed with the perfectly au fait manner in which the duties were performed; ever in readiness, the soldier was instantly put in motion when occasion demanded celerity of movement'.[4] The French army might be retreating; they might be demoralized; but they were still far from defeated.

By the 15th, Joseph had established his headquarters at Pancorbo, and the following day he was at Miranda del Ebro with the three armies finally brought together and positioned in the surrounding area. Consequently, once Wellington's intentions became clear, it would be a simple matter to concentrate the troops. The Army of the South straddled the Ebro, with three divisions on either side. This made them the French rearguard, although an attack by Wellington, depending upon the direction from which it came, could put them in the van. The Army of the Centre was downstream from Gazan, and Reille, with his three divisions, having now been re-joined by Sarrut, was using his cavalry to search the upper reaches of the Ebro in order to locate the Allies.

The French were now 60,000 strong, a much healthier situation than only days before, but d'Espinchal was not alone in feeling dejected. No army chooses to retreat except out of necessity, and a retreat being enforced by an enemy who had consistently wrong-footed his opponents was the worst kind of necessity.

The immediate objective for the French was to ascertain Wellington's wider intentions. Finally, on the 17th, Maucune, whom Reille had posted with his division at Frias as part of his effort to locate the Allies, reported the presence of Allied cavalry on the north bank of the Ebro near Puente Arenas, while other bodies of troops of indeterminate strength were following them. This certainly suggested the probability that Wellington was making a wide turning movement that might take him as far as Bilbao and would certainly disrupt the vital communications with France. In response, Joseph now ordered Reille to march towards Osma, from where he could advance either to Valmaseda or Bilbao, should Wellington have made that his objective. Gazan was to take two of his divisions and his cavalry to Espejo, both as support for Reille and to watch the north bank of the Ebro.

Of course, as Jourdan noted in his memoirs, these movements came too late, since Wellington was already advancing in a different direction. On the 16th the headquarters column, led by the Light Division, ended the day near Medina Pomar, after passing through country that was said to resemble Switzerland from the sublimity of the mountains and the beauty and fertility of the valleys. The next day they found themselves following a much more challenging route, not so much for the terrain but also because of 'the frequent halts and counter-marches in consequence of our having mistaken the road', with the result that they did not reach their allotted encampment until 4 pm. The Light Division, it should be added, were as short of bread as the rest of the army, and also, like the rest of the army, the men seized everything edible in gardens and fields. Initially, if they were caught, they were punished,

> but when our supplies of bread had entirely failed, it was thought proper to make up deficiency, by purchasing some bean-fields for the use of the men; and fatigue parties were told to gather the produce. I never shall forget the observation of a Pat as he trudged along sulkily on this duty. 'By J---s,' said he, 'I suppose they'll be after sending us out to grass next.'[5]

The supply problems also persisted in Graham's column, and stripping the bean plants, where available, was the only sensible recourse. There were worse problems, however. On the night of the 16th, when they were camped on gravelly ground, a tremendous rainstorm blew up:

... the tent pegs were uprooted and down came our house on top of us. Each man was eager to have a sleep, and each and all wished to have the tent pitched again. Yet no-one would stir, so there we lay; the water soaking through left both men and accoutrements in a miserable plight on the bugles calling us to renew our labour at daylight. The sight of the men encamping from under the tents exceeded anything, almost anything, that could be conceived in the shape of misery. Benumbed with cold, drenched to the skin, hungry as wolves, without the means of any kind of comfort, or the most distant hopes of relief.[6]

Yet when they finished their march on the 17th, what should await them but half a pound of wheat per man, which, said Douglas, was a very welcome guest.

Nor was John Douglas alone in his objection to the inclement weather. William Gomm wrote to his sister: 'We have had the weather of November – ever since we crossed the Ebro, and it is likely to continue. "Neuf mois d'hiver, et trois mois de mauvais temps" seems to be the character of this climate.'[7]

Tomkinson rarely commented on the weather in his journal. Instead, he took a keen interest in the movements of the French. On the 17th, he recorded that the enemy 'had shown nothing in our front, and have troops considerably to our rear of the Ebro, on the Burgos road. Our crossing to the left has been quite unexpected by them. We hear that it was their intention to fight on the main road, near Breviesca, and they have kept a division at Frias for the purpose of observing our movements on the Ebro.'[8]

By the 17th, the Allies were marching virtually in one column. Only Girón's Galicians were following a different route, towards Bilbao in order to disrupt French communications and disturb the Biscay garrisons. The plan now was to advance through the mountains to Orduña, by which turning manoeuvre they would avoid the difficult pass of Salinas on the Great Road to France. Then news arrived that two French columns were preparing to march, one from the direction of Vitoria, the other from Frias. These were Reille with Lamartinère's and Sarrut's divisions on his way to Osma and Maucune, whom Reille had ordered to abandon Frias, on his way to join the Army of Portugal. A change of arrangements was required.

The significant arrangements for what would happen on the 18th principally concerned the Light Division and Graham's column. Wellington required that:

> The Light division (without its artillery) will move by La Boveda to San Millan. Major-General Alten will place the division in a favourable position in the neighbourhood of San Millan, and will put himself in communication with the troops at Osma.
>
> The squadron of Major-General V. Alten's brigade will move with the Light division.
>
> These troops will move at 4 A.M.
>
> Major-General Alten will push forward his advanced guard from San Millan to the neighbourhood of Villanueva, and will send patrols by Espejo towards Puente Larra ...
>
> Major-General Sir Thomas Graham will put the troops under his orders in motion at 4 A.M., and will march in two columns to Orduña, the left column moving by Villafio and the Peña Vieja; the right by Villalba, the Peña Nueva and Tartanga. The whole of the artillery will move with the right column.

There was also a route for the Fourth Division which 'will move from Oteo at 6 A. M., and will proceed by San Martin and Venta Mamblija to Osma'. This division would be joined by the artillery of the Light Division, and the cavalry, with the exception of Alten's, Anson's and Bock's, would also move in the same direction.[9]

On the 18th Graham set off northwards towards Orduña, as ordered, but instead of keeping to the route he had been given, he chose to follow a shorter, if more challenging, one by way of Murguna. This meant that as Reille was approaching Osma, Graham was debouching in the path of the two divisions of the Army of Portugal. Reille had no choice but to make a stand, otherwise Maucune would be cut off as he marched from Frias.

In response, Graham sent forward the light battalion of the King's German Legion from the First Division to occupy the high ground on the right, where Captain Norman Ramsey RHA was also posted with his guns. In addition, two squadrons of cavalry were sent to protect the artillery. For John Vandeleur, who was not on covering duty, there had already been a moment of drama.

> I was on piquet with the advance. I patrolled to Osma, where, just as I arrived, I saw about 12 dragns. coming towards us. I had but three men, we halted and they halted. I took them for Spaniards but they fired a shot and retired. Col. Ponsonby came up with the remainder of the picquet, and ordered me to skirmish, which I did with them for 2 hours, supported by Capt. Webb, who had his horse wounded. They retired about half a mile into a thick wood, where they had a number of sharpshooters concealed. I followed no further than the edge of the wood. The col. then ordered up the German riflemen, who drove them back on the left. It then became an infantry business …[10]

John Douglas described how they met the French 'near the crossroads leading to [Bilbao] from the village of Orma. Here our old animosity kindled into a flame, and to work we went. The French appeared to be in good heart and played their part well, but getting flanked by our taking the village of Orma, they cut off the engagement and made direct for Vitoria after a very light skirmish.'[11]

Tomkinson, whose squadron was one of those protecting the guns, had a clear view of the ground and, perhaps, the better understanding of what was happening so often denied to combatants in the thick of the action. Noting that the French had just moved to Osma, he continued:

> The enemy showed about six thousand infantry, with six squadrons of cavalry, and on seeing we had troops up, halted a mile in rear of the village. The 1st and 5th Divisions, with Pack's and Bradford's brigades, formed in our rear of Osma, about two miles. Osma lies in a plain, surrounded on all sides with steep hills, the enemy occupying the foot of them on the Vittoria road, while we held those to the right of the Bilbao road, and the valley in the bottom of the opposite range. This range is very steep and commands the village as well as the position the enemy took up, and over which the light companies from the 1st Division were detached.
>
> This movement, with the 4th Division coming up on the hills to our right, caused them to move, after a little skirmishing, from the detachment made to the left, and a considerable cannonade from those on the right, as well as from our guns.

As the enemy was moving off, the 5th Division was passed from the valley along the range of hills to the right, and came up with the enemy's rear with their light troops. There was a considerable fire on both sides, but little done.[12]

The 4th Division had actually been in pursuit of Reille without offering any immediate threat, but the unexpected arrival of Graham's troops convinced Reille that discretion was the order of the day. He managed a fighting withdrawal, although James Hale of the 9th, in Hay's brigade, saw it somewhat differently:

> … at length the enemy began to retreat so rapidly, that our division was halted, and the light companies dispatched in pursuit of them. So we continued advancing, driving them before us like a flock of sheep for nearly two leagues giving them a few shots when convenient. They would give us a few shots sometimes, but we pursued them so closely, they had no time to give us many, for only five of our company were wounded on this occasion and, night coming on, that put an end to our pursuit.[13]

The cavalry might have been *les beaux sabreurs* of the armies of the day, but for Lieutenant William Hay of the 12th Light Dragoons, also posted to cover Ramsey's guns, Osma presented him with a very different experience, 'one of the most irksome and trying duties a dragoon can be exposed to – covering guns. There you have to sit on your horses, exposed to the fire of artillery, and losing horses and men.'[14]

The encounter between the Army of Portugal and the Allied left at Osma was not the only spat to occur on the 18th. A potentially more disastrous affair for the French happened at San Millan. According to Surtees, it was about midday when the advance guard of the Light Division, comprising the 1st German Hussars and the 2/95th, came upon a French piquet. Leach described how, 'as we were feeling our way through an intricate, thickly wooded country, we stumbled on a party of French Hussars'. The Germans immediately attacked and took about thirty prisoners. They also brought back the news that the French were at hand. This, of course, was Maucune's division, which had been on the march since daybreak, following the road from Frias which happened to lead obliquely to the one along which the Light Division was advancing.

Maucune had called his first brigade to a halt at San Millan because the second brigade, which was slowed down by the divisional baggage, had become detached. The first brigade, as it waited, was positioned behind a stream, with its front protected by several houses, and there seems little doubt that some of the troops were taking the chance to refresh themselves.

Leach continued:

> I know not where Lord Wellington's headquarters had been the night before, nor from whence he came; but in an instant he appeared on the spot, and directed the first and third battalions of our corps, supported by the remainder of General Kempt's brigade, to attack a brigade of French infantry, which we had pretty nearly caught napping at San Millan. We engaged them briskly in front, while some of our companies assailed both flanks. This drove them in confusion from the village, with the loss of some baggage.[15]

At this inopportune moment, Maucune's second brigade

> suddenly made its appearance through a pass on our right; upon which the greater part of our division was immediately formed on the height overlooking the valley. They marched along in loose and straggling order, to all appearance totally ignorant of our proximity, which circumstance was extraordinary, as we had a distinct view of them, and they could hardly have missed hearing the firing in the affair with their leading battalion. The head of their column had, in fact, almost come abreast of the right of our position, before they discovered their predicament. On perceiving it, they closed their ranks rapidly, and struck off the road towards the mountains on the right. The rifles of our brigade, supported by the 52nd regiment, were immediately pushed after them.[16]

Cooke's account continues Blakiston's narrative. 'The 52nd, at a run, brought up the left shoulder and actually formed line facing to the rear. They encountered the enemy of the crest of the hill. The enemy, the moment they met that regiment, turned round, threw off their packs, and fled to the mountains, keeping up a running fight. The 2nd brigade was now engaged front and rear.'[17]

With both of Maucune's brigades now on the run, the baggage train, which had been in position between the two brigades, was left at the mercy of the attackers. The escort tried to protect it but were beaten off and had no choice but to flee. What then happened was inevitable. The first to reach it were the 1st and 3rd 95th of the second brigade, leaving Surtees of the 2/95th feeling righteous indignation, but not because he was critical of such plundering: '... although my brigade, by beating and dispersing the enemy at the village, had been the principal cause of its capture, yet those whose hands it fell into had not the generosity to offer the least share of it to us, but divided it amongst themselves.'[18]

Blakiston also disapproved, although for a different reason. 'A good deal of plate, all Spanish, was found in the officers' trunks – a clear proof of the brigandish propensities of persons who ought to have set a better example, but who, I believe, differ from the privates only in being more accomplished rogues.'[19] He would discover soon enough that French officers were not the only ones with a taste for plunder.

It would seem that General Alten had some reservations about the way the spoils had been distributed. Two days later, as the Light Division was waiting for other units to close up, 'The horses, mules, and baggage, which had been captured from the enemy by the Light Division on the 18th, General Alten directed to be sold by auction in the camp this day, and the money produced by the sale to be divided amongst the troops, before any more heads were broken by a collision with our French neighbours.' According to Leach, 'a vast amount of female dresses' were found amongst the plunder. 'That a universal feeling of regret for the fair females who had thus lost their wardrobes pervaded all minds, I am ready to declare, but as there was no remedy for their misfortunes, abundance of purchasers were found.'[20] One is left to wonder what the troops did with this finery.

As for the French, Maucune brought as many as he could collect to Espejo, where he joined Reille. The remainder, whose flight had sent them more seriously astray, made their own way to Vitoria over the next two days. Jourdan commented that '[Maucune's] division suffered a considerable loss and would have been completely destroyed if they had fought with less valour'.[21] 'Valour' may not be the word that one would associate with Maucune's troops on this occasion, at least as presented in the Allied versions, but 'considerable loss' may well explain why the division would not take part in the Battle of Vitoria.

Joseph and Jourdan now recognized that Wellington had turned their right. They also appreciated that they could not hold their present position for much longer. At a meeting of the generals commanding, Reille advocated that they should abandon Vitoria and advance along the Ebro to Navarre. They should then urgently call in Clausel, or even Suchet. Joseph, of course, was basing his hopes on Clausel, who, if he had obeyed the king's order, could reach them before Wellington forced a general action upon them. As for Suchet, he had already been summoned to join the main army, which suggests that the marshal's ongoing conflict with the Anglo-Sicilian force was either not known of, or was underestimated, by the king and his senior officers. Sir John Murray had failed at Tarragona but his withdrawal had happened too recently to be known to either Joseph or Wellington. Even so, there was no chance that Suchet would be disengaging in order to join the main army. Reille might believe that, thus strengthened, they could confidently take the fight to the Allies, choosing their own ground in the process. Joseph, however, was unwilling at adopt such a drastic change of plan. If he were to do so, he would have failed to fulfil the most significant of his brother's instructions, that he should maintain communications with France, which meant protecting the route to Bayonne before all else. Furthermore, should he redirect his force to Navarre, where progress would necessarily be slow and difficult, he would have to abandon the civilian convoy, including all the spoils brought from Madrid and elsewhere, and even the five million francs which had just arrived to pay the troops. Such a move would also endanger Clausel, who would unwittingly come to Vitoria to find it held by the enemy. As far as Joseph was concerned, they had no choice but to proceed to Vitoria.

Very early on the 19th, d'Espinchal, as busy as ever, carried an order to Reille to hold a position on the Bayas at Subijana. This would enable him to cover the Puebla defile on the route from Miranda to Vitoria. Mermet's cavalry would actually hold the defile. D'Erlon would then bring the Army of the Centre through it and into the valley of Vitoria, to be followed by Gazan with the Army of the South.

Wellington, who was actually closer to Puebla than either Gazan or d'Erlon, had also made his arrangements for the 19th. Graham's column, including Anson's cavalry, was to begin its march as soon as possible after daybreak, making for Orduña by way of Berberana. His task was to open up the route for the rest of the army, so it was important that the rear of his corps and its baggage was pushed well away from Berberana in order to avoid creating a bottleneck. The Fourth Division was to march at 4 am and make for the road to Escote. Half an hour later the Light Division and Alten's cavalry were to march to the left of the Great Road towards Salinas de Paul and Pobes. Two brigades of the Second Division, which had been moving in support of the Light Division, were to make for Villanañe, where they would wait for further orders. Hill was to put the rest of his troops in motion once Graham had cleared the Great Road and would then move towards Puente Larra by way of Osma and Espejo. The Third Division's objective was Berberana, and the Seventh Division's was Villalba de Loza. As for the cavalry, D'Urban's brigade was to move to Carcamo and take position at the head of the Fourth Division when Cole arrived there. The rest of the cavalry would be given their orders the following morning. As for Girón, the order which was sending him towards Bilbao had been cancelled and he was now to advance towards Orduña, with his advanced guard at Amurrio, thus bringing him in closer contact with Graham.

Further orders were issued on the 19th, not just for the cavalry. The gist of these was to bring the various units further forward into more concentrated positions, although the instructions for the Fourth and Light Divisions were more specific. 'The movements of these two columns are to be combined, and they will, as far as circumstances permit, keep up a constant communication with each other, and favour each other's advance in case of opposition on the part of the enemy.'[22]

Both Wellington's and Joseph's arrangements were initially implemented as ordered. D'Erlon reached and passed through the Puebla defile, followed by Gazan. They could hear the sound of distant gunfire, however, because Reille had found his position threatened by the Fourth and Light Divisions. Mr Larpent, who had hurried the previous day to watch the action at Osma through his telescope, was once more on the scene.

He and other civilians attached to headquarters

> ascended a high hill on our right, which commanded the whole scene of action, and there with our glasses we could distinctly see everything. As soon as the light division had got almost round the hill on our right from the direction of the nearby Frias road in order

to be ready to advance and turn the French position, our fourth division advanced to the village here, and the skirmishing began from the houses and a chapel on the river. In about half an hour our fellows entered the village, and we got about three field-pieces into play close to it. We then saw the French, who were in considerable force on the other side, and formed into a crescent on a hill near, begin to move off at first gently, but soon in quick time, and a part of our division was very soon formed beyond the village over the river. The skirmishing thus went on all the way up the road and hill beyond to another village half a league further on the hill, where the French were drawn up in greater force; when our men got up, however, the enemy went off pretty quickly, and were last night in great force, some say fifty thousand, in a plain about a league and a half from this, and about half way to Vittoria.[23]

Swabey arrived late in the action, but 'when we overtook the columns in our front we found them engaged and the enemy retiring before them; no great execution was done on either side. It was a terribly wet and disagreeable day, we halted for the night, encamping in a ploughed field at Subijana, crossing the Bayas. Towards night about 600 prisoners were brought in, increasing the enemy's loss to nearly 2000 up to this date.'[24]

The Light Division, having played a peripheral part in dislodging Reille, now passed through Salinas de Paul, where

the division was halted to enable the men to refresh themselves. Every man carries a cup, and every man ran and swallowed a cup full of [water from a beautiful clear stream] – it was salt water from the springs of Salinas and it was truly ludicrous to see their faces after taking such a voluntary dose. I observed an Irishman, who, not satisfied with the first trial, and believing that his cup had been infected by something in his haversack, he washed it carefully and then drank a second one, when, finding no change, he exclaimed, – 'by J-s, boys, we must be near the sea, for the water's getting salt.'[25]

Kincaid was not the only one to be amused by this remark because Simmons also recorded it in his journal, and one can imagine how quickly it would have circulated around the battalion. It is also a reminder that however serious the business of war, there was always humour to lighten the mood.

Graham's column had a frustrating day. As Tomkinson recorded in his journal, 'We assembled on the Bilbao road, a league in rear of Osma, before daylight, and were pushed half a league towards Orduña by mistake. We marched to Jocano, and although only two leagues from Osma, did not arrive before 6 p.m. It rained the whole day, which rendered the roads – always bad – almost impassable.'[26]

This may explain why John Aitchison was feeling so disgruntled.

We are now within 30 miles of Vittoria, which I hope we shall reach in a day or two, but probably not without opposition. As yet the enemy have given us little fighting – we passed the Ebro unmolested on the 15th by the bridge of San Martin and have been very much harassed ever since – yesterday our column had an affair with them at the pass of Osma, which we gained in about 4 hours, but Ld Wellington with the Light Division had an affair also near Espejo – they made 250 prisoners and took much baggage – *we took neither* – the fact is we do not manage well – our country man Genl G. who commands us has shown himself a good deal too old – he is as far as concerns himself extremely active but he harasses the troops beyond conception and in the field he displays little science and still less decision.[27]

It should be added that Aitchison was in the habit of criticising senior officers. He had found Wellington wanting throughout the Burgos campaign, and he was writing after a day when they had been on the march for nearly 14 hours while progressing only 12 miles.

While the Allies were drawing closer to Vitoria, the French were taking possession of what would become the battlefield. Leith Hay had much to say about the situation:

After a long and fatiguing march of thirty-two miles, the 'Army of the South' entered Vittoria on the evening of the 19th. A more crowded town has seldom been witnessed: the court of Joseph Bonaparte, his guards, the various convoys from the interior, the head-quarters of the 'Army of the Centre,' and some of the cavalry, already occupied its buildings, or added to the confusion of the streets; the numerous staff and civil departments of Comte Gazan's army, formed a most embarrassing addition to the already unmanageable assemblage.

The convoy with which I had left Madrid had not yet proceeded beyond Vittoria; nor did it appear to have been the primary intention of the enemy to abandon the country on the left bank of the Ebro, and many of the Spanish refugees had consequently hoped the capital of the province of Álava would, for a time, terminate the very unwilling pilgrimage they had from necessity been induced to make. The passage of the Ebro by the allied army awakened the military and civil authorities from these dreams; and upon visiting some of the Spanish families with whom I had previously been acquainted, they were found making preparations for accompanying the cavalcade destined to move the following day on the road to Bayonne. At night Vittoria was illuminated in honour of the soi-disant king. As this was the result of orders, and as either French officers or their adherents occupied every house, there could be no difficulty in accounting for this tribute of respect. During the evening and night, the armies were placed in position, covering the town; peasants were compelled to assist in throwing up temporary field-works, into which were conveyed upwards of one hundred pieces of artillery.[28]

The French had finally accepted that unless they were prepared to stand and fight, outnumbered as they were, they would have no choice but to continue their retreat along the Great Road and out of Spain. There was still the chance that Clausel would arrive before Wellington made a move, which would improve the odds, but that depended as much on Wellington holding back or Clausel making a rapid advance. It had become increasingly obvious, as the campaign developed and the Allied commander was able to make them dance to his tune, that their ejection from Spain had been his sole objective. Thus he had constantly manoeuvred on their left, forcing them to make retrograde movements. His position was such that he could even block the Great Road if they lingered at Vitoria without offering battle. This would force them into the mountainous wastes of Navarre, where it would be impossible to support an army. By making a stand, they had the choice of ground. The question remained, however, what were Wellington's intentions? Would he engage in more manoeuvring which might allow Clausel to reach them in time; was he even intending to march to Bilbao; or was he preparing to strike the decisive blow?

Chapter 5

The Eve of Battle

During the evening of 19 June Joseph received a letter from Clausel which informed the king that he had left Pamplona and was making his way to Logroño, which was a two-day march from Vitoria. Joseph immediately responded by ordering him to march with all speed for Vitoria. That message never actually reached Clausel, and to make matters worse, that general received information suggesting that Joseph's army was on the upper Ebro, which he now made the objective of his advance. As for Foy, who had also been summoned to join the main army, he had called in his troops but had been more intent on extracting the French garrison from Bilbao than hurrying to join Joseph. On the day of the battle he was at Mondragon, over 20 miles from Vitoria.

In his memoirs, Jourdan stated he was fully convinced that if Wellington were to attack before the arrival of Clausel, the king's forces would be in great danger. This belief was based on a false assumption that the Allied army was twice the size of the French, although Wellington did indeed enjoy a numerical advantage. He also recognized that if they were defeated and no longer had access to the Great Road, even if they could still make their way to Pamplona by some other route, they would first have to retreat along tracks that were a challenge, if not an impossibility, for the passage of guns and wheeled vehicles. Presumably, he had conveyed these concerns to Joseph, because the king was now considering some other options. They could take a position on the Heights of Salinas which would allow more time for Clausel to arrive before Wellington could strike, since they would be able to hold him at bay more effectively than in their present position. Yet, ironically, because of the false reports which were now governing Clausel's movements, such a move would have prevented him from joining the main army. Also the Heights were singularly unsuitable for the operation of cavalry or for the sustenance of an army, which, if Wellington did not respond to the challenge, would mean further retreat, while sending a clear message that Joseph was ready to abandon his kingdom without a fight, a kingdom for which he felt more concern that he is sometimes given credit. There was also cause for some guarded optimism. Wellington would have to approach their present position by tracks that would undoubtedly slow him down, hence their conviction that he could not be in position to attack before the 22nd, by which time Clausel should certainly have arrived. Having reflected on all these points, Joseph decided to hold the position at Vitoria.

One further decision was taken, however, in an attempt to ensure an accessible line of retreat, should the French be forced back on Vitoria. As Leith Hay observed, the town was crowded not only with French army officers and staff and their baggage but also with the civilian convoy and all the paraphernalia attached to it. During the afternoon of the 19th, a large part of the convoy left Vitoria on the road to Irun, escorted by the garrison of the town, which properly belonged to the Army of the North, under the command of General Emmanuel Rey, who had been the governor of Burgos and could obviously be spared as he had no command in any of the three armies. The departure of the convoy was an impressive sight: 'the carriages and waggons extended as far as the eye could reach, winding through the rich and beautiful valley.'[1] It is also worth noting at this point that the rest of the convoy was despatched early on the 21st, escorted by Maucune's division, which reduced the Army of Portugal to just two divisions. This has been picked up as a bizarre decision, since it deprived Joseph of a paper strength of 4,000 men, and can only be explained in relation to San Millan. Furthermore, since there still remained all the baggage, carriages and waggons of the senior command of three armies, with all the plunder that those officers and their juniors, as rapacious as themselves, had brought with them as they left their various areas of command, Vitoria still had the potential to prove a bottleneck should the French be forced to retreat by any other route than the Great Road.

To return to Joseph's decision to remain at Vitoria, it has been suggested that it was based on two assumptions, each of which was misguided. On the one hand, having recognized that Wellington had been manoeuvring by making a series of flanking movements, there seems to have been a belief that he would continue this strategy, in order to force the French out of their positions. Yet, even if that were his intention, and some in his own army believed it might be, it was unlikely that he would follow the wide sweep to Orduña and even as far as Durango (which would certainly force the French away from the Great Road and towards Navarre) when there was a more direct route from Osma, by way of Murguia, to Vitoria. The essential misconception seems to have been that any other route was too challenging for a large army. But that was to ignore the equally challenging terrain that the Allied army had crossed to reach the Ebro. On the other hand, the Salinas pass might have been a better position, despite its apparent drawbacks, because it would have forced Wellington to make a difficult decision. Either he would have had to attack an unassailable position or he could have held his ground and risked being overwhelmed by both Joseph's army and the reinforcements with Clausel and Foy.[2]

Once the decision was taken to remain at Vitoria, at least until Clausel and Foy arrived, Joseph needed to prepare for the possibility, however unlikely in the short term, of an Allied attack. Both the dispositions of the French army, and the implications of Wellington's strategy, are best considered in relation to the topology of the area. Leith Hay's description of the valley is a good starting point.

> Vittoria is situated on rising ground, surrounded at a considerable distance, by an amphitheatre of mountains. With the exception of the height upon which the city is built, the country in its immediate neighbourhood is level, and of slight elevation. Extending along the north-west front of the town, at the distance of a mile, runs the Zadorra, a considerable stream, over which there are erected several bridges; to the south-west the lofty and extensive heights of Puebla communicate with the high grounds domineering the route to Pamplona; while on the directly opposite side of the valley, which in that particular part becomes more widely displayed, rise the eminences above Gamarra Mayor and Abechuco.

Leith Hay added that 'every thing about [Vitoria] had become eminently interesting from the situation of two powerful armies having arrived in close contact, under circumstances that rendered it nearly a matter of certainty that its neighbourhood must become the arena of very serious conflict'.[3]

The amphitheatre referred to by Leith Hay is roughly horseshoe shaped, with the town of Vitoria at the north-eastern, open end of the valley. The distance from the town to the Puebla de Alanzon defile at the far end of the valley, where it narrows between steep hills, is about 12 miles. The width, once the valley has opened up, is about six miles. In other words, this was an extensive arena for a battle. While the Heights of Puebla mark the southern end, the western and northern rim is dominated by the Sierra de Badaya. The river Zadorra flows across the province of Álava, passing Durana to the north of Vitoria and then turning in a south westerly direction before meandering on to Puebla de Aranzon, where it leaves the valley. From there it flows on to Miranda de Ebro. Within what would prove to be the limits of the battlefield it is crossed by ten bridges, of which the most significant are at Nanclares, Villodas, Tres Puentes (which, as the same suggests, was a clutch of three bridges), Ariaga, Gamarra Mayor and Durana. There was a scattering of small villages, little more than hamelts, in the valley. On or near the Zadorra were Nanclares, Villodas, Tres Puentes, Margarita, Crispiana, Gobeo, Yurre, Gamarra Mayor, Gamarra Menor and Durana, while Abucheco lay further back on the far side of the river. Most of these would prove significant to the movements of the two armies. At the foot of the Puebla Heights lay Subijana de Álava, Zumelzu, Esquivel and Gomecho, the first of which would see particularly fierce fighting. More centrally placed were Ariñez, La Hermandad, Zuazo, Gomecho, Ali and Armentia. All these settlements were potential defensive positions for an army under pressure and obstacles to an attacking force.

The terrain looks flat from the high ground but actually undulates, although not excessively. In 1813, some of the valley was under cultivation, while other parts were wooded, and in places it was intersected by deep ditches or trenches. There are two ridges of higher ground: one rises quite steeply from the Zadorra, south of Margarita, and extends to Zumelzu at the foot of the Puebla Heights, passing in front of the village of Ariñez; the other runs parallel from la Hermanded to Esquivel, with the knoll of Ariñez as its focal point.

Vitoria was, and still is, the point of intersection for several major roads. The Great Road, so crucially important to the French, came up from Burgos, passed through the town and then came close to the Zadorra at Gamarra Mayor and Durana. Crossing it at Vitoria was the Bilbao to Logroño road, while a lesser road from Subijana de Morillas to Salvatierra and Pamplona also passed through the town. It was a busy place under normal circumstances. On 20 June, it was a seething cauldron of activity.

During the morning of the 20th, great excitement, attended with feverish and unsteady feeling, seemed to have taken possession of the inhabitants and their numerous visitors. They had ascertained the near approach of the allied army, and in the act of occupying so extensive a position as that selected by Marshal Jourdan, great activity and constant movement were perceptible; troops passed through the town, and the sound of artillery and carriage wheels became incessant. The immense convoy that had left Vittoria appeared to have produced slight effect in relieving the crowded state of the town, the streets still presenting scenes of the utmost confusion, without any effort being apparent, by which order was sought to be restored.[4]

Early in the day, Joseph had proposed to Jourdan that they should ride over the ground and reconnoitre the positions of the three 'armies' in detail. Unfortunately for Joseph, and for French fortunes, Jourdan was taken ill during the morning with a sudden fever which kept him bedridden. Since Joseph was not expecting an imminent attack from the Allies, he decided to postpone this detailed reconnaissance until the morning of the 21st. As a result, Gazan's, d'Erlon's and Reille's troops remained in the positions they had taken up upon their arrival in the valley the previous evening, or in Reille's case, early in the morning of the 20th, as wet, tired and hungry as the Allies were in their encampments.

Thus the Army of the South, which formed the first line, occupied ground from the steepish ascent in front of Margarita to Subijana de Álava, at the foot of the Puebla Heights, a front of about 4,000 yards. Leval was on the right, closest to the river, holding the ascent from the Zadorra and extending left with his whole division, except for a company of voltigeurs who were guarding the bridge at Villodas. To his left was Darricau, who had positioned one of his two brigades in the front line, while the other was to be held in reserve behind Leval's division. Beyond him, Conroux's two brigades were positioned with Subijana de Álava to their front and Zumelzu to the rear. Occupying the foothills of the Puebla Heights was Maransin's single brigade, while Villatte's division was posted in front of Gomecha as a reserve for the whole line, along with Pierre Soult's cavalry. Gazan had also set up outposts at the Puebla de Arlanzon gorge and on the Puebla Heights, the first a likely access point to the valley, the second ideal for an outpost. He had also decided that cavalry would be of little use in any action. Although he held Soult's hussar division in reserve and used Avy's light cavalry from the Army of the Centre to patrol the river below Leval's position, he released the rest of his cavalry, Tilly's and Digeon's dragoons, to the Armies of the South and Portugal respectively. This left Gazan with about 28,000 men and 54 guns to hold his extended line, which meant there would be little depth.

Over a mile further back from Gazan's line, although closer to Villatte and Soult, were d'Erlon's two infantry divisions. They were in position behind the second ridge and the village of Gomecha, Cassagne's on the left and Darmagnac's slightly further back on the right, in front of Zuazo. The position of d'Erlon's cavalry is less certain, but it seems to have been posted on the flatter ground in front of Vitoria. From later events, it may be assumed the Tilly was further to the left than Treillard. D'Erlon had about 14,000 men and 24 guns in this more concentrated position. Cassagne's division was about twice the strength of Darmagnac's, however

The Army of Portugal was the weakest of the three armies, as they were deployed on the day, although Reille had thirty guns. When Reille positioned his troops in the early hours of the 20th, they occupied ground between Ali and Armentia, forming a third line. At this point Maucune's division was still with them. Reille also had a strong complement of cavalry, Boyer's and Mermet's from his own corps, and Digeon's from the Army of the South, who would prove to be a vital addition to his strength. The King's Spanish Guards were officially part of the Army of the Centre, but possibly due to doubts about their competence they were deployed behind Reille's line as a final reserve. In addition, 2,000 loyal Spaniards, under the command of the Marquis de Casapalacios, were sent to Durana, to hold the bridge that allowed the easiest access to the Great Road from the Bilbao road. They completed a force which totalled about 60,000, including the Spanish, although it has to be conceded that there is considerable difference of opinion here, not helped by the fact that the last returns before the battle are dated 1 May.

During the evening of the 19th, while the French were debating the best response to the situation Wellington's movements had created for them, the Allied commander was making his own arrangements for the following day. His principal aim on the 19th had been to take the French by surprise before they had time to manoeuvre into a strong defensive position. Had Reille been dislodged from his position on the Bayas before the Armies of the Centre and the South had marched through the Puebla defile, this aim would probably have been realized. Reille had stood his ground, however, and then skilfully brought his own troops across the Zadorra under Allied fire. Instead, Wellington now concentrated on bringing his forces into position for a carefully planned attack. Furthermore, having been informed of Clausel's departure from Pamplona, he knew that time was of the essence.

His arrangements were as specific as ever. Hill was 'to move the right column of the army into the neighbourhood of Pobes, keeping it on the right bank of the Boyas [Bayas] near Pobes'. This would place his column on the right for an advance towards Vitoria and would leave him in a good position for a direct approach to the Puebla defile, and thus into the valley. Picton was to bring 'the 3rd division at daybreak towards Morillas and Subijana, leaving the baggage at Caracamo to follow when ordered'. The reserve artillery was to stay with the baggage, but the Third Division would finish its march about two miles to the north-west of Hill's column. Dalhousie and the Seventh Division, with its baggage, would also march 'at daybreak from Berberana, by Guillerta, Sta. Estella, and Jocano, to Apricano', which would put them some four miles due north of Hill. Finally, Graham was to 'order Major-General Pack's and Major-General Bradford's brigades to Murguia, and will move the remainder of the left column of the army towards the same point as soon as one of the centre divisions of the army reaches Apricano. The Spanish corps of Major-General Girón will move to Orduña.' Graham was being directed to a position on the Bilbao road, well to the north and considerably detached from the rest of the army, with Girón in support ten miles further back. The troops not mentioned in these arrangements, that is to say, the Fourth and Light Divisions, were to remain in their present positions, and headquarters would also remain at Subijana de Morillas.[5]

Although the arrangements directed Picton to Subijana and Morillas, the map clearly indicates that latter must have been intended, since it placed the Third Division between Hill's and Dalhousie's forces rather than bringing it to the position that the Fourth Division was already occupying. Since on the 21st the Third Division, followed by the Seventh Division, would follow a route that took them to Anda, it is obvious that there had been further movement for these two divisions. It is also significant that Graham was to make his movements in concert with Dalhousie.

On the left, Tomkinson, as specific as ever, recorded the movements of Graham's column on the 20th and also gave his own opinion of them.

> The left column marched three leagues [from Jocano] on the banks of the Bayas to Marginia [Murguia]. The brigade was pushed a league on the main road, and occupied for the night Olano, and adjacents. The Spanish infantry under Longa, are a league in our front, and one league only from Vittoria. The enemy made a reconnaissance of them this evening, in which they kept their ground, and a battalion of Caçadores was ordered up close in consequence of the firing. I think we are pushed too far, as the enemy may be aware of our advance on the road, which is the main one from Bilbao to Vittoria, and I fear have seen the officers who went to look at the affair.[6]

Jourdan later admitted that 'reconnaissance in the direction of Margina [Murguia] encountered only some troops from Longa's corps with which they had a weak engagement'.[7] He had failed to recognize that Longa's corps had been deliberately placed at the head of the column and some distance from it to mislead the French into dismissing these troops merely as irregulars acting on their own initiative. Jourdan certainly gives no indication that the reconnaissance party was aware of the presence of British officers.

Jourdan referred to 'a weak engagement', but Captain William Hay of the 12th Light Dragoons told a rather different story.

> The evening before our brigade halted, about six miles from the enemy on the river Bayas, the Spaniards under General [Colonel] Longa, a guerrilla chief, had been sharply engaged during most part of the day.
>
> On our arrival on the encampment ground, I was ordered by General Ponsonby to take with me three men and go and report myself to General Longa, keeping up communications between him and our advance.
>
> On reaching his outposts, I found him still contending with a considerable body of French dragoons, who seemed inclined to force the Spaniards back from the position occupied by them in a small

village close to the river Zadorra, and I made my presence known to the officer in command.

One of the particular directions I received was not to allow myself to be seen by the French troops if I could avoid doing so. However, the enemy kept advancing and the Spaniards retreating in the most shameful way, before their cavalry. By-and-by Colonel Elly, quartermaster-general of the cavalry arrived and did all in his power to rally the Spaniards, and persuade their officers to charge the French on the main road, so as to give the infantry a chance of advancing and taking possession of some stone walls on the outskirts of the village; but all he could say was of no avail, and it appeared very evident that if not checked the Spaniards would be driven back on our pickets. In this moment of great excitement the old colonel turned to me, and asked if I would not take command of the Spanish cavalry, rally them, and drive the enemy back.

There follows a description of how Hay collected 150 Spanish dragoons, gave the command to advance and, with his three men of the 12th very much to the fore, led them forward, whereupon the Spaniards, both officers and men, followed. This charge soon dispersed the French. Hay concluded: 'Nothing but an example was wanting by the Spanish soldiers, who are as brave a set of men as need be, and their officers generally as great cowards as live.'[8]

There are several problems with this colourful account. The identity of the Spanish cavalry that Hay refers is unclear. According to the generally-accepted order of battle the cavalry of Penne Villemur and Julian Sanchez were in Longa's division, yet Sanchez was definitely operating independently. Nor would Hay have been likely to confuse lancers and dragoons. As for Penne Villemur, he had been with Girón earlier in the advance, and since there is no mention of him being on the battlefield the next day, it may be assumed he was still with the Galicians. Furthermore, if we assume that Hay is right and that one or other of these units was with Longa, then allowing for Longa's four infantry battalions, which totalled about 3,000 men, any engagement with such a force would hardly be weak. In addition, Tomkinson's account (above) suggests that Longa coped without assistance, even from the caçadores who were sent forward as a precaution. We may draw the conclusion, therefore, that while Hay was probably one of the officers Tomkinson referred to, and may even have been unable to resist the temptation to get involved, his account suffers from the exaggeration of memory and his own ego. It is a useful reminder that eyewitness accounts, particularly those recalled many years later, should always be treated with caution.

To return to Tomkinson's concern that they had been pushed too far forward, this had some validity. Joseph and Jourdan may have dismissed Longa's men merely as a guerrilla band, but Reille certainly entertained the possibility that Allied forces were on the Bilbao road. He had been given responsibility for protecting the French left flank, as it rested on the Zadorra, since a rupture at this point would jeopardize any French withdrawal. This had already led Reille to change his position and bring his troops closer to the river well behind d'Erlon's position. He had also sent patrols from Digeon's dragoon division to reconnoitre the area beyond Vitoria and to the north of the river, particularly along the Bilbao road. Digeon, who thus encountered Longa, reported back this encounter with s strong Spanish force, which stood its ground when challenged, so that it was the dragoons who retired. This left Reille uneasy, with the result that once again his troops, or at least some of them, found themselves on the move in the middle of the night. Leaving Lamartinière on the left side of the river, in a position from which he could intervene as required, Reille brought Sarrut's division and Curto's light cavalry from Mermet's division across the Zadorra and along the Bilbao road as far as Aranguiz. While the infantry took position in the village, Curto established outposts to their front.

The one Allied unit the French definitely located on their various scouting missions, of which there were many in addition to Digeon's according to d'Espinchal, was Morillo's, but since this position seemed to be occupied only by a small number of tents, it was thought merely to confirm that any Allied advance would come from the far end of the valley. The idea that Wellington was preparing a four-pronged attack certainly did not figure in Jourdan's calculations of how best to mount a strong defence.

The 20th was another excessively wet day, and that, coupled with long marches and short supplies, was enough to depress anyone's spirits. By focusing on a range of comments written on or about the 20th we are able to recognize just how many and varied were the different feelings and expectations on the eve of a battle that not all of them anticipated. John Rous, for example, wrote to his mother during the evening, telling her that 'for the last week we have always marched at 4 o'clock am and not halted on our ground for the night till nearly six o'clock pm, in addition to the pleasure of this we have had an unusual quantity of wet weather and the men have had flour instead of bread, in fact our army never before experienced what we have lately, at this season of the year'. Then, having described recent events, he added somewhat uncharitably: 'The 1st Guards are still at Oporto, where I hope they will remain the whole year; they have seen three retreats and have never seen an advance, we fancy that their appearing is the omen of bad luck.'[9] Rous certainly gave no indication that he believed a battle was imminent, even though he noted how close they now were to the French. He was not alone in expecting the turning movements to continue, a point to remember, perhaps, when assessing the uncertainties entertained by the French with regard to Wellington's intentions.

John Douglas remembered being in what was for him in an oddly negative frame of mind. 'We pursued our march, halted on the 20th to allow the commissary to come up if possible, but no, and as a last shift we were obliged to send out parties through the country to try to collect a little grub. This day was spent in gloomy forebodings and many a long look out for rations, but in vain.'[10] Presumably, the depressed mood was the result of hunger and being soaked but 'gloomy forebodings' certainly suggests some recognition of what lay ahead. Douglas, however, had been serving since 1809, starting with the Walcheren campaign, while Rous, although commissioned in 1810, had only arrived in the Peninsula in the summer of 1812.

George Bell in his later memoirs, based on journals written at the time, shared the retrospective sense of so many of the veterans that they had served in an exceptional army. Thinking back to the previous few days, he asserted that:

> Our army, swelling in numbers, came rushing in from hill and vale and valley, like roaring streams from every defile, foaming into the basin of Vittoria. When the king was conjecturing the quickest way to put the English army hors-de-combat, and at what hour he might consistently partake of the banquet he had ordered in Vittoria, Wellington was making his arrangements to cook him before sunset.

In contrast, 'We little knew of what was to come the following day, except from our men, who were fixing their flints, chaffing and talking of the "frog-eaters" who could not be far off. They said they nosed them from their backie and inions. I declined the tent accommodation, and slept soundly on the sod.'[11] This despite the fact that he had suffered a serious attack of the ague that day.

Hill's column, in which Bell served, were no better supplied than the rest of the Allied force, particularly his Portuguese troops. Indeed, Hill earned an unusually sharp rebuke from Wellington when he sought permission to feed them, since they were consistently worse supplied than the British. Wellington had issued specific orders that the attached Spanish and Portuguese corps must supply themselves, but starving soldiers would not be the most effective men to lead into battle. The division in question was Silveira's which, as Hill pointed out, 'for some days have been on very reduced rations. The day before yesterday they had only three quarters of a pound of meat and yesterday nothing, and have no prospect for this day. To give them bread, I am aware, is out of the question but I beg to know whether your Lordship will permit me to give them some meat.'[12]

Wellington's reply was curt and to the point: 'You may assist the Conde d'Amarante as you please, but let the Conde know that it is an exception to a rule to which I am determined to adhere, and that he must make his commissaries exert themselves.'[13] Wellington knew very well that the problem did not originate with the commissaries, but rules were rules.

David Robertson of the 92nd also spent a hungry night, ignorant of how close they were to the French.

> On the afternoon of the 20th, we halted for the night; and as Lord Wellington always kept every movement secret from the army, we were not aware of the proximity of the enemy – there being only a range of mountains between the two armies. There was one disagreeable circumstance that frequently took place during our campaigns. Whenever the army had to make a rapid march, some way or other, the Commissary always wanted the means of getting the bread conveyed to us; and it often happened on this march, as well as on former ones, that when we came within a short distance of the enemy, we were generally two days' bread deficient.[14]

Meat was always available because, in effect, it marched with the army but meat without bread made for a poor repast.

A brigadier who had the comfort of his troops at heart, though, could sometimes find a way to offer some consolation for the shortages. Even if he could not supply bread, there were other things that also mattered greatly to many of the soldiers. Such a man was Lieutenant Colonel the Honourable Henry Cadogan, in command of the first brigade of the Second Division. 'We continued to advance until the 20th of June; when reaching the neighbourhood of Vittoria, we encamped upon the face of a hill. Provisions were very scarce. We had not a bit of tobacco, and were smoking leaves and herbs. Colonel Cadogan rode away, and got us half a pound of tobacco a man, which was most welcome.'[15]

As the arrangements made clear, the Fourth and Light Divisions, under Cole's command, were spared a march on the 20th because they were already in the position Wellington's strategy required of them. There were still duties to be performed, of course, and a hussar officer recorded how 'we visited the outposts that evening, which were held by a brigade of Portuguese dragoons, closely supported by the 4th division. When we got to the picquet, a flag of truce, as it turned out to be, had come to the outposts, and driven in the vedettes. The Portuguese had made a proper kettle of fish of it', as will be seen.[16]

John Blakiston certainly appreciated a day's rest from marching.

> On the 20th we halted for the first time since we quitted the neighbourhood of Salamanca, having marched 270 miles in eighteen successive days. I am aware that if measured on the map, our march will not appear so long; but then it must be considered that the latter part was through a mountainous country, where the windings of the road always render the actual space traversed much greater than the direct distance between two places. The troops were, of course, a great deal fatigued, and began to evince the usual consequences of a long march in worn out shoes and sore feet; but notwithstanding this, and the privation they had undergone in the scarcity of provisions, they were in high spirits.

He added the proviso that however pleased they were to have the enemy on the run, they would have preferred him to turn and make a stand, a wish that was soon to be granted. Against this, he also made the point that 'To a mind possessing the common feelings of our nature, few things can be more awful than the eve of an expected battle; and I claim no community of feeling with those persons who have not experienced, on these occasions, some awkward sensations about the heart', feelings which kept him awake for the greater part of the night.[17]

Apprehension was a feeling that others also experienced that night. Sergeant William Lawrence of the 1/40th in the Fourth Division had been much impressed by the strength of the French position, which gave them the advantage of high ground, as well as forcing the Allies to cross a river by narrow bridges before any attack could be launched. This had led him to conclude that 'On reconnoitring the enemy's strong position much doubt was entertained as to our success, our army being much fatigued after its tedious march and likewise being very short of provisions. This latter circumstance caused many to set off that night in search of something to eat; but the only thing I with several comrades could find was some broad beans …'[18]

Surtees, being in the Light Division where confidence tended to run high, did not share Lawrence's doubts.

> During the next day, while we halted here, it began to be whispered that the enemy had concentrated his forces in and around Vittoria, which was distant from us about ten or a dozen miles, and that the divisions of our army had that day approached nearer together, which indicated a determination on the part of our Chief to try his hand with King Joseph, should he be bold enough to stay where he then was.
>
> Many, of course, and various would be the reflections which occupied the minds of different individuals, composing the two armies; but I speak from experience, that those are of a much more pleasing nature which a conspicuousness of superiority and a good prospect of success inspires, that those a retreating army are compelled to entertain.[19]

It is no surprise to discover that Dalhousie's column on the centre left was also short of supplies. John Green of the 68th commented somewhat ironically:

> This day [the 20th] we encamped about sixteen miles from Vittoria, and our commissary served out to the brigade a mixture of wheat,

> barley, rye, oats, and straw. We were now put on a level with the horses and mules, for they had the same sort of provisions; but neither the horses nor the mules could eat their corn with greater eagerness than we eat ours. My comrade and I sorted out grain, and then rubbed it between two stones: it thickened our soup, and made it more nourishing.

He added, almost as an afterthought: 'The two armies were now in sight of each other.'[20]

Things were no better in the 51st, but even short commons could be an excuse for some banter with a well-liked officer, in this case Major David Roberts, as Wheeler reported to his family. During the afternoon,

> as he was wont to do, [he] came round our camp to take a peep at the camp kettles. I with some of my comrades were smoking a pipe in our tent when the major peeped saying very good humouredly 'Well my boys have you any bread to give away.' We answered 'we had no bread but if old Bob, meaning his favourite horse, wanted corn we could supply him with plenty.' He smiling replied 'Never mind my lads there is plenty of bread down there' pointing with his stump towards Vittoria. 'And by this time tomorrow we shall have plenty.'

Wheeler was much struck by the fact that within a day 'a half-starved army of British and Portuguese' would have totally defeated 'the soldiers of the "Great Nation," Napoleon's Invincibles'.[21]

While the men in the ranks might ponder what lay ahead, acknowledging or repressing doubts and fears, or simply choosing to live in the hungry moment, for Wellington and his staff there was the important business of reconnoitring. Wellington conducted his own discreet reconnaissance, being careful not to draw attention to himself. Other parties received some unwelcome French attention. Thomas Browne of the Adjutant General's Department noted in his journal that

> The greater part of the Day was passed in reconnoissances on the French position, as they now appeared to have taken one up, as if to stand & fight a battle – They fired on our reconnoitring parties, & resisted the attempts of our picquets to drive in their outposts. Enough had however been observed, to enable Lord Wellington to make his dispositions for attack.[22]

There was one man who could give Wellington information on the French which no reconnaissance party would have been able to obtain. While Andrew Leith Hay had been wandering about the streets of Vitoria, observing the chaos, an aide-de-camp had arrived with a summons from General Count Gazan. Gazan was no longer in Vitoria, so Leith Hay was able to scrutinize the French reserve park of the French armies as he made his way to join the general. 'In point of number I had never seen so many pieces of field artillery assembled, nor can I conceive anything more regular, beautifully arranged, or in better order, than was this very imposing display of cannon.'[23] Leith Hay suspected that he had been meant to see it, because the colonel who was escorting him to Gazan pointedly drew his attention to it before ordering him to be blindfolded, as if the guns were to be his last impression of the imperial army.

When he arrived at Ariñez, he discovered that Gazan, who had spent most of the night of the 19th completing the arrangements for the following day, was still sleeping off his exertions. When he appeared, Leith Hay learnt that a letter had arrived from Wellington, accepting the proposed exchange of prisoners, and assuring the French general that he had already written to require the release of Artillery Captain Cheville. As a result Gazan was happy for Leith Hay to be escorted to the nearest Allied troops. While an escort party was put together, Gazan's staff 'conversed with great cheerfulness and apparent cordiality'. Leith Hay also received an ironic request from the Countess Gazan that, although it was

> an impossible contingency … in the event of her being captured by the allies, that I would exert my good offices to obtain for her a favourable reception. This sally occasioned considerable mirth, which was not diminished upon my departure, an event witnessed by the whole staff. Mounted on a very diminutive horse, my eyes bound up, the appearance of a low and small cocked hat then worn by the British army, and the constant subject of derision in that the enemy, all contributed to complete, in their opinion, a most grotesque figure; nor were the French officers restrained in the mirth thereby drawn forth. They, however, closed the scene by protestations of kindness and good wishes.
>
> … At length, in a valley shaded by trees, a picquet of Portuguese cavalry appeared, upon observing which, the French trumpeter

began to exert his lungs, and a white pocket handkerchief was waved as an emblem of peace. All proved ineffectual; the picquet, alarmed at the array evidently approaching direct to their post, treated with disregard the signals made, and, mounting with precipitation, galloped back, circulating a very unfounded alarm in the infantry camp. Under the circumstances, it became necessary to advance with caution, until we encountered troops inclined to remain, and discover that it was merely a flag of truce paying this unexpected, and apparently, to the Portuguese, not very welcome visit.

Having been handed over to some British staff officers by his French escort, Leith Hay was immediately escorted to headquarters by Sir Lowry Cole.

> An aide-de-camp having communicated my arrival from the enemy's army, I was immediately received by Lord Wellington, and with delight communicated to him the information derived from a residence with the imperial troops. The important fact of the French generals being determined to make a stand in their present position, from every circumstance I considered perfectly decided, and adduced reasons for that opinion.
>
> Having marched with the different armies, obtained information from each, and learned probably more than was intended of their relative situations and numerical strength, my observation, although defective, carried with it a certain authenticity seldom to be derived by a commander-in-chief on the eve of fighting a general action.[24]

A letter from Gazan to Wellington emphasized that he was acting under the agreement they had made, but until the French officer left England Captain Leith Hay must continue his parole. This was a disappointment 'but to have been exchanged under any circumstances was an instance of good fortune', particularly as it was the first such exchange that Wellington had been able to effect. And the parole was observed. Leith Hay spent the battle close to Wellington and there was a moment when the commander-in-chief, looking for someone to carry an urgent message, was about to give it to Leith Hay, only to remember that he could not even perform this duty because of his parole.

Wellington's own reconnaissance had shown him that the French presented all the appearance of an army preparing to stand and fight. Leith

Hay's information confirmed that appearance was not misleading. The Allied commander had already developed his strategy for the following day, and now issued his arrangements, which may be summarised as follows.

Since Hill's column would be the first to attack, it would commence its advance at daybreak to the Great Road near La Puebla, marching in the prescribed order of Morillo's corps, the Second Division and Silveira's Portuguese. Alten's cavalry brigade would follow Morillo, and the rest of the cavalry of the right column, would bring up the rear. Once the column was in more open ground, the cavalry would move out, to be used as circumstances required. Morillo's corps was to ascend the high ground (the Puebla Heights) in order to turn the enemy's left flank, while being careful to maintain contact with the rest of the column.

The Light Division was also to move at daybreak, initially following the course of the Bayas through the pass that led to Subijana, and then making for the camp of the Fourth Division and on to Nanclares. A squadron of the 15th Hussars would act as the advanced guard, while the rest of the cavalry and Major Gardiner's horse artillery would follow the infantry. Once the Light Division had passed their camp, the Fourth Division would follow the rest of the hussars, while being followed in turn by the 18th and 10th Hussars. Bringing up the rear was the reserve artillery, General Ponsonby's brigade and the Household Brigade. This column was to march to its left and, upon approaching Nanclares, await further orders. Wellington had already decided to attach himself to the centre-right column, for reasons which become clear once the course of the battle is considered.

There was a separate order for D'Urban and his Portuguese cavalry, who were to advance some distance to the right of the road and move forward towards the Zadorra in parallel to the Light Division as it neared Nanclares.

As for the centre-left column, the Third Division, followed by the Seventh Division, were also to march at daybreak to their left, advancing to Anda and then, turning to their right, to Los Guetos. From there detachments were to be sent towards Nanclares on the right to establish communications with similar detachments from the centre-right column. A further order, which was undoubtedly an unpleasant surprise to General Picton, put Dalhousie in command of the column. Both men had been gazetted major general on the same day in 1808, but Dalhousie had subsequently advanced to lieutenant general. For Picton, with a far more impressive Peninsular record, this slur on his reputation, as he undoubtedly interpreted it, explains his later loss of temper when he found himself hamstrung by Dalhousie's apparently dilatory behaviour.[25]

The left column was to move by the left from Murguia towards Vitoria. Graham was to establish communications as soon as possible with the column to his right, with Los Guetos as the point of contact, while the Third and Seventh Divisions would do the same towards Murguia when they approached Los Guetos.

There then followed a further order which seems to have created some ambiguity in Graham's mind:

> The movements of the Earl of Dalhousie and Sir Thomas Graham's columns are to be regulated from the right; and although those columns are to make such movements in advance as may be evidently necessary to favour the progress of the two columns on their right, they are not, however, to descend into the low ground towards Vitoria or the great road, nor give up the advantage of turning the enemy's positions and the town of Vitoria by a movement to their left.

The centre left would reach the Zadorra after a difficult advance and from a considerable distance while Graham would be much closer from the start and following an easier route. Yet, as he interpreted the order, he was to avoid becoming engaged in the vicinity of the town, and certainly to make no move unless it was co-ordinated with Dalhousie's.

Finally, Girón was ordered to march to Murguia and wait there for further orders. These subsequently brought him to the battlefield, but not until too late to have any effect on the action.[26]

To sum up, from right to left, Hill's column would make the first move by crossing the Zadorra at Puebla de Aranzon and then focus on the Heights and the villages on the lower slopes. Cole, having come to Nanclares, would judge his next move by Hill's progress. This would bring him across the Zadorra, in position to attack the right of the Army of the South. Dalhousie, having debouched into the valley and crossed the river, would be able to strike at Margarita, the pivotal point of the three French armies. Finally, Graham's advance would put the left column in position to block the Great Road, which was the French escape route.

Thus, for the Allies, a victory depended upon the synchronization of the four widely-separated columns. For the French, outnumbered by a force of 75,000 men, only standing their ground and repulsing, or at least holding off, the enemy could bring any kind of success, even if it was that of a safe withdrawal.

Chapter 6

The Waterloo of the Peninsula: the Battle of Vitoria

The Day Begins

The Allied bugles sounded before daybreak on 21 June, rousing the troops to a wet, dark morning. As dawn broke and the army prepared for battle, the clouds would disperse, giving way to warmth and sunshine. As ever though, food was the immediate concern. At Murguia, both Hale and Douglas were relieved to receive a ration of bread, 'half a pound for each man, but nothing else, but however, that with a drop of good water was very acceptable, for we had been without bread for three days'.[1] Douglas noted that it had arrived in the nick of time because before it could be divided up the order to stand to arms was given. He and his comrade decided to save half for when they camped for the night, a resolution that they abandoned when they realized there would be plenty when the battle was over – for whoever survived. 'On this the bread underwent a plunge bath in the stream, which caused it to go down a little quicker and easier and this concluded our repast in strong hopes of a second course in a short time.'[2] An interesting synthesis of realism and optimism.

Less fortunate was Robertson, with Hill's column. 'Some flour was procured in a village near the camp, and the bakers were set to work to prepare it for food; but just as they were wetting the flour, the divisions were ordered to fall in, and of course the bakers had to desist.'[3] He was far from the only one who would march into battle on an empty stomach. Nor were their opponents replete with supplies, the convoy having already consumed much of what was to be found in Vitoria.

Charles Cadell of the 28th, also in Hill's column, may or may not have eaten that morning but he remembered how a staff officer recommended them '"to get our breakfast and have our baggage packed as soon as possible."'

The Waterloo of the Peninsula: the Battle of Vitoria 111

> There was an unusual scene of bustle in the bivouack; but what most convinced us that some work was to be done, was when we saw the favourite black charger, fully caparisoned, of our chief, Sir Rowland Hill, (who was always cool in action as on a field-day) and the chestnut of Sir William Stewart, the brave leader of the British division of Hill's corps, whose soldier-like manner, when calmly, in the hottest fire, giving his orders, with his usual lisp, and gently switching the mane of his horse with a white cane, must be remembered by all who served under him.[4]

Another officer alerted to the certainty of action was August Schaumann of the Commissariat. He was personally acquainted with Colonel Miguel Álava, the Spanish military attaché. At dawn, while Schaumann was still drunk with sleep, Wellington and his staff rode past, out early to reconnoitre. Álava halted for a moment.

> 'Schaumann, hurry up and get mounted, there will be interesting things to see to-day. This morning Lord Wellington is thinking of making a heavy attack upon King Joseph, who is said to have taken up a strong position with his whole army in front of Vittoria. If he makes a stand there, it will be a great battle.'
>
> I dressed quickly, and after issuing the necessary orders to my staff, had breakfast. The whole bivouac was busy preparing to move, but no-one knew whither. I rode in the direction that Lord Wellington had taken, and soon found myself on the slope of some rocky heights. Below I could see a long and narrow valley covered with cornfields, and broken by plantations, clefts, ravines and villages, but the town of Vittoria was not visible, as it lay concealed behind another range of hills. In the clefts of the rocky slope on which I was standing I noticed a number of red patches, the odd appearance of which struck me as rather curious. But when I looked through my field glasses I recognised them as a brigade of infantry, who were sitting quietly on their knapsacks under cover, waiting for orders.

Schaumann also had a good view of the French.

> On the dominating height on the right of the French centre [the Knoll of Ariñez], there fluttered a large white flag. It marked the

spot where French headquarters, and consequently, King Joseph, were posted. It is an imposing sight to behold a strong enemy army in order of battle. Lines and columns are in process of formation. Generals and aide-de-camps gallop busily up and down the dark lines, and here and there a gun is fired as a signal.[5]

One of the escort who accompanied Wellington on his reconnaissance was the dragoon officer who subsequently wrote *The British Cavalry on the Peninsula*, his squadron having been designated for the task. Wellington galloped past them and drew close, almost too close, to the French vedettes posted on the Zadorra.

> The first shot fired that day was at his lordship. As the day cleared Lord Wellington repaired to an eminence, from which the posts and most part of the French position could be seen. The covering squadron of course followed, and the writer had the satisfaction of sitting within a few yards of the great chief during the whole time he was directing the attack.[6]

Thomas Browne, another who was close to Wellington throughout the action, later recorded in his journal that on the 21st,

> the Day broke beautifully – a bright Sun & clear sky, which as the dawn advanced shewed the glittering arms of the French on the same position as had been occupied by them yesterday. They were under arms, & Officers galloping about in all directions with here & there a group, as if assembling round some Chief & receiving his directions – All being prepared, the British got the order to attack every part of the enemy's line about eight o'clock.[7]

Since Hill's column would be the first to go into action, it was the first to leave its bivouac. By 7.30 am the Second Division, Morillo's Spanish corps and Silveira's Portuguese had reached the high road to Vitoria. For Moyle Scherer, it was an experience not to be forgotten. The troops, having marched through the village of Puebla,

> amid the *vivas* of the inhabitants, with our music playing and colours flying, we, in half an hour more, halted in the presence of the French army, which was formed in order of battle, on a position of great strength … The battle array of a large army is a most noble and

1. The Marquis of Wellington. (*Royal Military Chronicle*)

2. Major General Sir Rowland Hill, commander of the Allied right column. (*Royal Military Chronicle*)

3. General Sir Thomas Graham, commander of the Allied left column. (*Royal Military Chronicle*)

4. Joseph Bonaparte, King of Spain. (*Author's collection*)

5. Marshal Jean-Baptiste Jourdan, French chief of staff. (*Author's collection*)

6. General Honoré Charles Reille, commander of the Army of Portugal. (*Author's collection*)

7. General Count Honoré Théodore Gazan, commander of the Army of the South. (*Author's collection*)

8. General Jean-Baptiste Drouet, Count d'Erlon, commander of the Army of the Centre. (*Author's collection*)

9 & 10. Two views of the battlefield of Vitoria from opposite sides of the valley. (*Private collection*)

11. The battlefield of Vitoria as depicted by Andrew Leith Hay. (*Author's collection*)

12. The bridge at Tres Puentes. (*Author's collection*)

13. The Battle of Vitoria (Heath and Sutherland). (*Private collection*)

14. The Death of Colonel Cadogan (J. Atkinson/Ackerman's Lithography). (*Courtesy of Colonel Henry Cadogan*)

15. The Fifth Division at Gamarra Mayor. (*Private collection*)

16. Allied artillery at Vitoria. (*Private collection*)

17. The Battle of Vitoria, final stages of the action (F.C. Lewis). (*Private collection*)

18. Memorial to the Allied victory at Vitoria. (*Author's collection*)

imposing sight. To see the hostile lines and columns formed, and prepared for action; to observe their generals and mounted officers riding smartly from point to point, and to mark every now and then, one of their guns opening on your own staff, reconnoitring them, is a scene very animating, and a fine prelude to a general engagement. On your own side, too, the hammering of flints and loosening of cartridges; the rattle of guns and tumbrils, as they come careering up to take their appointed stations; and the swift galloping of aid-de-camps in every direction, here bringing reports to their generals, there conveying orders to the attacking columns, all speak of peril and death, but also of anticipated victory; and so cheeringly, that a sensation of proud hope swells the bosom, which is equal, if not superior to the feeling of exultation in the secure moment of pursuit and triumph.[8]

These final thoughts were obviously retrospective in the context of Vitoria. Yet in a campaign that had very much proceeded to the Allies' advantage, there can be little doubt that Wellington was in command of troops, British, German, Portuguese and Spanish, some battle-hardened veterans, others new to the game, who had confidence in their commander and in their own abilities. At this point, they were still the fine army of Wellington's proud claim, so far removed from the rabble that had staggered back to Portugal nearly eight months before.

The Allies were not alone in these early-morning activities. The first notable activity on 21 June on the French side, apart from Reille's change of position in the middle of the night, was the departure of Maucune's division as the escort for the second convoy of refugees and the spoils of occupation. They set off at about 3 am for Pamplona. A few hours later, in fine drizzle which soon gave way to sunshine, Joseph and Jourdan, who had now recovered from his brief indisposition, carried out the reconnaissance that had been postponed from the previous day. They rode to Zuazo, from where they could survey the valley and their dispositions. From their perspective, their left rested on what Jourdan subsequently described as a chain of mountains, in other words the Heights of Puebla, and their right extended to the Zadorra. There was one particularly notable elevation, extending from the Great Road to the Zadorra. Jourdan believed that it would have been better crowned with guns than deploying them at Ariñez, or at Aranguiz, up on the Bilbao road. Jourdan also claimed in his memoirs that Reille certainly believed that Aranguiz would not receive serious attention, despite Longa's probing the previous day. Impressed by the potential strength of this ridge, Joseph, presumably prompted by his chief of staff, decided that it should be occupied by the Army of the South, while the Army of the Centre should occupy an indeterminate position between the Army of the South and the Army of Portugal. With d'Erlon's right on the Zadorra, near Yurre, the gap between him and Reille, which was disturbingly wide, would be closed. If the three corps were concentrated in this manner, they would not only each be more secure, but any one would be able to come to the support of the others. It would also facilitate the effective command of the different armies once the battle started.

As Jourdan commented in his memoirs, if these new dispositions had been taken up the previous day (as they probably would have been but for the marshal's sickness), they might well have prevented the catastrophe that eventually overtook the French. Gazan had already informed Joseph that he thought the enemy was on the move, even before the king had begun his reconnaissance. Now, when he received the order to change position, he sent the emissary back with the message that it was too late to change his dispositions because it was obvious Allied troops were coming into the valley and he expected to be attacked at any moment. As a result, Leval remained on the high ground in front of Ariñez. When Joseph rode up, Leval also informed him that the Allies (presumably the first sighting of Cole's column) were on the move. This and his own observations justified Gazan's reluctance to move, particularly as the new position would isolate the troops he had posted on the Heights of Puebla.

To return to Jourdan's claim that Reille was not expecting action at Aranguiz, it has to be questioned why he should have placed one of his two divisions there (Maucune having already departed with the second convoy). Sarrut's division held the village and had also extended to the right to occupy some higher ground. From this position they could intercept any movement to either Ariaga or Gamarra Mayor. Since Reille had posted Lamartinière and his cavalry, in which he was strong, on the Vitoria side of the Zadorra, he would seem to have been preparing to resist an attack along the Bilbao road, or to move in support of the Army of the Centre, should the need arise.

Joseph and Jourdan now rode forward to the Knoll of Ariñez, which would be their vantage point for much of the battle. Scouts were coming in to confirm that the enemy was now well past the Zadorra and the village of Puebla. As Leval had suspected, further reports indicated that a large body of men was advancing towards Nanclares and Villodas. In other words, the Allied attack had been building up while the king and his chief of staff were still trying to improve a faulty defensive position.[9] But at least the attack, for such it undoubtedly was, was coming from the direction that the French command had anticipated, that is to say, from the south-west by way of the passes at Puebla de Alanzon and south of the Sierra de Arrato. This was further confirmed when Maransin reported that the column on the right had divided in two, with one part keeping to the lower ground while the other was heading for the Heights. Despite Joseph and Jourdan's hope that they would not have to fight before the arrival of Clausel, a battle was about to be forced on them.

In d'Espinchal's opinion, the battle was lost before the French had fired a single shot. The day was to prove one of the most damaging to the French armies in Spain, and the disaster had to be attributed to the bad dispositions and obstinacy of Marshal Jourdan, who refused to respect the observations of the generals. Instead, he continued to defend a defective position, which would have been difficult for an army three times as strong to hold. 'How otherwise could an army of elite troops, fighting with such energy and courage, lose so comprehensively? Because of the improvidence of one man.'[10]

Presumably d'Espinchal did not know of, or chose to ignore, Jourdan's sickness the previous day. If there was one man responsible for the defective position, then it was Joseph Bonaparte. It was unfortunate that both he and Jourdan had shared the complacent belief that no Allied attack was imminent; although it has to be conceded that Wellington himself had helped to feed that belief. Yet it may be assumed that if Jourdan, at least, had realized that Wellington was very much in attacking mode, he would have reconnoitred at daybreak, which would have allowed time for Gazan's change of position.

The specific defects in the French position also need to be considered. Sir Charles Oman was particularly scathing in his assessment, pointing out that, it was as well known to every practical soldier then as it is now, that a normal river-position cannot be held by a continuous line of troops placed at the water's edge. For there will be loops and bends at which the ground on one side is commanded and enfiladed by higher ground on the enemy's side. If troops are pushed forward into such bends, they will be crushed by artillery fire, or run danger of being cut off by attacks on the neck of the loop in their rear. Unless the general who has to defend a river front is favoured with a stream in front of him absolutely straight, and with all the commanding ground on his own side (an unusual chance), he must rather look to arranging his army in such a fashion as to hold as strong points all the favourable sections of the front, while the unfavourable ones must be watched from suitable positions drawn back from the water's edge.[11]

Oman pointed out that the judicious positioning of artillery and equally judicious strengthening of all the defensive points, such as villages and woods, even the preparation of trenches, although it would not prevent the enemy from crossing the river, would facilitate effective counter-attacks. Perhaps even more telling is his reference to bridges and fords. No bridges had been destroyed, although some barriers had been erected. As a result, the bridge at Villodas was to prove a particular problem. No accurate identification of fords had been undertaken. If further evidence were needed that an attack was not expected, or that it would be delayed fortuitously until Clausel arrived the following day to swing the balance in favour of the French, this neglect provides it.

According to Leith Hay, the French had made some effort to place their guns in the most advantageous positions, and then defend them by forcing the local peasants to labour through the night of the 19th on temporary field works. Their main concern, however, seems to have been to protect the vital route from Burgos to Bayonne, but from the direction of Burgos rather than from Bilbao. Wellington was equally aware of the significance of this route to the French and of the effect it would have on their options if it were blocked. That would be the task of Graham's column, of course, and, as noted, the purpose of sending Longa forward on the Bilbao road to convince them that only a party of guerrillas was operating in that area. The result was that Reille alone suspected there could be more troops behind the Spaniards, although it is debatable whether even he appreciated the strength of the force that was advancing on his depleted corps, positioned as it was to hold a front that extended more than two miles.

Hill Opens the Ball

Cadell had noticed that Hill's favourite horse was being saddled up ready for action and had drawn his own conclusions. For Thomas Howell of the 71st, in the ranks, recognition of the day's significance came gradually.

> Next morning, we got up as usual. The first pipes played for parade; the second did not play at the usual time. We began to suspect all was not right. We remained thus until eleven o'clock [in fact, very much earlier]; then received orders to fall in, and follow the line of march. During our march we fell to one side, to allow a brigade of guns to pass us at full speed. 'Now,' said my comrades, 'we will have work to do before night.' We crossed a river; and, as we passed through a village, we saw, on the other side of the road, the French camp, and their fires still burning, just as they had left them. Not a shot had been fired at this time. We observed a large Spanish column marching along the heights on our right. We halted, and drew up in column. Orders were given to brush out our locks, oil them, and examine our flints.[12]

Hill's column actually left their bivouacs soon after 5 am, crossed the Zadorra and marched through the Puebla de Aranzon defile to the village of La Puebla. Here they halted for a careful inspection of arms and ammunition. At this point, John Patterson of the 50th tells us,

> ... the sudden apparition of an aid-de-camp arrested our attention. This important person, riding up to Colonel Cameron, who was on our right, a conference ensued between them, when presently the cry of 'Halt!' resounded from one flank to the other. We were in full march at the time, and had passed a narrow bridge that crossed the little river Zadorra.
>
> Half an hour unravelled the wondrous mystery, and told us what the noise was all about. Notes of preparation responded to

commands; ramrods ringing, snapping locks, and hammering flints, hinted rather plainly as to the nature of the business in which we were about to be engaged.[13]

Colonel Cadogan also instructed his brigade, of which the 50th were the senior regiment, that they should now strictly observe silence both on the march and when they went into action. Only when they received an order to charge should they cheer. Once the enemy had been overwhelmed, they were to observe silence again.

The 71st would be the first into action, so James Hope of the 92nd, the third battalion of Cadogan's brigade, had time to ruminate over the scene before him. He noted how,

> the left of the French army occupied in force the Heights of Puebla. The centre the village of Subujana de Álava. Their centre right was posted on a height, which commanded the valley of Zadora. The height was crowned with infantry, flanked, and otherwise defended by at least 100 pieces of cannon. A little further to the right there was a thick wood, the importance of which was not overlooked by the enemy. Some battalions of infantry were posted in it, to keep the communication open between the troops of the right centre and right wing, which extended to some distance beyond Vitoria. To the left of the centre there was another wood, the skirts of which were lined with cannon, and numerous bodies were from time to time thrown into it. In short, their position and numbers were truly formidable; but neither of these circumstances tended to depress the spirits of our soldiers.[14]

What Hope could see was, for the most part, the Army of the South, with some suggestion of the other troops beyond.

Hill now sent forward Morillo's Spaniards and the 1/71st, along with the light companies of the two British brigades of the Second Division, led by Cadogan. Their task was to ascend the western end of the Heights, which were occupied in force by French light infantry. It was no easy ascent. The Heights

> consisted of a precipitous mountain ridge, of considerable elevation; and upon the summit of which, the space for operations was so confined as hardly affording compass for the troops to move in sections.

> To the eastward, the hill was scarped in such a way, as to be nearly perpendicular with the valley; while, on the western slope, where the ground was not so steep, it was broken into deep and hollow chasms, inaccessible even to the riflemen [of the 5/60th], who found it a task of no small difficulty, to thread the mazes of the tangled brushwood at the top, tumbling every now and then upon the sharp-edged fragments of the rocks, very much to the detriment of their heads and limbs. Even upon the apex of the range, our footing was painfully uncertain; our men got many an upset into holes, that lay like traps or pitfalls in our way.[15]

This account by Patterson relates to the troops that subsequently followed the Spaniards and the 71st, but the natural difficulties of the ascent remained the same. Add to this the wild broom, sprouting oaks and other hardy plants which grew on the Heights and it is easy to grasp why this was such unsuitable terrain for military action.

The 71st and the light companies were on the left and led the advance, while Morillo's Spaniards were to the right of them. As the troops clambered up, the Spaniards made better progress and were the first to engage with the enemy, enjoying considerable success as they put pressure on the French voltigeurs. Indeed, there was considerable praise for Morillo and his men, particularly from Patterson.

> These hardy fellows cleared everything before them, pressing their adversaries onward from the rising grounds that branch away from the base of the Sierra de La Puebla, to the bottom of the valley. Volumes of smoke, and a loud rattle of musketry echoing from these hills, proclaimed in a very convincing manner with what obstinacy they fought. *Morillo* himself was there – that was quite enough. The man's whole existence was one of danger and desperate enterprise, in all their wild variety. He was no stranger to the ground whereon he was then performing; familiar with the duties of a well-tried soldier, and long inured, as well as to brave the most perilous undertakings, he could not be employed in a business more congenial to his feelings.[16]

Morillo, according to Patterson, was a fighter through and through and a man who inspired total loyalty. Even when he later received a serious wound, he refused to leave his troops. There can be little doubt that Hill, who knew him well, appreciated that he and his 'hardy fellows' were the ideal harbingers of what the French were about to receive. But Morillo did not have the strength of numbers to overwhelm their opponents, particularly when Jourdan, realizing what was happening, ordered Gazan in Joseph's name to send Maransin's brigade to reinforce the voltigeurs. By this time, though, the 71st and the light companies were also on the summit, piped on their way to the tune of 'Hey Johnny Cope'.

This attack, combined with that of the rampant Spanish, forced the French voltigeurs to give ground. With the western end of the Heights in Allied hands, the two remaining battalions of Cadogan's brigade, the 1/50th and the 1/92nd, prepared to ascend the Heights by much the same route as the 71st. They were under the command of Colonel John Cameron of the 1/92nd, who would soon find himself in full command of the brigade, Colonel Cadogan having been wounded early in the struggle. His determination to remain near his men of the 71st rather than be carried to the surgeons has become one of the most famous images of the battle.

> Their commanding officer, the Honourable Lieutenant Colonel Henry Cadogan, fell mortally wounded while leading his men to the charge, and being unable to accompany the battalion requested to be carried to a neighbouring eminence, from which he might take a last farewell of them and the field. In his dying moments he anxiously enquired if the French were beaten; on being told that they had given way at all points, he ejaculated, 'God bless my brave countrymen.' And immediately expired.[17]

At the same time, Maransin's brigade, the only brigade of the 5th Division of the Army of the South on the battlefield, had ascended the heights to join the voltigeurs, to be replaced behind Subijana de Álava by St Pol's brigade from Darricau's division. Gazan, however, had failed to implement Jourdan's order to the full. Maransin's brigade was supposed to have been supported by a division, presumably Villatte's, since it was being held as a reserve. As a result, Maransin's troops were now under as much pressure as the voltigeurs, who were falling back on them.

If the French were forced off the Heights, there would be nothing to stop the Allies from advancing to the end of the ridge and then turning northwards towards Vitoria, which would enable them to drive both

Gazan's and d'Erlon's forces to the Zadorra. By this time Jourdan knew that as well as the enemy troops at Nanclares and Villodas, there was another body at Mendoza. The Armies of the South and Centre would be caught in a pincer movement. Furthermore, the Allies would also be able to cut the road to Logroño, which would endanger Clausel. As a precaution, therefore, against the possibility that Allied troops might be advancing along this road, Jourdan sent Tilly's dragoons to reconnoitre, and then ordered Cassagne, from the Army of the Centre, to follow Tilly and take position near the village of Berostigueta. To strengthen the position on the Heights he sent Jean-Pierre Rey's brigade from Conroux's division to support Maransin, while St Pol prepared for an attack on Subijana.

The orders received by the 50th and 92nd caused some confusion as the two battalions ascended the steep incline. Hope of the 92nd vividly described what happened. Although his later version[18] is more coherent, as one might expect, the letter he wrote to his friend six days after the battle undoubtedly conveys more accurately the experience as it was lived.

> During these operations, the 50th and 92nd were ordered to support the attack on the heights. These troops had nearly gained the summit, when they received an order to return. We had descended about half-way, when a third order arrived, for the 50th regiment to proceed to their first destination, and the 92nd to attack a French battalion of infantry, posted on a ridge a little in their front, and which acted as a corps of communication between the troops of the left wing and those in the wood to the left of the centre.
>
> Through fields of wheat, which rose above many men – over ditches thickly lined on each side with thorns and briers, the 92nd regiment marched to meet their foes. Having arrived at the foot of the ridge on which the enemy had been posted, the Highlanders were ordered to load, and prepare to charge. With a firm pace they ascended, every moment expecting to be met by their antagonists: – conceive, then, their surprise, when, on arriving at the top of the ridge, they found that the enemy had precipitously retired to another during their advance.
>
> Two Spanish guns having, by great exertion, been got to a position on the right of the 92nd, that regiment was ordered to form close column, and cover them. These soon drew on the regiment the heavy

fire from a battery which the enemy had planted on the left of the wood, and which caused it the loss of a serjeant and several privates.

The enemy, who, till now had not discovered the importance of the heights they had lost, detached about 7,000 men from the centre to re-take them. This movement brought on a series of severe skirmishes, which in the end proved extremely ruinous to the enemy.[19]

Far from not recognizing the importance of the Heights, Jourdan had simply not expected an attack along them. Once he was aware that the Allies had not only ascended them but were pushing back the troops posted there, he first sent the order to Gazan to reposition Maransin's brigade, and then to send in St Pol's brigade, as already noted. The position had become increasingly critical, though, so he did what Gazan should have done and ordered Villatte's 3rd Division of the Army of the South, presently positioned at Gomecha, to move to the eastern end of the Heights by way of Esquivel, which would prevent any sudden attack on him, and stop Hill's advance. These were the troops Hope identified, and whom Thomas Howell met at much closer quarters.

The 71st and Morillo's Spaniards had reached a ravine which bisected the ridge and had with difficulty climbed down and then up the opposite slope. Four companies were detached from the 71st and posted among the rocks. They then became aware of 'a heavy column, dressed in greatcoats, with white covers on their hats, exactly resembling the Spanish'. But these newcomers were not Spanish; they were some of Villatte's troops who now

> gave us a volley, which put us to the right about at double quick time down the hill, the French close behind, through the whins [dialect for furze or gorse]. The four companies got the word, the French were on them. They likewise thought them Spaniards, until they got a volley that killed or wounded almost every one of them. We retired to the height, covered by the 50th, who gave the pursuing column a volley that checked their speed. We moved up the remains of our shattered battalion to the heights.[20]

Hope's account takes the encounter a little further.

A very deep ravine runs between the two heights, from the bottom of which, to where the 50th were posted, the ascent was extremely abrupt. – To this point the 71st were retreating, and the 92nd advancing. To this point the march of the enemy's columns was also directed, and they had attained to within a few yards of the summit when the 92nd arrived. By their great superiority, the enemy had succeeded in turning the left wing of the 71st, and had cut off its communication with the 50th. This was the existing state of affairs when the 92nd entered the lists, whose presence on the right of the 50th restored every thing to its former state – the united efforts of the three regiments, under the direction of the Highland Chief [Colonel Cameron], compelled the assailants to seek for safety in a precipitous flight.[21]

Although the troops had been given the usual sixty rounds of ammunition, by this stage of the action the 71st in particular had virtually exhausted their supply, which demonstrates the intensity of the fighting. Richard Heneghan of the Field Train was now ordered to replenish the troops' cartouche boxes, a duty he would have to carry out a second time. He would later reflect on the vast amount of ammunition expended during the battle compared to the relatively light casualties, calculating that over three million rounds had been fired to kill or wound some 8,000 of the French.[22]

Villatte's troops would regroup and return to the attack at least twice more, but with no greater success, and thus, as David Robertson concluded his account of the part played by the 92nd, 'having secured our right, and prevented the enemy from extending farther, we had little more to do, save to watch the movements of the French'.[23] Hill had attained his first objective, which was to secure the Heights of Puebla.

As Patterson tells us, they were indeed spectators. By the time the Allied position on the Heights was secure, other Allied columns were in action; and

> raised far above the plain on which the hostile enemies were contesting, we had almost a bird's eye view of the whole field of action, spread out, as it were, like a map beneath our feet. The reverberation of the artillery among the rocks, by which we were surrounded, the echo of the continued rolling of musketry, the confused noise and din of the battle's turmoil, the varied bright and polished arms, accoutrements,

and trappings of the combatants, as they shone resplendent in the rays of a brilliant sun, – the rapid movement of the Cavalry to and fro, – the manoeuvring of the infantry, together with an endless variety of circumstances connected with the pomp of war, formed on the whole a scene of awful grandeur, unrivalled by anything that the imagination of man could fancy.[24]

To retrace the course of events as they involved Hill's column, when the first brigade was sent to engage the French on the Heights, the second and third brigades, under Brigadiers John Byng and Richard O'Callaghan, remained on the far side on the Puebla defile. As the action on the Heights intensified and it was obvious that Gazan was under orders to send more troops to stop the Allied advance, Hill reciprocated by sending O'Callaghan's brigade forward to put pressure on the Army of the South. They advanced about a league at double-quick time. Then, having passed through the defile, they were permitted some breathing space before being ordered to wheel to the right and advance along the lower slopes to the village of Subijana de Álava, where the two battalions of St Pol's brigade, the 21eme légère and the 100eme de la ligne, from Darricau's 6th Division, were defending the village. Most of them were posted in strength a little to its rear, taking advantage of the cover offered by the woods that lay behind Subijana. The British troops forced their way into the village, where they found themselves under fire from the guns of Conroux's division. According to Captain Moyle Scherer of the 34th, there were fourteen in total but they had little effect. He had also expected the French to put up a strong resistance.

> I could never persuade myself that they would resign so important a post as the village without a struggle; and when we got close to it, and began to find the ground difficult and intersected with walls and banks, I expected every moment to be saluted with a murderous discharge of musquetry, and to see them issue forth; and I had prepared my men to look for, and disregard such an attack. Not a soul, however, was in the village, but a wood a few hundred yards to its left, and the ravines above it, were filled with light infantry. I, with my company, was soon engaged in smart skirmishing among the ravines, and lost about eleven men, killed and wounded, out of thirty-eight.[25]

According to both Charles Cadell of the 1/28th and George Bell of the 2/34th, the French made several attempts to take possession of the village, all of which were repulsed. The latter, in a retrospective account which undoubted bears little resemblance to the feelings of this young ensign on the day, described the fierce fighting in the churchyard, so that

> some open graves were soon filled up with double numbers; indeed, churches and churchyards were always a favourite resort for this peculiar amusement. They were places of strength, and contended for accordingly; and here our battle raged with more violence and contention. We had possession – nine-tenths of the law in battle – but, hardly pressed front and flank, I thought we had killed more of our neighbours here than was needful; but as they cared little for life in their excitement, they would be killed. As Colonel Brown said, 'If you don't kill them, boys, they'll kill you; fire away.'[26]

It would be interesting to know what Bell wrote in the journal upon which his memoirs were based.

The adversaries who launched the counter-attacks were the 55eme and 58eme de la ligne of Schwitter's brigade, and the contest took on the pendulum swing that so often happens in such contests. Rey's brigade, the other brigade of Conroux's 4th Division, was also drawn into the fight, until a stalemate was reached which held up O'Callaghan's brigade, but also pinned down an appreciable number of French troops. Byng's brigade and Silveira's Portuguese were now sent to join O'Callaghan's battalions, although Hill decided that rather than forcing the issue he would hold the ground he had gained and wait upon the events that were happening elsewhere.

The Arrival of the Centre Columns

The movements of General Cole's centre-right column, comprising the Fourth and Light Divisions supported by most of the Allied cavalry, very much depended on Hill's progress to the right and the effect it had on the French. Ideally, it would lead to the enemy drawing in troops to counter the threat that Hill posed, which would be the measure of Hill's success. Weakening the right of the Army of the South would render it vulnerable to the advance of Cole's command.

Both of Cole's divisions were brought forward ahead of time, ready for the moment when they would start to put pressure on Leval's division, now at some distance from the other divisions, which had been drawn towards the Heights by Hill's movements. Once they had left their own encampment, the troops of the Light Division passed through the camp of the Fourth Division, who would soon follow them. They marched through Subijana de Morillo and other villages until they ascended some rising ground, which allowed them to assess the French position from the perspective of their own. Somewhat helped by the benefit of hindsight, John Blakiston recognized that

> the position of their wings [the Armies of the South and Portugal] was strong; but the only strength of their centre consisted in the river and in a height about half gun-shot from it, which commanded the valley for some distance. Their reserve was judiciously posted in the rear of their centre, on some heights near the village of Gumecho. I do not know whether the river Zadorra was fordable or not; but most probably it was; for in the length of the position, there were not less than four bridges, not one of which the French had attempted to destroy. The banks, however, were precipitous. This position was, I think, too extended, being little less than ten miles in length, but its main defects were; first, that it faced the wrong way; and next, that the only roads by which the enemy could retreat lay at one extremity of their line, so that, if defeated, their left wing stood a good chance of being cut off.[27]

This last comment is worth remembering when considering Gazan's conduct towards the end of the battle.

Having considered how the French might have improved their dispositions, suggestions that would have created more concentrated dispositions, Blakiston came to the conclusion that 'nothing could have justified their giving battle in such a situation, when the mountainous country in the rear must have offered them some impregnable positions, unless it was the necessity under which they felt themselves of covering Vittoria, and of endeavouring to secure the junction of Clausel's division'.[28] This final, pertinent comment emphasises the extent to which Napoleon's determination to suppress the guerrillas in Galicia and Navarre that caused Joseph so disastrously to delay his summons to Clausel may well have brought about the catastrophe which was about to happen.

Blakiston was not the only one who subsequently remembered what they had seen as they found themselves with a clear view of the valley. John Cooke was able to locate Joseph, surrounded by his staff, still positioned on the Knoll of Ariñez, from where he could follow the progress of the right and centre of his own army. Cooke also noticed, as he surveyed the ground, that there were no obstructions, not so much as a bush, 'to prevent the sweeping of their artillery, the charging of their cavalry, or the fire of their musketry, from acting with full effect on those who should attempt to pass the bridges in their front, which was absolutely necessary for us to carry before we could begin the action in the centre'.[29]

Timing was vital at this point. Not only whatever headway Hill was making on the Heights, with its attendant effect on the dispositions of the Army of the South, but also the progress of the Third and Seventh Divisions, would determine the next movements of the Allied centre right. Hill's troops were already doing well. The centre-left column, however, which had more difficult terrain to cross, had yet to appear. Wellington took the opportunity, therefore, to move a little closer to the river in order to get a more precise understanding of the French dispositions in this part of the valley. William Surtees took the opportunity to draw as close as he dared, in order to hear what the 'big-wigs' were saying. To his surprise, one of the staff officers declared, after inspecting the scene through his glass, that it would be impossible to make much impression on such a numerous and strongly posted army, and could only conclude that the officer in question must be a natural pessimist.

Not surprisingly, the French soon became aware of Wellington's more exposed position and

> instantly detached a corps of voltigeurs, who, rushing down to the river, dashed across the bridge at the village of Villodas, and immediately took possession of a small woody height on our side of the river, from whence they opened a fire on his lordship and those that were with him. This, of course, could not be borne; and as my battalion was the leading battalion of the column and nearest to hand we were ordered (with two companies of our 1st battalion, which stood next to us) to take our arms, and drive these fellows across the river again.[30]

Kincaid also referred to this skirmish, although in slightly different terms. 'The three battalions of our regiment were, at the same moment, ordered forward to feel the enemy, who lined the opposite banks of the river, with whom we were quickly engaged in a warm skirmish.' The significance of 'at the same moment' is that it refers to Kincaid hearing 'a sharp fire of musketry' to his right, which was the head of Hill's column attempting to force the Heights of Puebla. 'The affair with Sir Rowland became gradually warmer, but ours had apparently no other object that to amuse those who were opposite for the moment; so that, for about two hours longer, it seemed as if there would be nothing but an affair of outposts.'[31]

The two divisions now moved further forward until they were within a mile of the Zadorra. Under direction from Wellington, the Light Division, still in the lead, left the road and drew together in close columns, while sheltering under some rocks nearby. The Hussar Brigade dismounted and took post on their left while the Fourth Division moved to the right, closer to Nanclares. The dead ground of the undulating foothills effectively hid these movements from the enemy, but Wellington could see enough of French movements, particularly those of Tilly's and Cassagne's divisions, to know that sizeable bodies of troops were being drawn out of position to the point where they would soon be beyond the parameters of the action. Less satisfying, though, was the non-appearance of Dalhousie's column and the silence along the distant Bilbao road that suggested Graham had yet to come into action.

At about 11.30 am or noon (the time given varies from account to account), Wellington led the Light Division to a position directly opposite the right of Leval's division by way of a hollow road which hid their advance. They were now within 200 yards of the bridge at Villodas and Cooke understood, from what he could hear, that the bridge would have to be taken at the point of the bayonet, with the inevitable casualties. He also observed that across the river the French gunners were standing by their guns, lighted matches in hand and consoled himself with the thought that at least they could be picked off by the riflemen.

At this crucial moment a Spanish peasant, Jose Ortiz de Zarate, approached Wellington and informed him that the bridge at Tres Puentes was undefended. Wellington immediately sent Kempt's brigade, with Ortiz as their guide, to test this information. The river between Villodas and Tres Puentes describes a sharp hairpin bend, while the path along it is shadowed by overhanging rocks. With the benefit of these two natural features, the brigade was once more able to advance undetected.

> The brigade moved off by threes at a rapid pace along a very uneven and circuitous path, concealed from the observations of the French by high rocks, and reached the narrow bridge which crossed the river by the hamlet of Yruna. The 1st Rifles led the way, and the whole Brigade followed. We passed at a run, with firelocks and rifles ready cocked, and ascended a steep road of fifty yards. At the top was an old chapel, which we had no sooner cleared, than we observed a heavy column of French on the principal hill, and commanding a bird's eye view of us. Fortunately, a convex bank formed a sort of bridgehead behind which the regiments formed at full speed, without any word of command. Two round shots came amongst us: the second severed the head from the body of our bold guide, the Spanish peasant. Our post was most extraordinary. We were at the elbow of the French position, isolated from the rest of the army, and within 100 yards of the enemy's advance. We were occupying part of their position on the left of the river without any attempt being made by them to dislodge us. The sound of a shot from any direction, scarcely struck on the ear. We were in momentary expectation of being immolated, as I looked over the bank I could see King Joseph, surrounded by at least 5,000 men, within 800 yards of us. The reason he did not attack is inexplicable; it cannot be accounted for by the most ingenious narrator.[32]

The only logical explanation is that Joseph and Jourdan were so convinced that Hill's was the van of a concentrated attack that they disregarded the stray brigade at Tres Puentes. They were aware of the advance of the two divisions of Cole's column, and assumed that they would unite with Hill. In his memoirs Jourdan suggested that Hill's attacks, on Villatte and on Subijana de Álava, were made to enable the Fourth Division to cross the Zadorra at Nanclares. He granted that it was unfortunate, but he was convinced that it need not have proved a disaster because Leval's division was in firm possession of a position that would enable him to prevent the junction of the two columns. Then, along with Conroux's and Darricau's divisions, to his left, he would be able to attack Hill. As extra surety, Joseph ordered the return of Cassagne's division.[33]

Cooke was not alone in his surprise:

> General Sir James Kempt expressed much wonder at our critical position and our not being molested. He sent his aide-de-camp at speed across the river for the 15th Hussars, who came forward singly and at a gallop, up the steep path, and dismounted in rear of our centre. The French dragoons coolly, and at a very slow pace, came within 50 yards to examine the strength of our force, when a few shots from the Rifles induced them to decamp.

Kempt's brigade could advance no further and had no choice but to await the arrival of the Third and Seventh Divisions to their left.

> I observed three bridges within a quarter of a mile of each other, at the elbow of the enemy's position. We had crossed the centre one, while the other two, right and left, were still occupied by the French artillery. At the latter, the enemy had thrown up an earth entrenchment.[34]

The 'dragoons' were Avy's chasseurs, presumably sent to check the strength of the brigade and to dislodge them if they could. Apart from this isolated unit of cavalry, and Leval's division, still holding the high ground in front of Ariñez, this part of the battlefield was strangely lacking in French troops. With Gazan's other divisions now well to the Allies' right, Cassagne, who had been temporarily attached to the Army of the Centre now returning from the Logroño road, the next troops were Darmagnac's, back towards Zuazo. This was the moment to attack Leval, but where were the troops to carry out the attack?

The Fourth Division had reached Nanclares some time before but it would be some considerable time before they crossed the river by the narrow bridge, while Vandeleur's brigade was held at Villodas both by the French guns and the obstructions to the bridge. Wellington was still waiting on the higher ground above Nanclares for some indication that either Dalhousie, with the centre-left column, or Graham, advancing along the Bilbao road, was coming into action. He would have been able to see Dalhousie, while Graham's encounter with the French would be signalled by the sound of musketry or artillery fire. Yet he could neither see nor hear anything. These were critical moments for the Allied commander as the chance to strike a potentially fatal blow was in danger of being lost.

The Third Division, having spent the night around Carcamo (without tents, according to General John Colville), was roused at daybreak by the call of the bugles, and the troops were on the march as the sun rose. After an advance of about two leagues, they filed to the right and began the ascent of a steep hill which would give them an excellent view of the valley of the Zadorra and of the French army, drawn up for battle, from its summit.

The valley 'lay immediately in our front, intersected with corn fields and vineyards, and shaded with many smiling villages, conspicuously among which stood the town of Vittoria, situated some miles to our left'. This pleasant scene, however, also encompassed

> the legions of France, confident of victory and ready to receive us. Their confidence was not altogether without foundation – their hopes of success resting on the superior force they had to the Allies – the position they held was formidable, and indeed of such a nature, as might have appalled most troops. The dark, deep, and rapid Zadora flowed along the bottom of the heights they occupied, which were fortified with breastworks and redoubts, and strongly lined with cannon; while a broad and level plain intervened between the contending hosts, across which the assailants had to pass in front of their most deadly foe. Such was the commanding and formidable position of the French army, in the morning of this ever memorable day.

It is questionable whether William Brown was thinking of superiority in terms of numbers or of the quality of the experienced French soldiers, as so many of them were despite Napoleon's depredations. If the former, then he was mistaken: if the latter, he was merely demonstrating the respect for the enemy which the British soldier so often expressed. What cannot be questioned is that from Brown's perspective, and in respect of the number and disposition of the French guns, the position must have looked daunting. Brown, however, could glory in the fact that the French would be swept away 'like chaff before the wind' before the day was out.[35]

At some point during this ascent the sound of gunfire became evident. A local inhabitant appeared to inform Daniell, who was presumably towards the rear of the column, 'that the battle between the Inglezes and Franzeses was beginning'. By the time Daniell reached the summit, above the village of Mendoza, he could see that the battle had indeed begun. 'The troops under Sir Rowland Hill were just commencing their attack upon the heights of Puebla and the position of the enemy above Subujana, while the light and 4th divisions advancing immediately on their left so as to support this attack, were preparing to force the passage of the Zadora.'[36]

The Third Division were now on the south side of Monte Arrato and were in position to launch their own attack, while their commander, General Picton, was chafing against the delay. Although the leading brigade of the Seventh Division, William Grant's, was also well forward, the other two brigades, Edward Barnes' and Carlos Lecor's, were some way behind. Dalhousie, who, according to Daniell, was anxious to lead the assault, cited Wellington's orders to justify waiting for his missing troops rather than advancing further with Grant's brigade. These orders, he claimed, required him to co-ordinate his movements with what was happening to his right, and not to be drawn in until it became evident that he should do so. In other words, he was now waiting for specific orders from headquarters.

Picton, however, was not a man for doing nothing when action was the order of the day. He could see that the French were unprepared for an attack from the direction of Mendoza and having to wait upon Dalhousie meant that both his frustration and his temper were mounting dangerously. He now

> inquired of every aide-de-camp whether they had any orders for him. As the day wore on and the fight waxed louder on the right, he became furious, and observed to the communicator of these particulars. 'D—n it! Lord Wellington must have forgotten us.' It was near noon and the men were getting discontented. Picton's blood was boiling, his stick was beating with rapid strokes upon the mane of his cob. He rode backward and forward, looking in every direction for the arrival of an aide-de-camp, until at last one galloped up from Lord Wellington. He was looking for Lord Dalhousie – the 7th Division had not yet arrived, having to move over different ground. The aide-de-camp checked his horse and asked the general whether he had seen Lord Dalhousie. Picton was disappointed; he had expected that he might at least move now, and in a voice that did not gain softness from his feelings, answered in a sharp tone,

'No, Sir: I have *not* seen his Lordship, but have you any orders for *me*.' 'None,' replied the aide-de-camp. 'Then, pray Sir, what are the orders that you *do* bring?' 'Why,' answered the officer, 'that as soon as Lord D. shall commence an attack on that bridge,' pointing to the one on the left (Mendoza), 'the 4th and the Light are to support him.' Picton could not understand the idea of any other division fighting in his front, and drawing himself up to his full height said to the astonished aide-de-camp, 'You may tell Lord Wellington from me, Sir, that the 3rd Division under my command, shall in less than ten minutes attack that bridge and carry it, and the 4th and Light may support if they choose.' Having thus expressed his intention, he turned from the aide-de-camp and put himself at the head of his men, who were quickly in motion toward the bridge, encouraging them with the bland appellation of 'Come on, ye rascals! Come on, ye fighting villains.'[37]

In response, the men of Thomas Brisbane's brigade ran cheering down the hill towards the river, whereupon they inevitably attracted the attention of the French artillery posted there. This was not the only problem that confronted the division.

On gaining the river side, it was found unfordable, by reason of the strength of the current, and the depth of water. This was a very unfortunate circumstance, for we were now sorely galled by the enemy's cannon shot from the heights, and annoyed by the fire of their light troops, stationed on the opposite bank. We then moved to a bridge, some hundred yards higher up, but which was found barricaded with wood. From an isolated hill in front of the chain of heights, and about two hundred yards from the bridge, the enemy kept up a heavy cannonade, mowing down our ranks, and literally making lanes through our columns. The bridge being found impassable, to ford the river was once more attempted; but all our efforts in this proving of no avail, orders were given to counter-march, and force the bridge. Being hemmed in between a high thorn hedge and the end of the bridge, we had not space left for this evolution, so that the column got into confusion. This was a dreadful moment. From the enemy's cannon the shot flew quick, our men fell fast, and nothing less than total destruction seemed inevitable, when a round shot from the French struck the barricading, and threw the planks of which it was composed to a considerable distance. Our troops, like lions pursuing prey, immediately rushed on the bridge, and without any orders being given, cheering as they went, flew up the road.[38]

Leaving Brown and his comrades on the French side of the river, the problems of the Seventh Division now need to be addressed. Like the Third Division, they were on the march from their camp at an early hour, but ahead of them lay a much more difficult advance. According to John Green, 'We did not march by the direct road, but crossed the country, and climbed several hills that were almost inaccessible, and descended others that were very dangerous by reason of their steepness.'[39] And steep hills were always a challenge for the artillery.

William Wheeler, while coping with the same route as Green, for their battalions were both in Grant's brigade along with the Chasseurs Britanniques, later shared his rather different experience with his family.

> We had not proceeded far when the company which I belonged to was ordered out to scour a wood on our right flank. We extended and marched through without falling in with the enemy, but we fell in with plenty of cattle, sheep and goats. We haversacked a few sheep and ran against an old shepherd, we soon relieved him of all he had, viz a four pound loaf, some cheese and about a quart of wine. The poor old fellow cried. It was no use, we had not seen a bit of bread these eleven days. The old man was not far from home and could get more.[40]

According to Oman, the reason that two of Dalhousie's brigades were so far behind the leading brigade was because the guns had blocked their path. These were Michael Cairnes' guns, and he gave a rather different version of what happened in a letter to his stepfather.

> The 3rd and 7th Divisions (forming a column under Lord Dalhousie, not a little annoying to Picton) had made a very fatiguing march of 3 leagues over the steepest mountain we have yet crossed, when Lord D. who was out to the front sent back to us to move on with all speed. Unluckily the Portuguese and 2nd British Brigade of our Division had mistaken their road (if it could be so dignified, for it was no road at all) by passing over (instead of skirting as ordered)

a hill on our right, so that they did not arrive until very late in the action. Our first brigade however were in their place & so (*nous nous flattons*) were we.[41]

Despite the difficulties of the terrain, Cairnes had obviously worked hard to keep up with the leading brigade, that is to say, Grant's brigade. Unfortunately, the numbering Cairnes gives to the brigades has subsequently caused confusion. Grant's was actually the second brigade but, for whatever reason, this was the brigade that headed the advance.

Picton had cut a strange figure as he led his 'villains' to the river. 'Old Picton rode at the head of the third division, dressed in a blue coat and a round hat, and swore as roundly all the way as if he had been wearing two cocked ones.'[42] As for Dalhousie, he had no choice but to follow with Grant's brigade, since there was still no sign of either Barnes or Lecor.

According to John Blakiston, with his Portuguese battalion of the Light Division,

> about this time, that is to say, about one o'clock, [we] crossed the bridge of Nanclares, and took post on an eminence a little beyond it, nearly opposite to the height occupied by the enemy's centre; in doing which we were somewhat incommoded by a few guns which were brought down to the bank of the river to bear on our flank. The 4th division followed, and formed on our right. Being halted here a short time, we were enabled to look around us. To our right the 2d division was warmly engaged with the enemy's left wing, which kept retreating before it, and on our left we perceived the 7th and 3d divisions, which had just debouched from the mountains.[43]

Leith Hay, no doubt itching with frustration that honour prevented him from becoming involved in the action, could only watch and marvel at

> one of the most animating scenes ever beheld: the whole country appeared filled with columns of troops: the sun shone bright: not a cloud obscured the brilliant and glowing atmosphere. From right to left, as far as the eye could reach, scarcely the most diminutive space intervened between bodies of troops, either already engaged, or rapidly advancing into action; artillery and musketry were heard in one continued uninterrupted volume of sound, and although the

great force of French cannon had not yet opened upon the assailants, the fire had already become exceedingly violent.[44]

For Cooke, the arrival of the Third Division brought some relief for Kempt's brigade from 'an awkward state of suspense' as they had watched the French drawing off towards Vitoria, which, of course, was the movement of some of Gazan's divisions to halt Hill's advance. Then they saw

> the head of the 3rd Division rapidly debouching from some rocks on our left near the hamlet of Mendoza. The battery of Trespuentes opened on them, and was answered by two guns from the horse artillery on the right of the river. Some companies of the Rifle Corps sprang from the ground where they lay concealed, darted forward and opened a galling fire on the left flank of the enemy's gunners, at great risk to themselves of being driven into the water, for the river ran on their immediate left, while the French cavalry hovered on their right. So well did this gallant band apply their loose balls, that the enemy limbered up their guns and hastily retired, and the 3rd Division, at a run, crossed the bridge of Trespuentes [Mendoza?], cheering but unopposed.[45]

The arrival of Picton and the threat of yet more Allied troops closing in meant that Leval's situation was now critical. His division was amongst the weakest of the French army, and he would soon be seriously outnumbered as the leading brigade of the Seventh Division, the other brigades of the Light Division, and the Fourth Division had crossed or were preparing to cross the Zadorra. The two other divisions of the Army of the South, Conroux's and Darricau's, had both been reduced to a single brigade when St Pol's and then Rey's brigades were sent to strengthen the counter-attack against Hill. With Maransin's single brigade already greatly weakened and Villatte's division engaged with the 71st and Morillo's Spaniards, there were few troops to spare to support Leval. Furthermore, the Army of the Centre had been dangerously weakened when Cassagne's division was sent to the Logroño road against any Allied troops that might advancing from that direction.

The troops closest to Leval were Darmagnac's at Zuazo, two miles to his rear. That gap needed to be closed. Leval was ordered to retire past the village of Ariñez to the high ground beyond it, while Henri Schwitter's brigade from Conroux's division and Victor Rémond's from Darricau's marched in parallel with Leval before also taking position on the same ridge. Recalling Villatte was more difficult. By now he was some distance along the summit of the Puebla Heights and heavily engaged. Extricating his troops would be dangerous enough, but he would also have had to bring them across the front of Hill's force in order to take up a new position. At least there was every expectation that Cassagne would soon be back in position.

In effect, the French were now forming a new line even as an increasing number of Allied troops were coming into action. Darmagnac was ordered to move forward from Zuazo and occupy Margarita. Should that prove impossible, he was to put troops into La Hermandad. This would then anchor the French position on their right. From there the line would extend to Gomecho and on to the high ground behind the village of Zumelza on the left.

As Oman pointed out, this was a dangerous manoeuvre at a time when the enemy was building up his attack. Furthermore, the units withdrawing to the high ground beyond Ariñez had no infantry reserve to form on, but only the cavalry of Pierre Soult and Anne-François Treillard. Also, the various units were coming from so many different directions that making a co-ordinated move would be difficult, particularly for those which were already engaged. Nor, at this point, was any attempt made to close the gap between the Army of Portugal and the rest of the French forces. There was also good reason by now why Reille could not have changed his position even if he had been ordered to, as will be seen.[46]

Even as the French began these movements, Picton had already sent his other two brigades, John Colville's and Manley Power's Portuguese, both of which were still on the right bank, to explore the river for a ford. They finally found one about 300 yards upstream. Crossing the river proved a challenge and took longer than Picton probably anticipated, but once the two brigades were on the left bank, they were in position either to occupy Margarita, which would outflank Leval, or support Brisbane's brigade as well as Kempt's brigade. For these two units, their nearest opponents were Leval's division, which, having been forced from the high ground between the Zadorra and the Great Road by Picton's sally, was now, as ordered, occupying Ariñez and the rising ground towards the

Knoll. The village itself was held by Georges Mocquery's brigade, with the 103eme de la ligne from Victor Remond's brigade to its left, while Jacques Morgan's brigade was positioned on high ground to the French right of the village, where the divisional guns were also posted. It was both a strong and a crucial position.

Wellington, for his part, was already in position to give the orders for the Allies' next moves, which were designed to outflank the French on their right, even as they were still establishing their new positions. Colville was to focus on Margarita, while the rest of the Third Division was to attack Leval at Ariñez. Power's brigade on the left was to ascend the hill at Ariñez, while Brisbane's, on the right, with Kempt's brigade in support, was to take the village. The 1/95th was sent ahead and the Greenjackets were able to clear the French light infantry out of their path. They successfully penetrated into the village itself, only to be overwhelmed by Mocquery's superior numbers and forced to retreat. At the same time, Brisbane's brigade became the targets of the French guns and were driven back, which earned them a sharp rebuke from Picton.

Every battle abounds with stories of near misses. For John Kincaid, his came at this point. 'During the few minutes that we stopped there, while a brigade of the third division [Brisbane's] was deploying into line, two of our companies lost two officers and thirty men, chiefly from the fire of artillery bearing on the spot from the French position. One of their shells burst immediately under my nose, part of it struck my boot and stirrup iron ...' At which point the near miss descended into farce, because the shell had 'kicked up such a dust about me that my charger refused to obey orders; and while I was spurring and he capering, I heard a voice behind me, which I knew to be Lord Wellington's, calling out, in a tone of reproof, "look to keeping your men together, sir".' Kincaid could only surmise that Wellington had assumed him to be a young officer 'cutting a caper by way of bravado' and such was his embarrassment that he could not bring himself to turn round and look.[47]

Brisbane now had his brigade back in line and brought it forward. The 88th began their attack by swinging round to the south of Ariñez, even though the approach was made difficult by the proximity of more rising ground, and the 74th advanced in a direct line against the village. At the same time, Power's brigade attacked to the left and was soon engaged with Morgan's brigade. The Allied troops found the walls of the village lined with defenders who sustained a running fire against them, inflicting heavy casualties, particularly on the 88th. They, however, held their fire until they were within 50 yards of the French, whereupon they delivered a volley and then charged. This, coupled with the attack from the 74th, caused the defenders to effect a hasty departure. The third battalion of the brigade, the 45th, had turned their fire on the 103eme de la ligne, which joined in the rapid withdrawal towards Gomecha. As the rest of Leval's division pulled back, Morgan's brigade disengaged from their struggle with the Portuguese and joined the retreat.

Picton's successful attack has been posited as the most decisive action in the whole battle since it created a gap in the French line. This was exacerbated by the direction of Leval's retreat which seems to have taken him back in the direction of Zuazo rather than towards Gomecha on the Great Road where Cassagne had now arrived, his troops no doubt wearied and frustrated by their quixotic march to Berostigueta.

In response to Joseph's orders, d'Erlon had sent the Dutch general David Chassé's brigade from Darmagnac's division to Margarita where they arrived in time to set up their defence while Colville was still advancing on the village. Darmagnac also sent his other brigade, Neuenstein's Germans, into La Hermanded. As he did so, Grant's brigade, still the only one from the Seventh Division to have reached the battlefield, crossed the Zadorra. Vandeleur's brigade from the Light Division was still dismantling the defences the French had erected at Villodas but it was only a matter of time before they too would cross the river and join the action.

In a letter to his brother, Colville described his part in the battle as

> detached service, not having received from anybody an order from the time I commenced till the time I discontinued action, then taking up a defensive position on account of my being threatened with being turned by an overwhelming force, when Lord Dalhousie sent me a Brigade of the 7th Divn. to support my right. As far as my observation and feeling went at the time, I should say indeed this was the only support I directly received the whole day, though this of course does not argue against my being otherwise assisted by the attacks made relatively to my position, though without being immediately in concert with me.[48]

Colville also sent a report to Picton, since he had not been under the immediate supervision of the commander of the Third Division. He could only regret the heavy losses suffered by his division in the attempt to gain possession of the two villages of Magarita and La Hermandad and then hold them against any French counter-attack, but he also praised the conduct of the officers and troops, with particular commendation for Lieutenant Colonel Hugh Gough and the 87th, who behaved 'in a style of gallantry and good order that in my opinion nothing could excel'. What the report fails to mention, however, is the names of the villages that were taken. It is clear that initially Colville's battalions, particularly the 83rd, were successful in driving back the enemy during the early stages of the advance. When they came under enfilading fire Colville had to order a charge, which successfully dispersed the French. By this point, the other battalions had come up and the division was able to drive the French out of Margarita, but the French retired in good order to La Hermandad, and from this position they were able to pin Colville's troops down with a heavy cannonade.

La Hermandad was one village too far, as Colville explained to Picton.

> I had at first hoped that the village was in the possession of the light companies under Lt. Col. Lloyd, but on closing to it found it not to be the case, and that it was too late for me to attempt it with fatigued troops, as the enemy had already arrived at it. I therefore satisfied myself for the time with only securing the Brigade by placing it's left on the river, and covering its front by light infantry (who now for the first time joined me in very small numbers) placed behind trees and on the mill dam.[49]

In his memoirs, Jourdan implied that once Ariñez and Margarita were in Allied hands the fate of the French hung in the balance.

> We have said, this last division [Darmagnac's] was moving in the direction of Tres Puntas. Arriving at Magarita, it engaged with two English divisions, which had already thrown some troops to the left of the Zadorra. Count d'Erlon recognising the importance of stopping the progress of the enemy to that point, which would force the retreat of Leval's division, called Cassagne's division forward. The action was very lively and could have had a fatal result if Count

d'Erlon had been defeated, since the enemy would easily have been able to extend to the rear of the Army of the South and separate it from the Army of Portugal.[50]

Although Chassé had eventually abandoned Margarita, as has been seen, his next position at La Hermandad had prevented Colville from driving a wedge between Gazan's and Reille's forces. This may explain Jourdan's brief optimism that the situation could yet be saved, or that the French could still extricate themselves in their own time. Joseph, however, had just received a report from Reille which not only created more uncertainty but undoubtedly snuffed out whatever optimism Jourdan had felt.

> This general reported that he was being attacked by infinitely superior forces and that he could make out large numbers which were advancing from Murgina [Murguia]. Indeed, he had discovered the presence of two English brigades under the command of General Graham, the Spanish corps of Longa and the Galician army under Girón, and to oppose them only had two weak divisions and 1500 Spanish, being the remainder of the troops of that nation still in the king's service. It was not very probable that with these inferior forces he could prevent the enemy from crossing the bridges at Arranguiz and Ariaga, and make themselves masters of communications with Salvatierra, the only point by which he could retire.[51]

Graham's Intervention

To recapitulate, Reille was holding a position along the Zadorra which extended from the bridge at Ariaga to the bridge at Durana, this last being on the Great Road to Bayonne. In effect, therefore, he was protecting the line of retreat. Sarrut's division, with Jean-Baptiste Curto's cavalry, was at Aranguiz, a forward position which protected the Ariaga bridge. Lamartinière's division, supported by Pierre Boyer's and Julien Mermet's cavalry, focused on Gamarra Mayor, an access point to the Great Road, which was heavily defended by both men and barriers and covered by guns on both sides of the river. The Spanish troops under the Marquis de Casapalacios at Durana had a half-battery of guns. Casapalacios also had stray troops under his command, including men from the Army of the North who had been on garrison duty. Reille had posted his infantry, something under 13,000 men in total, to guard the most obvious targets for an Allied attack. There was one further bridge he might have defended, at Yurre, on a road that also led to Ariaga and on to Vitoria, but this seems not to have been considered. As well as his own 3,500 cavalry, posted as indicated, he also had Alexandre Digeon's division, about 1,500 strong.

Reille had sent Curto's cavalry out early to reconnoitre the Bilbao road, and learnt that a large body of troops was advancing from Murguia. This confirmed the information that the deserter had given, if such a man existed. Reille then rode out himself to double check and could see quite clearly the varied uniforms of Graham's definitely multi-national force. He also recognized the vulnerability of Sarrut's position. It is one of the ironies of the contest between Graham and Reille that neither wanted a battle of attrition. Whereas Graham definitely seems to have interpreted his orders as an instruction not to become embroiled in any unnecessary fighting, Reille intended to preserve his own troops at any cost, except permitting the enemy to cross the Zadorra. Consequently, when Graham was finally in position to assess the French troops ahead of him and located Sarrut's division at Aranguiz, he came to the conclusion that to engage them unnecessarily would lead to a protracted struggle. Instead, he would cautiously feel his way forward. Essentially, his task was to get his troops across the Zadorra, drive back the Army of Portugal and block the major French line of communication to Bayonne. Furthermore, he was to act in concert with the troops to his right where, so far, there was only silence. Thus his conduct was more circumspect than it might have been without Wellington's ambiguous order. As for Reille, it was important that, as the third line, he should preserve the integrity of his force.

Tomkinson, writing in response to his understanding of Reille's dispositions, certainly did not share Graham's circumspection. In his opinion, 'Nothing could be more fortunate than the Spaniards [Longa's] showing themselves last night, and the enemy in the reconnaissance they made yesterday on them not seeing our column. The force they had placed on Gamarra Mayor, and Abucheco, and on the heights to our left, was thought quite sufficient to retain them against the Spaniards.'[52] Yet, bearing in mind the task Reille had been given and his resources, he may be thought to have used his troops to their best advantage under the circumstances. Knowing the importance of the Great Road to Joseph and Jourdan, it has to be questioned why they had not thought to defend it in greater strength. Maucune's division, of course, could have made a crucial difference.

Both Douglas and Hale refer to some high ground that they reached some time between 9 am and 10 am, according to the latter. From this position they could look down on Vitoria, giving them

> a fine view of the greater part of the French army, for they had formed all ready for combat along the river for three or four miles each way. On one side of Vitoria is a plain or a sort of marsh, on which place they were like a swarm of bees, for the whole of their baggage, together with three waggon-loads of money, (which they had got to pay the army), were formed up all regular, in readiness to follow our army, for they thought to drive us down the country again, in about the same manner as they did from Burgos, or at least, they told the inhabitants of Vittoria that such was their intention, and so it plainly appeared, for we hardly ever knew them to exert themselves as they did at this place.[53]

Still Graham waited for an indication of action on his right and still there was nothing. By about midday, though, he could see another indicator that told him the Allies were not only in action, but successfully so. He could see Hill's troops at the western end of the Heights of Puebla. This persuaded him to move forward and drive the French out of Aranguiz. As he advanced, though, he realized that both infantry and cavalry were abandoning the position. Reille knew that fewer than 6,000 men would not be able to halt the Allied advance. He pulled them back to a new position at Abucheco, where Sarrut posted Jean-Baptiste Menne's brigade, and at the river, where François Nicholas Fririon's brigade was now positioned. He also brought his cavalry south of the river, deploying his two dragoon units, Digeon's and Pierre Boyer's, behind Sarrut and Lamartinière. The light cavalry, Mermet's two brigades were in position to protect the flanks of the two infantry divisions.

The first units that Graham sent forward were Longa's Spaniards and Pack's Portuguese. The former was to take Gamarra Menor before moving on to Durana, which was the key to blocking the Great Road. This village, unlike the other two villages that would have to be taken, Abucheco and Gamarra Mayor, was on the left bank of the river. Pack was to attack the high ground above Gamarra Mayor, to clear the way for the Fifth Division's advance on the heavily-defended village. At the same time, the First Division, along with Spry's Portuguese brigade from the Fifth Division and Bradford's independent Portuguese brigade, were readied for an advance on Abucheco.

Tomkinson summed up the situation from his position as a spectator.

> In our front the enemy have from 4,000 to 5,000 infantry, and about six squadrons of cavalry, occupying strong hills to the left of the road, and with reserves in the villages of Gamarra Mayor and Abucheco, covering the passes over the Zadorra river, which, for the security of their right, and their main road to retreat by on Tolosa, it is necessary for them to retain.
>
> A squadron from the 16th, and two guns, were sent down the road a short distance, covering the formation of the troops to the left. The 5th Division, and Major-General Pack's brigade of Portuguese infantry, with a squadron from the 12th Light Dragoons, the whole under Major-General Oswald of the 5th Division, were detached to attack the enemy on the left, whilst we waited for the commencement on the right by Lord Wellington, regulating our movements by what might there happen.[54]

Another unwilling spectator, his unit like all the cavalry constrained by the ground, was Hay, who was certain that he had never been in such a position where

> we were enabled to see for miles, while we were unable to take part in whatever was going on …
>
> We were from time to time the mark for a salvo of artillery; but the attention of the batteries was directed principally against the moving columns of infantry, either contending for the passage of the river, or directed to clear the ravines of the French troops in possession; hence we were not much molested and had fair time for observation. Nothing could exceed the magnificent sight or the excitement with which one viewed the progress of our gallant men.[55]

Longa was soon in possession of Gamarra Menor after driving out a French battalion that had offered little opposition. He then became engaged in a much fiercer struggle for the bridge at Durana where, ironically, Spanish former guerrillas contested with what in a later period might have been called Spanish quislings. He would eventually force his way across the narrow bridge into the village, thus blocking the road to Bayonne, but that would be after a struggle that lasted several hours, during which he was held at bay by Casapalacios's guns. Once he was in the village and even after many of Casapalicios's troops had taken to their heels, he was still unable to proceed further because of the guns and Mermet's cavalry, which had ridden out in support. It mattered little. He had achieved his objective and only a major French counter-attack could have re-opened the road. That was not going to happen.

There can be no doubt, from the way he so carefully recorded them in his dispatches, that Longa's exploits earlier in the year had greatly impressed Wellington; and it may be presumed that his own judgement of the man, once he had joined the Allied army, influenced his decision to send him to Graham's column. It is notable that Longa alone managed to block the French from the one road that would allow them to get their guns and their baggage off.

This is to move ahead, however. The situation at Abechuco quickly resolved itself when the French withdrew from the village without offering much resistance to an attack by Colin Halkett's brigade. They joined the rest of the division at the bridge which, if taken, would eventually have brought the Allies to the Great Road. It might have been predicted, therefore, that Graham would now send the First Division forward to contest the Ariaga crossing. These troops, however, would remain inactive against a French force of roughly equal strength until much later in the afternoon. This undoubtedly explains why both Aitchison and Rous, in letters home, give so little detail of any part they may have played in the battle. It also suggests that Graham was still influenced by the uncertainty of Dalhousie's progress, as Tomkinson suggested, and also by Wellington's order to engage to no greater degree than could be considered necessary. The 'Gentlemen's Sons' and their comrades in the King's German Legion had to spend the time kicking their heels. And while they did so Reille felt sufficiently confident to detach Fririon's brigade and post it as a reserve at the village of Betonia.

It may be suggested that some of the hardest fighting of the day took place at Gamarra Mayor where a bitter and protracted street fight was followed by a struggle for the all-important bridge. Unlike the other contested villages, strong defensive measures had been taken to prevent any Allied ingress. The French were aware that, even more so than at Abechuco, possession of the bridge would quickly allow the enemy to block the Bayonne road. Consequently, the French had prepared their defences well, barricading the bridge and the streets while also covering the position with their guns. Now, Jean-Bernard Gaultier's brigade of Lamartinière's Division, comprising the 118eme and 119eme de la ligne, stood ready to resist the Allied onslaught.

Tomkinson, who had joined the squadron of the 12th Light Dragoons posted to the rear of Gamarra Mayor, watched as the Fifth Division

> attacked and carried the village at the point of the bayonet. The leading brigade was the 2nd Brigade under Major-General Robinson, consisting of the 4th, 47th and 59th, and were moving in an echelon of regiments from the left. There was either some shyness in the two leading regiments [the 47th and the 59th, both relative newcomers], or some misunderstanding of orders; but Colonel Brooke, perceiving it, called, 'Come on, Grenadiers 4th!' passed the other two with his battalion and carried the place, taking 2,000 prisoners and three guns.[56]

Tomkinson had this account from Brooke himself, and there seems little doubt that the 1/4th did overtake the other two battalions to arrive first at the village. Yet the casualty figures are heavy for all three battalions, which testifies to the sanguinary struggle that ensued as Frederick Robinson's brigade tried to force their way into Gamarra Mayor, and also to the bravery and determination of the French resistance.

The heaviest casualties in Andrew Hay's brigade, which had followed Robinson's, were taken by the Royal Scots, their losses being comparable with the casualties for the three battalions of the second brigade. Douglas's account makes clear why.

> We marched to the village of Gamara. We drew up in column within gunshot of the village, primed and loaded, uncased the colours, and on we went to the attack. As we stood in column, a Brigade of Portuguese [Pack's], on our right, had attracted the attention of the boys in the village, who let fly a few 9 pounders among them, one of which struck a tree and caused it to roll to the right of our regiment so smoothly that one of our grenadiers put out his foot to stop it, which shattered

his leg in such a manner that amputation became necessary, and he died in the operation … We moved to the village under no small fire. The road, being fine, enabled us to move in column of companies on our right. The country towards Vitoria was open, but somewhat defended by the zig-zag course of the River Zadora. On our left there was a large thorn hedge in full feather, through which the balls were whizzing very thick, as you might perceive the leaves and branches falling fast, and here and there a man.

We reached the village, which we named Gomorrah, as it was a scene of fire and brimstone. The enemy were driven through the village, and over the River Zadora. One wing cleared the houses and gardens on the right and then lined the bank of the river, keeping up a heavy fire on the advancing supports. The light company entered a house at the end of the bridge, from the windows of which a very destructive fire was then kept up, while as many as could pushed across and formed as they arrived close to an old chapel. We that had crossed had taken up a very favourable position and were picking them off in good style.[57]

Douglas was of the opinion that if the battalions that entered the village had been sent across the bridge, the French right wing would have been separated from the left. That is perhaps somewhat tendentious, however. Those troops who had managed to cross the bridge, the only ones to do so until much later in the afternoon, were soon forced back under heavy French fire, and any further attempts to cross were treated similarly. Even attempts to debouche from the streets that led to the river were causing heavy casualties. Robinson called a halt to his brigade until there was some artillery support, whereupon the bridge became a killing ground.

Hale was also in the thick of the action, although the 9th, arriving after the Royal Scots, took much lighter casualties.

The enemy made several bold attempts to force the bridge, in order to regain the village, but were repulsed every time with great loss; it was a very narrow street that led to the bridge, which was a great disadvantage to us, and their guns continued roaring tremendously, it was much in comparison to continual thunder, for they never ceased throwing shots and shells into the village during the action, by which most of the houses were very much damaged.[58]

The situation might best be described as a bloody stalemate, and so it continued for several hours, until events elsewhere forced Reille to deal with a totally transformed situation in which holding the line of the Zadorra was no longer his priority.

Defeated on all Fronts

Despite Reille's success in holding back Graham's column and Colville's failure to take La Hermandad, the French troops were now under severe pressure at all points. While the Third Division was pressing hard on Leval and Darmagnac, Cole was able to bring the Fourth Division across the Zadorra at Nanclares. He was followed by most of the Allied cavalry, although there was little they would be able to do, since they could only operate easily on the flattish ground that bordered the Great Road. The infantry continued to advance in echelon, led by Stubbs's Portuguese brigade, and closed up with Hill's left. On the Heights, Villatte, who had thrown all his resources into the struggle, was being forced back by Cadogan's brigade, now under the command of Colonel Cameron, and Morillo's Spaniards. It seems that Villatte was as yet unaware that the whole French army was making a retrograde movement.

Jourdan realized that 'The ruin of the army depended on the first post that was forced; there was nothing in reserve except the cavalry, for which the terrain permitted very little employment, which made it more embarrassing than useful. The danger was, therefore, imminent.' Jourdan ascribed to Joseph the decision to concentrate on drawing together the various French units, particularly those of the Army of the South, which had been pulled away from the Great Road and the Zadorra towards the Heights of Puebla and Subijana. It is more likely, however, that Jourdan's was the guiding voice, even if orders were given in Joseph's name. Gazan and d'Erlon were now ordered to withdraw towards Zuazo, as a central point for this new concentration. To make the point, Joseph now rode to the village, accompanied by Jourdan. He also ordered General Louis Tirlet, on the day in command of the French artillery, to set up a battery of forty-five guns to hold back the Allied advance and protect the different units as they made their movements in obedience to orders.[59]

By accident rather than design, the French had formed themselves into a new line, which now started further back at La Hermanded and extended to Esquivel. The troops of Darricau, Conroux and Maransin, which had disengaged from their fight with Hill as already ordered, retired until they were level with Gomecha. This made them vulnerable to a concentrated Allied attack, particularly as Conroux and Darricau needed time to unite their brigades, a task that was never fully completed. The French had most of their guns in this new position, not only the forty-five Tirlet had brought up from the reserve but also the guns of the Armies of the South and Centre.

The initiative was now firmly with Wellington. The best the French could do was to hold off the Allies while they effected a managed withdrawal. Wellington had already instructed Dickson to bring up the Allied guns, which had made little movement until now, as much because of the terrain as of the development of the action. This meant they were less widely dispersed than might have been expected. They were now to be positioned on the higher ground abandoned by the Army of the South, a development that gave Dickson particular satisfaction, as he later wrote to MacLeod.

> The nature of the country, and want of roads, was the means of throwing a large proportion of our Artillery together away from their Divisions, which I availed myself of, and by employing them in masses it had a famous effect. This was adjoining to the great road to Vitoria and the French brought all the Artillery they could to oppose our advance so that the cannonade on one spot was very vigorous.[60]

With each side now having about seventy guns in position, the result was that rare event, an artillery duel in the middle of a battle.

Even so, an immediate attack under cover of the bombardment was not feasible. Cole and Hill needed time to bring their units forward, and Picton's troops required some re-organization after their successful attack against Leval. This brief hiatus did not prevent Dalhousie from throwing Grant's brigade against La Hermanded. Although Grant was supported by Cairnes' guns, the French had superior artillery. Grant's four battalions were able to advance to within 200 yards of the French but were then brought to a halt. John Green, with the 68th, has given us a vivid account of the advance from the perspective of a man in the ranks.

I dont know that I ever saw the 68th regiment march better in line than they did into the battle of Vittoria every man was as steady as possible. We continued to advance until we reached a small wood: we then received a galling fire from the enemy. One of our company, named Taylor, received a severe wound, and several others fell dead at our feet. As I was loading my piece, a shot came and broke the ram-rod in my hand. I changed my musket immediately with a wounded man, and took my place on the right of the rear rank of my company. On the other side of the wood there was a division of the enemy's infantry drawn up ready to receive us, and when they came within a short distance, they poured a volley upon us which did great execution, wounding Colonel Johnson in two places, and killing several men. We continued to advance until we got through the wood, when the firing from the enemy became dreadful, and our men fell in every direction. I really thought that, if it lasted much longer, there would not have been a man left to relate the circumstance.[61]

They were finally brought to a halt by the battery, and had to take refuge in a deep ditch.

If Harry Smith is to be believed, Dalhousie now hesitated, discussing with his quartermaster-general what to do next. When Smith pressed him for orders, he replied, '"Better take the village." I roared out, "Certainly my lord," and off I galloped, both calling to me to come back, but "none are so deaf as those who won't hear." I told General Vandeleur we were immediately to take the village.'[62]

Whether it was Smith's decision to take it upon himself to convert a comment into an order, or whether Vandeleur was acting in response to orders already received, the sudden arrival of this brigade, so long delayed by the need to dismantle the defences at Villodas, made up Dalhousie's mind for him. Interestingly though, Green suggest that Grant's brigade had advanced 15 minutes too early for the Light Division, who were supposed to be acting with them. Whatever the truth of it, the 52nd and the Greenjackets plunged forward, sweeping up Grant's brigade as they passed, and launched an impetuous attack against the French defences. Neuenstein's German troops were quickly overwhelmed and made a scrambling retreat to the high ground behind them. Here they were able to form on Cassagne's division, although at some point they lost their commander who was killed when he fell from his horse.

Wellington's next move was to increase the pressure on the line which the French now presented to him, extending from Crispiana on their right to Zuazo and the high ground in front of Esquivel on their left. It was still strongly defended by Tirlet's guns, extending both sides of the Great Road, but increasingly vulnerable to flank attacks. As Jourdan commented, he and Joseph had an embarrassment of cavalry posted behind the infantry but it was no more use to them that the Allied horse was to Wellington. Vitoria was very much an affair of foot soldiers and guns. As for the French infantry, Cassagne now held the right in and about Crispiana while the other division of the Army of the Centre, Darmagnac's, was posted in and around Zuazo. Although not as thoroughly beaten as Leval's division, Chassé's and Neuenstein's brigades had taken considerable punishment at Margarita and La Hermandad, but had been able to reform and now stood their ground in what was the centre of the French line. Leval should have been holding Gomecha, but when he retreated from Ariñez he marched south-east rather than east, which would have taken him to the village. Instead, he had drawn closer to the rest of the Army of the South, still well to the left of the French position. Villatte, finally forced from the Puebla Heights, held the ground in front of Esquivel.

By about 4.00 pm Wellington was ready to launch the onslaught which he believed would force the French out of position and back to Vitoria, thus accelerating the withdrawal that had been taking place, move by move, since Leval was ejected from Ariñez. On the left was Colville's brigade, which had been able to move closer to Crispiana once La Hermandad had fallen. The Allied line then continued with Grant's brigade, still the only one from the Seventh Division to be involved in the action. Next to Grant were the other two brigades of the Third Division, Power's and Brisbane's. Stubb's brigade of the Fourth Division was on their right, with Byng's and O'Callaghan's of the Second Division on the extreme right. Cameron's brigade and Morillo's corps were in an ideal position, of course, to attack Villatte's flank. Forming a second, supporting line were the brigades of Vandeleur and Kempt from the Light Division, Anson and Skerrett from the Fourth Division, and Ashworth's Portuguese. The cavalry was drawn up behind the two lines of infantry, along with Silveira's Portuguese.

Jourdan later wrote his own, rather selective, account of subsequent events, which can be summed up as follows: the retiring French troops came under vigorous enemy fire but the cannonade from the grand battery soon brought the Allied columns to a halt. Jourdan fantasized that if they had had 10,000 lancers with which to attack the now-shaken troops, this part of the Allied army would have been destroyed. Then something went wrong. General Gazan, instead of leading his divisions towards Zuavo, inclined strongly to the right as if withdrawing in order to make contact with Villatte. He continued to follow the line of the Heights, thus leaving the Great Road and Vitoria far to what was now his left as he made his retrograde movement. Inevitably, a large gap opened up between himself and d'Erlon. The latter, understanding the direction of Gazan's march, did not halt at Zuavo but marched on to Crispiana. Thus, the drawing together of troops became a general retreat, with Salvatierra as the objective.

To this effect, General Tirlet was ordered to bring off the artillery park and then report that he was on the march towards Salvatierra. At the same time, and despite being pursued, the Army of the South continued to retire in good order. Other Allied columns were following d'Erlon, and would have come up on Reille's rear if d'Erlon had not managed to hold them at Crispiana. Now Reille, in turn, was forced to abandon his positions on the Zadorra. He retired along the left back once the rest of the army had drawn level with him.[63]

Two points emerge from this interpretation of why the French collapsed. Firstly, and by implication. it was caused when Gazan chose not to obey the precise order he had been given. Secondly, if that in turn led to d'Erlon's decision to keep marching when he realised he was no longer in contact with the Army of the South, and was also under Allied attack, then the French were not so much defeated by the Allies as forced into a rapid retreat by their own misadventures.

Significantly, Gazan saw things rather differently, as he made clear in letters written to Marshal Soult and to Henri Clarke. To Soult, who had previously commanded the Army of the South, he wrote in defence of his troops.

> The Army of the South fought as well as ever, and resisted for 8 hours the many attacks which were made by the combined Divisions

of Generals Hill & Graham [he means Cole] and only abandoned their position by the King's orders, when they found themselves completely out-flanked by the other English Divisions, which were led by Lord Wellington in person ... A retreat of this kind could not but cost us dearly, as I was still on the heights above the village of Ariñez when the enemy was master of Vitoria, and had captured our carriages and artillery Park.[64]

This certainly contradicts Jourdan, as does the letter to Clarke. Having described events up to the point where the French were feeling the effect of Picton's and Graham's attacks, he continued:

> This was the point of affairs when about mid-day the King ordered the retirement of the Army of the South, with the intention of taking up a position further back. The movement was executed in echelon, when the right of the Line, occupied by the 1st Division under General Leval, found itself completely out-flanked by the enemy, who had forced the passage of the Zadorra at the point defended by the Foreign troops of the Army of the South. General Leval fell back on the village of Ariñez and for a few moments held the upper part of it, with General Maucune's [Morgan's] brigade, while his other brigade, under General Rémond [Mocquery?], went to hold the defile behind it, which was already defended by Artillery.
>
> This was the position of affairs when a heavy fire from the Artillery of our centre, in position a little to the rear of the Ariñez plateau, checked the enemy sufficiently long to allow the Army of the South, which was on the left amongst the hills, time to effect its retreat behind Vitoria.
>
> Leval's Division covered the retreat on the main road and covered it with success, and several efforts of the enemy to break through failed.[65]

It is possible to match elements of these letters with Jourdan's memoirs, although much is left open to question. By exploring the Allied perceptions of what was happening to their opponents, it can be established that the sequence of events, from the point when Joseph realized that a change of alignment was urgently required to the French departures from the battlefield, was both more protracted and more complicated than either

Jourdan or Gazan suggested in their accounts. When the Allied line started to advance, the troops immediately came under heavy fire from the French guns. As Jourdan noted, there was a point when the line wavered and came to a halt, but once Dickson opened up with the artillery, the troops were immediately on the march, although not without continuing to take casualties. The Portuguese brigades of Power and Stubbs suffered particularly severely. The effect of the Allied guns soon became apparent, however, as the French artillery fire began to slacken. As Dickson wrote to Macleod, 'In none of our Peninsular battles have we ever brought so much cannon into play, and it was so well directed that the French were general obliged to retire 'eer the Infantry could get at them.'[66]

Heneghan, serving with the Field Train, was more specific in his memoirs.

> Ninety guns under the direction of Colonel Dickson, in a state of as perfect efficiency as could be displayed on the barrack field at Woolwich, were darting their destructive fire on the enemy's lines. From upwards of one hundred guns the compliment was returned, and for the space of more than half an hour, this brilliant battle of Artillery continued on both sides, presenting a spectacle of such magnificent fire-work, and attended by a thundering so terrible, as might have satisfied even Jove, as a display of his god-like powers.[67]

When the smoke cleared, 'The French could be seen abandoning every village, every height and every position, and falling back in confusion on Vitoria.'[68] Yet although it might be obvious to an unengaged observer like Schaumann that French were effecting a withdrawal, it was less obvious to those who were in the middle of this hell on earth, like Captain George Wood.

> It was now that the hurry, bustle and confusion of a great battle were experienced; such smoke, such noise, such helter-skelter! the cries of the wounded – the groans of the dying – the shouts of the victors – the dragoons and artillery flying – dust in clouds – caps, muskets, knapsacks, strewing the ground – baggage, carriages, waggons, and carts broken down. Such a spectacle might indeed cause a conquering army to exclaim, 'Oh! what a glorious thing is a battle!' but what must be the situation of the vanquished?[69]

More explicitly, Blakiston remembered the approach to the French guns when,

> the first time during the day, our regiment became exposed to a fierce fire of artillery, under which, however, we deployed in a very creditable manner. After remaining in this unpleasant situation for a short time, we were ordered to take ground on our left, and to join the remainder of our brigade in column behind the village of Gomecha, where we remained as a reserve, till the divisions on our right and left had dislodged the enemy from the heights in our front. We immediately moved up, and I then saw the first trophies of our success, in the capture of those guns, which a short time before, had poured destruction into our ranks.[70]

As will be seen, Blakiston was describing a crucial sequence in the advance, but attention first needs to be given to the left of the Allied line, where Colville had been able to eject the French from Crispiana, a victory which seems to have been achieved surprisingly easily, if the French casualty figures are considered. The 16eme léger, from Cassagne's division, which had been posted to hold the village, suffered losses of one officer and twenty-six men, numbers that do not suggest a desperate resistance by a unit that had so far done a great deal of marching but little fighting.

Once Crispiana was in Allied hands, the right flank of the Army of the Centre had effectively been turned. At the other end of the Allied line, although still somewhat detached, Cameron's brigade and Morillo's Spaniards, having forced Villatte from the Puebla Heights, were now threatening Gazan's left flank. They also understood what was happening elsewhere on the battlefield. Hope wrote to his friend on 27 June:

> From the summits of Puebla's blood-stained heights, we beheld, with pride and pleasure, the gallant conduct of our friends in the valley.
>
> So close was the terrible conflict, in many parts of the glorious plains of Vittoria, that the hostile combatants were often observed pointing their deadly weapons at each other, when the space between them barely permitted them to do so without crossing the muzzles of their pieces. The courage of the soldiers invariably rose in proportion to the exertions required of them. Wherever the bayonet

was directed, there every thing was forced to yield. At times, the fire of our small arms seemed to make but a feeble impression on our enemies; but, as soon as the two armies came close enough to make use of the steel, the French uniformly gave way.[71]

Both ends of the French line were now under sustained pressure, while the centre was also feeling the force of the Allied advance, which brings us back to Blakiston's account. Because Leval had failed to establish himself at Gomecha, there was a considerable gap between d'Erlon's and Gazan's troops. The Light Division was in position to send skirmishers forward. Taking advantage of ditches and some wooded terrain, they were able to pick off the French gunners, thus facilitating the further advance of the Allied centre. It also meant that both d'Erlon and Gazan were vulnerable to being turned on both flanks. As if this were not enough to discompose the French, many of whom may have already seen themselves as defeated, a rumour began to circulate that the road to Bayonne had been blocked.

Nor was it an empty rumour. Longa finally drove out the defenders and took possession of Durana at about 5.00 pm. This meant that the French escape route had indeed been blocked. All that could be hoped was that Reille would be able to hold off Graham's column long enough for the rest of the army to leave the battlefield in some sort of order. Victory could no longer be achieved; the only options were a managed withdrawal or complete collapse.

With Gazan pulling back and widening the gap that separated him from d'Erlon, that general had no choice but to withdraw to a new position between Ali and Armentia, taking most of the guns with him. Here he made yet another stand and, with artillery support, successfully held the Third Division at bay. Then Colville, with the support of Vandeleur and Grant, was able to get round d'Erlon's flank at Ali, while at the same time Cole and Hill were beginning to threaten his left flank. This forced him to pull even further back or lose the guns.

With the Allies pressing too close to make a contest for the Bayonne road feasible, Joseph now gave orders for a general retreat on Salvatierra. Once the artillery train and park were on the move, the Army of the South was to withdraw by way of the various tracks south of Vitoria. This would keep them clear of the Army of the Centre, which would use tracks running to the north of the town. Once past Vitoria, however, all these tracks led into the Salvatierra to Pamplona road, itself inadequate for so much traffic, so that the inevitable confusion was only delayed. As for the Army of Portugal, still holding Graham's column on the Zadorra, it was to maintain its position and thus prevent Graham from attacking d'Erlon's rear. Once the Army of the Centre was clear away, Reille could disengage and join the retreat.

There was one further complication, however, that Joseph and Jourdan had not allowed for when planning a controlled withdrawal. The civilians attached to that part of the convoy still in Vitoria which had already so hindered French operations had been spectators of the battle. Indeed, according to Wheeler, Joseph had ordered stands to be erected for them, while Heneghan noted that churches, towers, and even the roofs of the houses were crowded both with the inhabitants of Vitoria and those attached to the French cause in some manner or other. As the realization dawned that the French were on the verge of defeat, there was an inevitable outbreak of panic. The need to escape became the prime concern. Carriages and baggage waggons were set in motion. In no time at all the vital tracks were blocked by wheeled transport, which itself was struggling to make any progress. It also meant there was no hope of carrying off the guns.

Even as Gazan continued his withdrawal and d'Erlon set his own troops in motion, Reille was left in an increasingly challenging position. He needed to stand fast if the Armies of the Centre and the South were to make their escape. Yet not only did he still have to hold off Graham, but he also faced another Allied threat. As d'Erlon abandoned his position, Colville, Grant and Vandeleur were ideally placed to attack the Army of Portugal on its left flank and roll it up.

Until this point, Reille had sustained a determined defence of his three-mile front. With Lamartinière holding the Fifth Division at Gamarra Mayor, although suffering heavy casualties, and Casapalacios doing the same at Durana, mainly with his guns, the situation for Sarrut at Ariaga a stalemate of intermittent artillery fire and the whole line supported by three cavalry brigades, the Army of Portugal was secure for as long as the rest of the French forces held the enemy in check. If d'Erlon's right flank were turned, however, the Allies would be able to advance without opposition to Reille's position. That had now happened, of course, and Reille was suddenly very vulnerable. In order to save his own troops, he took the decision to retreat without waiting for d'Erlon to pass behind him.

His immediate challenge was how to extricate Lamartinière and Casapalacios. Menne's brigade from Sarrut's division was guarding the bridge at Ariaga, but the enemy at Abechuco was still giving no indication that a forward movement was imminent. On the other hand, Menne's brigade would be the first to suffer an attack from Colville's, Vandeleur's and Grant's advancing troops. Digeon was instructed to act as a cavalry shield so that Menne could withdraw, although not before the 15th Hussars had suddenly appeared on the scene from the direction of Vitoria and tried to ride down Menne's infantry. In response, Digeon launched several determined cavalry attacks and these enabled Menne's troops to make the narrowest of escapes. They had to leave behind not only all their guns but also their mortally-wounded divisional commander, General Sarrut.

In the meantime, Boyer's and Curto's cavalry had joined Fririon's brigade at the village of Betonio. This not only allowed Menne and Digeon to form on them, but also gave Lamartinière a rallying point as he withdrew from Gamarra Mayor. At the same time, Casapalacios's Spaniards had made for the hills, as hotly pursued by Longa as Lamartinière was by the Fifth Division, Pack's Portuguese and the two squadrons of the 12th and 16th Light Dragoons that had been attached to the division.

Once his troops were all in, Lamartinière's arriving in a state of panicked confusion, Reille moved a mile or so further back to the woods at Zurbano, where Graham's light cavalry would come upon them. Tomkinson recorded the part played by his squadron, which is worth reproducing at some length.

> On passing the river we turned to the right, on the road to Vittoria, a mile from which place we came up with the enemy's scattered infantry pursued by Major-General Pack's brigade, and made a few prisoners. We were now at the edge of the wood, and being a little puzzled by a deep impassable drain, it was necessary to ascertain how far the enemy had gone and what there was in the wood. This gave time for the brigade to come up, together with the heavy Germans, under Major-General Bock, and in ten minutes we were in march through the wood, which is for the most part open, though the trees are so close and low that infantry cannot be attacked by cavalry. Major-General Pack's brigade moved on with us, and a few of Colonel Longa's Spaniards.

The enemy collected in the wood a rear-guard of six squadrons and a regiment of infantry, as others scattered as light troops in all directions. With this force they occupied a plain about half a mile across, surrounded with wood and ending in a defile, thus keeping the head of the lane, along which we could alone get at them. The Spanish infantry got into a field of corn and down the lane, and on firing a few shots the enemy moved off, and we pushed on after them. My squadron was in advance, and on arriving on the plain, formed immediately and advanced to the charge. All was confusion, all calling 'go on' before the men had time to get into their places. We got half across before I was able to place them in any form, and had we been allowed one minute more in forming, our advance might have been quicker, and made with more regularity.

The enemy had about six squadrons in line, with one a little in advance, consisting of the élite companies. This I charged, broke, and drove on their line, which advancing I was obliged to retire, having had a good deal of sabring with those I charged and with their support. A squadron of the 12th was in my rear, and in the place of coming up on my flank, followed me, so that they only added to the confusion of retiring by mixing with my men.

When another squadron arrived on the scene, the confusion was further compounded, and the best that Tomkinson could do was 'to front and make a rally back'.[72]

The rest of the brigade now came up, and Hay, with the 12th, described how they advanced,

> first at a trot and then at a canter, and soon came in sight of the French cavalry. On seeing our advance, advantage was taken of some broken ground at the extreme end of the plain over which we were advancing towards them, to halt and form for our reception.
>
> As we drew closer this appeared madness, as their numbers did not exceed half ours. Our trumpet sounded 'The Charge,' when, on coming up to what seemed a regiment of dragoons awaiting their doom, their flanks were thrown back and there stood, formed in squares, about three thousand infantry. [The 36eme de la ligne of Fririon's brigade.] These opened such a close and well directed fire on our advance squadron, that not only were we brought to a

standstill, but the ranks were broken and the leading squadrons went about, and order was not restored until a troop of horse artillery arrived on our flank.[73]

The guns sent the Army of Portugal on its way, but in good order. This enabled Reille to keep his troops fairly well concentrated as they continued their retreat to Salvatierra by way of the various tracks or across the fields. The only attack they experienced as they made their way to the Pamplona road was some distant firing from Longa's troops. They had also managed to carry off two guns, the only ones saved from the battlefield.

It was to Reille's advantage that he had managed to keep control as he extricated himself from his positions on the Zadorra, while more a matter of luck that he had completely skirted Vitoria and the chaos that was developing there rapidly making it an impassable obstacle, just as Jourdan had anticipated. As a result, his troops would remain well clear of the other fleeing French and in relatively good order. The Army of the South, on the other hand, although it had been the first to retreat, also seems to have been the first to lose order. The pressure was coming from the Allied troops descending from the Puebla Heights, which put them in a position to cut off their line of retreat, and from the rest of Hill's column, along with Cole's, advancing from Subijana. The realization that the tracks they were following were leading them away from the Salvatierra road increased the panic. They were also moving across deeply entrenched ground. It was no wonder, therefore, that, as Cooke wrote:

> The enemy sacrificed all their cannon (with the exception of eight pieces), while withdrawing the right of their army behind the left wing under cover of this tremendous cannonade, which was their only chance left to quit the field in a compact body. This movement was executed in strange confusion in and about Vitoria ... The French managed to drag the eight pieces of artillery across the fields for nearly a league but, coming to marshy ground, they stuck fast.[74]

Gazan promptly gave the order to abandon the guns. Every unit was ordered to make its escape as best it could. The troops threw off their kit in order to hasten their departure. And in no time it was a case of *sauve qui peut*.

Sergeant Anthony Hamilton, like Cooke of the 43rd, having witnessed how 'in a moment the French army became a vast mob, without organization of any sort, and divested of every attribute of a military body', rejoiced that 'Never had any victory achieved by the enemy over the rude and undisciplined Spanish levies been more complete; never was an army reduced to a more absolute and total wreck than that which now fled from the field of Vittoria.'[75]

D'Erlon had initially been able to bring his troops in fair order to the south of Betonio as Reille was moving to Zurbano. The Third Division was in hot pursuit, however. William Brown of the 45th, although he generalized about both d'Erlon's and Gazan's commands, was actually involved in the harrying the former.

> Their centre and right, on abandoning the heights, moved through the valley, where they made an obstinate resistance at some villages, but from which they were ultimately dislodged by our troops at the point of the bayonet, leaving several cannon behind them. Retreating in open columns, and filing by companies, they occasionally halted, wheeled into line, and saluted us with several volleys of musketry, but they were instantly charged by our troops, who bore down everything that opposed them. The retreat of the enemy, which had hitherto been conducted in good order, now assumed the nature of disorderly flight. Pressed hard on both flanks, and closely pursued in the rear by our victorious army, their main body reached the vicinity of Vittoria, when a scene of confusion and dismay ensued which exceeds description.[76]

At this point, the inevitable question has to be, where was the cavalry, of which Wellington was particularly well supplied, having four British heavy brigades, five light and two Portuguese brigades, totalling over 8,000 men. With the French on the run, this was the moment to let them loose, so that they would drive the enemy into even greater disorder, and pick up prisoners while they were about it. As already demonstrated, the 12th and 16th Light Dragoons had already played their part in sending the Army of Portugal on its way, after the 15th Hussars had tried to cut off Menne's brigade. Yet only Anson's and Colquhoun Grant's brigades would play any significant part in these final stages of the battle, although Ponsonby's brigade seems to have been on the edge of the action.

The anonymous author of *The British Cavalry on the Peninsular* served with the 15th Hussars and subsequently wrote an account of the part they played in helping the French on their way.

> The hussar brigade was directed to the left of the town; the ground was flat, and apparently well suited to the operations of cavalry. In passing through it, we found it intersected by deep gulleys, so broad as to make it necessary to ride into them. The 15th Hussars were in front, and passed a dozen or more of these cuts in their passage round the town without meeting any opposition. A few French infantry might be seen here and there. When we had nearly completed the circuit, a gun was brought up within two hundred yards; we saw it unlimbered and loaded, and were in momentary expectation of a discharge. Our advance, however, was so rapid, although two of the gullies intervened, that the French had not even time to give us one shot, but passed off at speed.
>
> We now entered upon an uninterrupted plain of some extent, – it was a scene of confusion. We passed through a crowd of broken infantry, some threw down their arms, although probably some resumed them, and got a shot at the hussars when they had passed on. The leading squadron of the 15th charged some French chasseurs, upset them and completely cleared the foreground. It was then we perceived heavy masses of French cavalry, but Sir Colquhoun Grant discovered that he was accompanied by the single regiment which he had gallantly led into action. [This was the moment when they came up against Digeon's cavalry.] A staff officer had, most unwarrantably, stopped the other part of the brigade, and turned it through the town, and had not even given notice to Colonel Grant that he had done so.

Although Grant rallied the 15th, they were outnumbered as much as three to one by Digeon's brigade. As a result, there was nothing more than 'some skirmishing and cavalier sabreing' until Captain Webber Smith RHA brought up his guns and sent the dragoons on their way.[77]

The author subsequently reflected:

> The divisions of the French army were defeated in succession: the whole of the guns, save two, had fallen into our hands, as well as

the reserves of ammunition; consequently, the French infantry had nothing to depend on but the cartridges remaining in the soldiers' pouches, which, in many of the divisions, must have been very small. The cavalry of the enemy was very inferior in number to ours, and lastly, the retreat of the French lay through open country. Had the attack of the cavalry been unsuccessful, which is a most improbable supposition, the enemy could not have profited by our failure. But on the other hand, supposing the British horse to have driven the French dragoons out of the field, the infantry mob was at their mercy. Many thousands must have been made prisoners, and those who escaped would have only found safety in retiring from the high road, and in the hill country, would have fallen prey to the guerrillas. Is it possible that any one can be so unreasonable as to blame the British cavalry for not taking advantage of these favourable circumstances?[78]

These sentiments and the sense of indignation that the inaction of the Allied cavalry should be criticized were widely shared. As Oman pointed out, this inaction is evident in the casualty figures. Of the 155 killed and wounded, all but 13 were from Anson's and Grant's brigades. The anonymous writer believed it was because Wellington, having achieved his great victory, did not want the French to salvage something from their defeat by overpowering the Allied cavalry. There are more likely explanations, however. It has to be conceded that the terrain, until well past Vitoria, was unsuitable for massed cavalry movements. There may also have been reluctance among the senior officers to set their troops in motion when there was no direct order from Wellington to do so, having been castigated often enough for launching rash actions against the enemy. Furthermore, the nominal commander of the cavalry, Major General Bock, was out on a limb, attached to Graham's column. There can be no doubt, though, that it was an opportunity lost, as so many eyewitness accounts make clear, and the cause of great frustration.

Andrew Hartley wrote in his journal what so many others must also have felt: 'we expected & ardently wished to have an opportunity of charging their retiring Columns but this was denied us their Retreat was so rapid we could not come up with them.'[79] It is one of the ironies of Vitoria that the first time Wellington had cavalry to spare, he fought on a battlefield where so little use could be made of them.

Aftermath

There was another reason why so many of the French escaped, and both cavalry and infantry played their part in letting it happen. As has already been noted, once the word got back to Vitoria that the French were losing the fight, many of the remaining civilians who had followed the army thus far, bringing with them all their possessions, recognized that the time had come to leave. Once Gazan's troops were known to be in full retreat and considerable disorder, the exodus became a mass of frantic humanity, all struggling to make their own escape. In no time, the roads out of the town, and the town itself, were blocked by a disaster of wheeled vehicles. Even if escape was possible it was soon discovered that the tracks were totally unsuitable for equipages of any kind.

Leith Hay, coming up with Wellington, has left us a vivid description of what confronted them.

> Such a scene as the town presented has been seldom witnessed; but no time was permitted either to investigate into, to correct, the chaos that therein reigned. Every step that we took proved the decided nature of the déroute that had overtaken the French army. Cannon, overturned carriages, broken down waggons, forsaken tumbrils, wounded soldiers, civilians, women, children, dead horses and mules, absolutely covered the face of the country; while its inhabitants, and *others*, had commenced, diligently commenced, the work of pillage. Seldom on any previous occasion had as rich a field presented itself. To the accumulated plunder of Andalusia were added the collections made by the other armies; the personal baggage of the king, Fourgons having inscribed upon them in large characters, 'Domaine Extèrieurde S. M. l'Empereur:' waggons of every description; and a military chest containing a very large sum recently received from France for payment of the troops, but which had not yet been distributed; jewels, pictures, embroidery, silks, every thing that was costly and portable, seemed to have been assiduously transported, adding to the unmilitary state of these encumbered armies.[80]

Such an eminently portable treasure trove could not be resisted by men who were already high on the powerful drug of victory. Captain John Blakiston's Portuguese troops and the rest of the Light Division were neither better not worse than thousands of other Allied soldiers of all ranks. They had initially been in pursuit of the French but

> about dusk, the head of our column came suddenly on some wagons which had been abandoned by the enemy. Some one called out, 'They are money-tumbrils.' No sooner were the words uttered than the division broke, as if by word of command, and, in an instant, the covers disappeared from the wagons, and in their place were seen nothing but a mass of inverted legs, the superior members belonging to which were employed in groping for the dollars; for money it certainly was. The scene was disgraceful, but at the same time ludicrous. I was sent to endeavour to clear one of these wagons, in which I at length succeeded; not, however till the money had disappeared; when to my surprise, I discovered an officer at the bottom, with his hands full of the precious metal! I shall not mention his name or his regiment.[81]

This scene was replicated many times over. Moyle Scherer was employed for two or three days with the fatigue parties that were collecting the guns and caissons that the French had abandoned.

> The ground, for nearly a square league, was covered with the wreck of carriages, cars, chests, and baggage; and, here and there, whole fields were literally white with thickly scattered papers. In their search for money and valuables, the soldiers had ransacked every thing; they had torn out the lining of carriages, and cut open the padding; they had broken all the correspondence chests of the various military and civil offices, and had strewn out papers, returns, and official documents, that had been for years, perhaps, accumulating. You saw the finest military books and maps trod under foot, and utterly spoiled by the rain, that had fallen the day after the battle.[82]

Military papers were of no interest to the ravening pack, when there were pickings which represented wealth beyond most soldiers' imaginings. For Edward Costello, the problem was not how to procure this wealth but how to carry it off.

> ... I observed a Spanish muleteer in the French service carrying a small but exceedingly heavy portmanteau towards the town. I

compelled him lay it down, which he did, but only after I had given him a few whacks in the ribs with my rifle. On inspection I found the portmanteau to contain several small bags filled with gold and silver in doubloons and dollars. Although I never knew the exact amount, I should think it was not less than £1,000. As I had contributed most towards its capture, I took it as booty, and with my comrades gone in another direction, I had no one to claim a portion of it.

... My chief anxiety now was to secure my prize, but how was it to be accomplished? I could not carry the portmanteau because of the weight, so to bear the valuable load I took one of the many mules that were blocking up the road. A sergeant and two men of the 10th [Hussars] were passing, and being at a loss how to fasten the portmanteau, I resorted to them for aid. Incautiously, I rewarded them too liberally, and in giving them several handfuls of dollars, they got a glimpse of the gold, half of which they demanded.

Since the 10th Hussars were newly arrived in the Peninsula compared with his own years of service, and therefore less deserving, Costello immediately seized his rifle and cocked it. 'Retiring three or four paces, I brought it to me shoulder, and swore I would shoot dead the first man to place his hands upon my treasure. My determined air, and the ferocity of my appearance – my face was covered with perspiration and gunpowder – induced them to pause.' Fortunately, the sergeant came to his assistance, and helped him strap his treasure to the mule. Later he entrusted the money to the quartermaster, to some of the officers and even to some of the men in his company. From the last, he claimed, he received very little back.[83]

Not everyone was as happy with his new-found wealth as Costello. Some, like John Brown, were overwhelmed. Having secured 500 dollars and 90 doubloons, he then sat down at the foot of a tree to reckon up his gains.

[I] found myself far from being happy. This sum, which appeared to me immense, was far beyond what my most sanguine hopes had ever anticipated. The transition from poverty to comparative wealth was too sudden. If it had been a few dollars only, I would have been at ease, nay overjoyed, and would have spent it the first opportunity; but the sum I now possessed was too great to throw away at folly's shrine, and how to dispose of it to advantage was more than I knew … In fact, I was in a complete labyrinth of care, and for the first, and I fear the last time in my life, I experienced the misery of being rich.[84]

Eventually, the problem was solved for him. The following day, while they were on the march, the Third Division was halted and the men were ordered to open their knapsacks. Although no questions were asked, every last coin was removed. Brown does confess that, while it had caused him so much trouble while it was in his possession, the loss of this sudden wealth was equally painful. And it was probably matched by the experience of John Green and his comrades, who, having come across a paper parcel full of what felt like doubloons, opened it only to discover that it contained gilt buttons![85]

Not everyone was looking for wealth. One of the most sentimental discoveries was made by Moyle Scherer. As he rifled through the litter of papers, he came across a cache of twenty letters, written by a Monsieur Thiebault to his wife over an extended period of time. Just reading the letters gave him great pleasure. When he subsequently met some French officers, prisoners presumably, he asked after Monsieur Thiebault and learnt that he was the king's treasurer, who had been killed by a stray shot when he was with the baggage. (Other accounts suggest that he was killed deliberately as he tried to protect the military chest.) He also learnt that Thiebault's son was a prisoner.

> I made a package of the letters, and sent them to the son, accompanied by a note, to which I did not sign my name, that he might not be distressed, by knowing or meeting one who had read this affectionate correspondence; and I had the happiness of learning, that the recovery of these papers, these precious memorials of an amiable parent, having proved the greatest consolation to this unhappy young man.[86]

Of course, not everyone came near the treasure trove. The Fifth Division and Pack's Portuguese halted at Zurbano and the First Division also spent the night nowhere close to Vitoria, which denied them any share of the pillage. Hill's troops, likewise, did not approach the town. Yet there was more than enough to go round, even allowing for the fact that every camp follower, as well as many of the citizens of Vitoria and even some French soldiers, took their share of the loot. Soon a veritable market was set up.

> In the army six and eight dollars were offered for a guinea, it being impossible to carry the dollars. Mules, worth 250 dollars, were sold for three guineas ... All the Portuguese boys belonging to some of the divisions are dressed in the uniforms of French officers, many of generals. The camp of the infantry near Vitoria was turned into a fair – it was lighted – the cars, etc., made into stands, where the things taken were exposed for sale, and many of the soldiers, by way of adding to the absurdity of the scene, dressed themselves up in the uniforms found in the chests.[87]

Tomkinson does not reveal whether he was a customer at this fair.

Undoubtedly, for Wellington, the most galling aspect of the glorious free-for-all was the loss of the French military chest, five and a half million francs sent to Joseph's treasury. This was money that he could have used to repair his own military finances but now most of it was in the hands of his own 'scum of the earth'. That it rankled is demonstrated by a dispatch he sent to Lord Bathurst on 29 June:

> We started with the army in the highest order, and up to the day of the battle nothing could get on better; but that event has, as usual, totally annihilated all order and discipline. The soldiers of the army have got among them about a million sterling in money, with the exception of about 100,000 dollars, which were got for the military chest. The night of the battle, instead of being passed in getting rest and food to prepare them for the pursuit of the following day, was passed by the soldiers in looking for plunder.[88]

There was another kind of treasure that had fallen into the hands of the Allied soldiers. An army for which supplies had often been intermittent suddenly found itself in possession of a cornucopia of food and wine. Account after account details the feast that the writer enjoyed as darkness fell. According to Simmons, well supplied by his men, this was the best meal he had ever eaten, while Schaumann went one better. Having arrived at a hotel which was full of English officers, he first arranged the stabling of his horse and then in a large room, I found two long tables spread for a meal (tables at which the French officers had arranged to feast after their victory), and seated at them about 150 English officers of all ranks and regiments. Famished as we were, we devoured everything that was placed before us. The dishes consisted chiefly of roast mutton and various birds, and were very well cooked. But what was most welcome to our parched lips was the wine – Médoc, Burgundy and Champagne …

Being determined to sample all these wines, 'we tasted so often that not one of us remained sober. At last overcome by sleep, we ached for beds, and the landlord and his men were obliged to bring every available mattress, cushion and blanket down into the dining room.'[89] It was an excellent way to celebrate a victory.

So much for the triumphant Allies. Long before the Allied troops started their orgy of pillaging, Joseph and Jourdan had already made their escape from the scene of their disaster. Having withdrawn at about 6 pm from the high ground which had been their standpoint throughout the battle, they moved a little to the east of Vitoria even as their troops were being increasingly overwhelmed. Here they tried to restore some sort of order, as well as organize the departure of the artillery park. Both tasks proved impossible. By now, all the exit routes form the town were blocked, with the chaos already spreading well beyond. As for the soldiers, they simply paid no heed to king or marshal.

The sudden arrival of the 10th and 18th Hussars made their position perilous. Their only escort was two squadrons of the Lancers of the Guard, and although it seems possible that some other cavalry may have rallied to their assistance, it was still an unequal contest. As the lancers offered whatever defiance they could manage, Joseph hurriedly climbed into his carriage. Nowhere was passable, however. The hussars were threateningly close. In desperation, Joseph scrambled out of his carriage, hurriedly mounted a horse and, accompanied by his aides and Jourdan, joined his troops in making the best of his way to Salvatierra.

His carriage was soon plundered, setting the pattern for what would follow. The 14th Light Dragoons, who, like the rest of Alten's brigade, had played little part in the battle and had actually suffered no casualties, claimed Joseph's silver travelling chamber pot as a trophy. The 87th, of

Colville's brigade, who had played a notable part and suffered the heaviest losses in the Third Division, found a reward in a trophy of their own, the marshal's baton, discovered when they looted Jourdan's baggage. They would subsequently have to surrender it though, so that it could be sent as a trophy to the Prince Regent.

Others trying to make their escape, particularly the civilians, were less successful. Even those who managed to get their carriages out of Vitoria were soon trapped in the general chaos and found themselves at the mercy of the Allies. Yet, apart from Monsieur Thiebault mentioned above, there is no record of their being harmed. One, in particular had every reason to be grateful to those who came to her aid. Although Countess Gazan, the general's wife, had managed to leave the town, she had gone no distance before her carriage tumbled into a ditch. The first to encounter her was Thomas Browne. She had climbed out of her carriage and now

> declared to me in a scream who she was – I recommended her to re-enter the carriage, shut the door, & remain quiet – she said she would – There were, a Nurse and two little children of hers in the next carriage to her – It appears, that after I had ridden on she left her carriage, & in the hurry of the moment, lost the Nurse & Children ...[90]

When Mr Larpent came upon her, she was standing in the midst of broken carriages and other debris just outside the town. His first impression was of an elegant, well-dressed lady who introduced herself as the Countess de Gazan. She was anxious to save her carriage, horses and mules. With the assistance of two hussars Larpent managed to extricate the carriage and save four of the six animals. He then escorted the lady and her waiting-woman back to Vitoria and to the house of a friend before embarking on a search for her two-year-old son. This proved fruitless but a meeting with Wellington enabled him to carry back the message that the Allied commander would make sure the search for the child continued, and she was at liberty to join her husband.[91]

Although Larpent does not mention him, it is clear from Andrew Leith Hay's narrative and from some other sources that he also encountered Countess Gazan, since she was said to have enjoyed the assistance of both the judge advocate-general and one of Wellington's aide-de-camps. Leith Hay had spent the whole battle close to Wellington, although as a non-

The Waterloo of the Peninsula: the Battle of Vitoria 171

combatant because of his parole. Since he was the only Allied officer that she was acquainted with, she had been sending messages in the hope that one would reach him and he would befriend her in her present dangerous situation. He found her at the house of her Spanish acquaintances to which Larpent had escorted her. She told him that in the confusion she had entrusted her son to a gens-d'arme à cheval, who had disappeared in the crowd, and had also been separated from her servants. Leith Hay, like Larpent, searched the depot where the prisoners were being held, and where he found the servants, but there was no sign of the boy.[92] He continued to act as an escort to the countess during the following days, however, as a chance to repay the debt of gratitude he felt that he owed to her husband for his generous treatment of a prisoner, so unlike the attitude of Leval and Lamartinière.

There seemed little hope of finding the boy. Larpent heard subsequently that he had been killed between two carriages. Yet the story has a happier ending than might have been expected, according to Browne. Whereas Leith Hay simply stated that some days later she joined her husband and her child, Browne, after some acerbic comments about the speed with which she recovered from her loss and revelled in the attentions she received from the officers at headquarters, reported that

> the Child was afterwards found & restored to her. It had been seen on the ground, crying, by an English Cavalry Soldier, who took it up before him, carried it so for several Days, fed it with part of his rations, & had taken an amazing fancy to it – The Soldiers of his troop also made a great pet of it, & he parted with it at length, not without great reluctance.[93]

To return to the evening of the 21st, even without the cavalry to lead the chase there were infantry units enough to sustain the pressure on the fleeing French. As John Kincaid pertinently remarked, though, ordered troops will always be outpaced by disordered troops who have rid themselves of all the paraphernalia that might slow them down. Furthermore, desperation gives strength to tired legs. As darkness fell, Wellington called off the hunt, leaving the French to continue their flight. They had left behind not just their dead and wounded but also nearly 3,000 prisoners. This last, of course, is far fewer than an effective pursuit might have yielded. Nor were their casualties as high as might have been expected: 758 killed and 4,436 wounded. Similarly, the Allies had also suffered less than might have been expected, particularly when the numbers engaged are considered: 3,672 British, 921 Portuguese and 522 Spanish. For a battle during which there had been so much expenditure of ammunition, these numbers are surprising, and difficult to explain. Certainly, Richard Heneghan of the Field Train, who knew exactly how much ammunition had been expended by the Allies and could reckon the equivalent amount for the French, could not understand them.

They bring us to the darker side of any battle, however, and that should never be overlooked or forgotten, however glorious the victory. For all the reporting of their pillaging, eating and drinking, time and again the soldiers remembered their fallen comrades, as Edward Costello vividly described. After an evening spent drinking wine and brandy, come midnight one of them asked after a fallen comrade. Other names followed, and in each case the news was bad. Then a soldier called Treacy

> jumped up, and in a loud voice, called out to all, 'Hear me boys! Hear what I am going to say.'
>
> A deep silence followed. Treacy knelt on his knapsack, and squeezed his hands together in the attitude of prayer. 'May the Lord God grant that those fellows in yonder camp remain where they are until we have the pleasure of thrashing them for the gap they have this day made in our mess.'
>
> 'Amen! Amen!' responded a dozen voices, with an emphasis that would have done credit to a clerk in a country church, and, I am certain, with a better inclination for the desired object.[94]

Costello also remarked on the way his comrades reflected on the good qualities of their dead fellows and remained silent on their faults.

For Mr Larpent, who had arrived in the Peninsula during the retreat from Burgos, a pitched battle was a new experience that he was eager to witness. Along with Dr McGrigor and a few other non-combatants, he took position on a hill which was about a mile from the French and provided an excellent panorama of the whole battlefield. The group of spectators followed the action by moving from one hillside to another. Finally, sensing that a general Allied advance was now imminent, they

> advanced with the Household brigade constantly as they moved. We now began to see the effects of the guns. Dead and wounded men and

horses, some in the most horrible condition, were scattered all along the way we passed. These were principally cannon-shot wounds, and were on that account the more horrible. It was almost incredible that some could live in the state we saw them. From my black feather I was taken to be a doctor, and appealed to in the most miserable voice and affecting manner, so that I immediately took out my feather, not to be supposed so unfeeling as to pass on without taking any notice of these poor creatures. Our hospital spring-waggons were following us, and men with frames to lift up and carry off those near the road; some in the fields about crawled by degrees into the villages; but hundreds were lain without food or having their wounds dressed until now, two days afterwards.[95]

As much a battle tyro as Larpent was Thomas Playford of the Life Guards. He confessed in his memoirs that it was only then, as they advanced across the battlefield, that he became fully aware of the horrors of war, and offered himself the only relief he could think of, that his own sword had played no part.

> As we followed close behind the English infantry and artillery, we often passed over ground where dreadful carnage had taken place only a few moments before, and the sight of mangled human beings struggling in the agonies of death, with the cries and groans of the wounded laid in hopeless suffering beneath the feet of our horses, pained me very much, because I experienced a deep sympathy with these human sufferers. I could not bear to look upon the ground strewed with the dead and dying. But other soldiers could express their anxiety for close combat, and some could suddenly dismount, when an opportunity offered, and search the person of a dying officer for silver or gold.[96]

The men who had to try to deal with the horror Playford described were the surgeons. One such was 22-year-old Walter Henry who, like Larpent and Playford, was experiencing his first pitched battle. He was attached to the 2/66th, who formed the first provisional battalion with the 2/31st in Byng's brigade of the Second Division. As the troops readied themselves for battle, he was almost overwhelmed by the excitement of it.

> This was the first time I had seen a powerful army prepared for battle; and truly the sensation was exhilarating and intoxicating. I was young and ardent, and felt strong emotions in anticipating the approaching combat, and the probable discomfiture of those imposing masses. And though the reader may smile at the confession if good natured, and sneer if the reverse, I acknowledge that I was for a few moments half ashamed of my quiet profession; I longed to join in the impending struggle, and 'throw physic to the dogs.'[97]

When the action began, Henry found himself summoned to join the surgeons at Subijana de Álava, where O'Callaghan's brigade was taking heavy casualties.

> We collected the wounded in a little hollow out of the direct line of fire, but within half a musket shot of the village; unpacked our panniers and proceeded to our work. This Brigade had four or five hundred men killed and wounded in the course of an hour or two; so we were fully employed. A stray cannon shot, from a battery firing on the village, would occasionally drop amongst us, by way of an incentive to expeditious surgery; and after one of these unpleasant visitors had made his harmless appearance, a young chirurgeon of my acquaintance, who is still living, became so nervous, that although half through his amputation of a poor fellow's thigh, he dropped the knife, and another hand was obliged to complete the operation. But this was only a temporary weakness: at my suggestion he lay down on the grass, and did good service the whole day. Spring waggons were in attendance, in which we placed our worst patients and sent them to Puebla, where Dr. McGrigor, then at the head of the medical department in the Peninsula, had early in the day made the most judicious arrangements for their accommodation.[98]

As the situation at Subijana was brought under control, Henry was ordered to ascend the Puebla Heights and assist there. He 'reached the top of the mountain in time to witness the last moments of Colonel Cadogan of the 71st, whose death much resembled, and equalled in glory, that of Wolfe. After he received his mortal wound, he reclined with his back against a tree, beholding the progress of the battle, but with glazing eyes; and cheered, like Wolfe, by the defeat of the enemy.'[99]

The pressure on the surgeons was unremitting. Having given assistance on the Heights, he was then summoned back to Subijana, and witnessed a fierce contest between French tirailleurs, supported by artillery, and parties of Allied troops. There were heavy casualties. Henry counted 150 killed or seriously wounded in a field of less than two acres.

Once the French had withdrawn, 'Mr Wasdell, two other surgeons, and myself here set to work afresh, after swallowing some wine and biscuit; and we remained collecting, dressing, amputating, packing the wounded in the spring waggons and sending them to the temporary hospital till seven o'clock.'[100]

It is fair to say that the wounded had reason to thank not only the surgeons, like Walter Henry, for their unstinting efforts, but also James McGrigor for the excellent arrangements he had made in respect of carrying frames and temporary hospitals which did so much to improve their chances of survival.

As always happens in moments of crisis, some men proved themselves capable of great humanity to the enemy. Swabey, for example, thought nothing of lying between one of his own men and a wounded Frenchman as he waited for medical attention. The implication is clear. All were entitled to the doctors' care. For Augustus Frazer, there was the opportunity for even more active charity. Towards the end of the battle, as Reille was being forced to pull back from the Zadorra, Frazer found himself among the French wounded near Ariaga. As he wrote to his wife later that day: 'I had the opportunity of solacing the agonies, and probably the last moments, of the French general of division Sarrut, whom I helped out of the road, and laid against a bank, under charge of Bombardier Smith. I got the poor general some brandy, and sent him a surgeon. He said he was grateful, but dying. He was sadly wounded with case shot.' The following day, Frazer wrote: 'General Sarrut is dead. Poor Man!! I wish now I had taken his decoration of the Legion of Honour, but though I saw it, the general thanked me so warmly, and squeezed my hand with such earnestness, that I felt it would have been ungenerous to have taken the prize.'[101]

A much more pragmatic attitude is displayed in William Lawrence's encounter with a French soldier. It is not without a vestige of humanity but also shows keen awareness of his own interests.

I came across a poor wounded Frenchman crying to us in English not to leave him, as he was afraid of the bloodthirsty Spaniards: the poor fellow could not at most live more than two hours, as a cannon ball had completely carried off both thighs. He entreated me to stay with him, but I only did so as long as I found it convenient: I saw, too, that he could not last long, and very little sympathy could be expected from me then; so I ransacked his pockets and knapsack, and found a piece of pork ready cooked and three or four pounds of bread, which I thought would be very acceptable. The poor fellow asked me to leave him a portion, so I cut off a piece of bread and meat and emptied the beans out of my haversack, which with the bread and meat I left by his side. I then asked him if he had any money, to which he replied no, but not feeling quite satisfied at that, I again went through his pockets. I found ten rounds of ball cartridge which I threw away, and likewise a clothes-brush and a roll of gold and silver lace, but those I could not give carriage to. However, I found his purse at last, which contained seven Spanish dollars and seven shillings, all of which I put in my pocket except one shilling, which I returned to the poor dying man, and continued on my way up the hill.[102]

A Battle Won: A Battle Lost

It is a truism to state that some battles are won by the brilliance of the victors, whereas other battles are won because of the incompetence of the losers. There is obviously an element of truth in both parts of this statement when considering Vitoria, not only because of what happened on the battlefield itself but also because of the consequences for both the Allies and the French. For the former it was certainly a comprehensive victory, but not the crushing one it might have been. For the latter it was, without question, an overwhelming defeat and yet, as the expression goes, they lived to fight another day.

It is probably not surprising that, whether in their journals, their letters home or their memoirs, most combatants did not reflect in detail on how the battle had been won or lost. The conflict continued; the armies moved on; and the combatants moved on with them. On the Allied side there was plenty of self-congratulation. There was also much generous praise, particularly for the Portuguese, of which Thomas Browne's is typical. 'The conduct of the Portuguese troops in the battle of Vitoria had been admirable. Nothing could exceed their gallantry & discipline, & their loss was in full proportion to that of the British.'[103] Similarly, George Bell conceded that Morillo's Spaniards 'displayed unusual courage and fought well'. Patterson's more positive praise for Morillo and his men has already been referenced. As for the other Spanish corps on the field, Gomm wrote to his sister:

> I had almost forgot mentioning to you that we had a good deal to do with Longa, the famous guerilla, yesterday. His people behaved well, and were of much service. He is himself a young man; and for one so full of enterprise, and so little used to control, I thought his behaviour admirable, in falling so readily as he did into our plans – sometimes very opposite to his own.[104]

There was also praise for some individuals. Dickson, for example, in his letter to MacLeod, felt that he could not close 'without mentioning the valuable assistance my friend Frazer afforded during the whole business. I may truly say he flew from one troop to another, accompanying them into action, and attending to their supply, or looking out for roads for them to move. You who know Frazer so well can easily anticipate what he would be on such an occasion.'[105] At the same time, he offers no evaluation of the Allied victory, only noting that the French fought well until Allied pressure started to tell, whereupon they began to buckle.

Two men who did reflect on how the victory had been achieved were William Surtees and William Tomkinson. Surtees had been fighting the French since the Helder expedition of 1799, and thus had enough experience to pass judgement on them, and particularly on the French command.

> In looking back on the events of this day, I cannot help being struck with the bad generalship of those who commanded the French army. Marshal Jourdan, I understand, was Joseph's advisor on this occasion. He had always borne the character of an able General, but here he showed but little ability. Why did he so much weaken his force on the conical hill to support his left? Had he maintained his ground there, which is strong by nature, and they had rendered it strong by

art, he might have completely checked us on the right; for if we had advanced too far on that side, our wings would have been separated, which would have been a dangerous experiment; and I think Lord Wellington would not have hazarded it. And after leaving his first position, why did he not fight at every one of the beautiful little positions which he afterwards took up but never defended? This conduct is most unaccountable, for had he made a longer stand, even although he should be beaten, which no doubt he would have ultimately been, yet, by making this stand, he might have got off the greater part of his materiel, instead of which he carried off with him one gun and one howitzer only, leaving upwards of 250 pieces of ordnance in our hands. Most of his infantry left the field apparently unbroken; for only here and there they had stood to let our people get at them. It is true Sir Thomas Graham early cut off their retreat by the great road to France; but what then? This ought to have made them fight the more desperately, to enable them to get off the better by the Pamplona road. The infantry should have stood till the last, and not retired till fairly beaten out of the field. Nothing could be finer than the movements of our army.[106]

Despite the final sentence, it is clear from this evaluation that Surtees believed that the French, although unlikely to achieve a victory, could have managed a controlled retreat.

For Tomkinson, it was the movements of the Allied army before the battle, particularly the final movements that brought them to the battlefield, which secured victory.

Nothing can speak more for the judgement displayed in pushing on our advance, and the excellent arrangement in making the columns move to those points where they were required to attack. Had the left column moved with the remainder of the army, to the point on the main road before the enemy's position, and then been detailed to its appointed place, two days, or one at least would have been lost, and the divisions of the enemy in question [Clausel's and Foy's] might have joined. Most generals would, I think, have reconnoitred the enemy's position, having their whole force collected, and then have detached to the left. I look upon it as the best thing we have done connected with the whole advance.[107]

Put these two views together and it may be surmised that Allied strategy won the battle and French tactics lost it. On the French side, we have already seen that Jourdan held Gazan responsible for the defeat, when he failed to follow orders at the first crisis point. Jourdan also believed that if Gazan had sent Maransin's brigade to the Puebla Heights at the first appearance of the Spaniards and then supported him with a division, Morillo could have been swept aside before other Allied troops completed the ascent. This would have enabled the French to come down from the Heights and attack the Allied flank in the valley.[108] As a result, Hill's column would have been defeated before the other Allied forces had crossed the Zadorra, and the French would have enjoyed a victory or would at least have been able to hold the position until the arrival of Clausel.

Since the focus here is on the earliest stages of the battle, it is relevant to consider Gazan's description of what happened. In the letter to Clarke, already quoted, he explained that as soon General Maransin reported that

> a strong column was debouching from the Puebla defile, one half moving to the low-lying '*Grande Route*,' and the other half ascending the hill by the '*Petite Route*,' which leads from Puebla to Subijana de Álava. The Army of the South stood to arms at once, and struck camp. The 12th Regiment, Légère, was sent up the hill to help the outposts of [Maransin's] Brigade, and every disposition was made to resist the attack.

Once the Allied column had debouched and had started to ascend the Heights, 'General [Maransin] was ordered to move with his other Regiments to help the 12th Légère, and the 21st and 100th Regiments of the 6th Division under General Daricau marched to support [Maransin's] Brigade.'[109]

The one conclusion to be drawn from this difference of opinion as to whether or not Gazan offered an inadequate response to Morillo's ascent of the Heights is that the French command had neither expected an attack along the Heights nor prepared for the possibility, except by placing some voltigeurs in sufficient strength to observe and report, but in insufficient strength to stem a determined attack.

Hippolyte d'Espinchal, of course, had already blamed Jourdan's obstinacy for the debacle, a view he posited even before he started his account of the battle. He was pleased to report, therefore, that the next day 'The King was distressed by the misfortune that he had brought about by following the suggestions of Marshal Jourdan, who, for his part, reproached himself for his unforgiveable mistakes; but, unfortunately, he recognised it was too late and he lost his mind.'[110]

It was more comforting to praise those who had fought so well, despite all the mistakes. Supreme among them, in d'Espinchal's opinion, was the commander of the Army of Portugal, 'who deserved admiration for the way he had held off the masses of a victorious army with his weak corps. Two horses were shot under him, his coat was pierced by two musket balls, and his hat, knocked from his head by a shell.' That evening he arrived at the bivouac with nothing but the horse he was riding. Yet he was calmly imperturbable and d'Espinchal could only admire his insouciance. 'Count Reille, not more than 35 years old, had acquired great talents in the school of his father-in-law, Marshal Masséna, and he was rightly considered as one of the finest generals of the Empire.'[111] It is unlikely that many would have disagreed with this judgement, even among the Allied officers.

While Tomkinson ascribed Allied success to the strategy that had brought the army so effectively to the battlefield, General Maucune held the opposite view of the French. Having left Vitoria very early on the 21st with the second convoy, he reached Mondragon later that day. Here he found General Foy on the march towards Vitoria. Maucune told Foy;

> No-one is in command; the King is in a state of continual indecision; we are aware that the English army has been manoeuvring by the left since the start of the campaign. We want neither to fight nor to retire; we do not even have a plan. Vitoria is encumbered with artillery materiel and carriages. Everything that has been tried against the English has failed. The troops are good but they have lost heart because they are badly led. We are in danger of a great catastrophe.[112]

Not surprisingly, there was an anxious wait for news. According to Captain Nicolas Marcel of the 69eme de la ligne;

We did not know anything yet of the affair at Vitoria: we had seen neither fugitive nor courier on the road we occupied, but the joy on the faces of the Spanish townspeople and peasants made us think we had not been victorious; many soldiers of the regiment, who had undoubtedly heard the news from the women, told their officers that the Spanish couriers had announced everywhere that our army had been routed. Towards evening, General Foy, on whose face one could read his concern, gave the order to depart.

During the night fugitives from the battle brought in the first certain news. 'The English had debouched where no-one could have expected them to arrive; our troops, attacked from behind and not having the time to receive any orders, fell into a terrible state of confusion: only the two divisions of the Army of Portugal had fought with heroic courage; all the rest, infantry, cavalry, artillery, were seized with terror.'[113] It was indeed the catastrophe that Maucune had predicted.

In the two centuries since most of these judgements were passed, many commentators have added their own interpretations as to why, from the Allied perspective, the result of the Battle of Vitoria was unsatisfactory because it failed to deliver the killer blow which would have rendered Joseph's forces incapable of mounting any kind of fightback. The French had suffered a devastating loss of materiel but they were still a fighting force that managed to cross the Pyrenees some 55,000 strong, ready to continue the conflict. Oman concluded: 'That the battle of Vitoria was the crowning point of a brilliant strategic campaign is obvious. That in tactical details it was not by any means so brilliant an example of what Wellington and his army could accomplish, is equally obvious.'[114]

The consensus view would probably run along the lines that a complex plan in which timing was absolutely crucial was always susceptible to less than complete success if even one element failed. From the moment Hill launched his attack, the other three columns were required to make their own movements in accordance with what was happening on their right. Cole being held up at Nanclares was a hitch, but one that was solved when Wellington sent Kempt's brigade upstream and they were able to cross at Tres Puentes. Far more serious was Dalhousie's failure to appear, particularly as Graham was supposed to be timing his approach to the Zadorra in accordance with his. Yes, the centre left was required to advance across the roughest terrain of all four columns, country unsuited for guns. Yet, as Oman pointed out, Cairnes managed to catch up with Grant's brigade, while Barnes' and Le Cor's brigades were never seriously engaged, as their casualty returns demonstrate: no losses in Barnes' brigade and only six in Le Cor's as against 328 in Grant's. Oman identified poor staff work, and therefore a failure on the commander's part, as the cause of the two brigades losing their way when they 'did not take the path assigned to them, and went right over, instead of skirting, the summit of Monte Arrato, making an apparently short (and precipitous) cut, which turned out to be a long one'.[115] To add to this failing, Dalhousie only attacked (with his one brigade) when he received a specific order to do so. Yet, by the irony on which the fate of an army may depend, because of Dalhousie's delayed arrival which kept Picton leashed until that general's patience ran out, Jourdan was able to conclude that no attack would be made on his right and he could send troops to the Heights to deal with Hill.

As for Graham, who has also been found wanting, his over-cautious approach certainly seemed difficult to justify to Fortescue, who wondered why he did not force the passage of the Zadorra. He could have attempted to ford the river, which was shallow in parts; and, instead of concentrating on the bridges at Gamarra Mayor and Ariaga, he might have sent support to Longa once he had taken the bridge at Durana.[116] The answer seems to be that, like Wellington, he believed Reille to have four divisions of the Army of Portugal, and there was also the problematic instruction that he was not 'to descend into the low grounds towards Vitoria or the great road, nor give up the advantage of turning the enemy's position and the town of Vitoria by a movement to [his] left'.[117] Orders stating what not to do are more challenging to implement that those that give clear instructions for action. Perhaps, as an exacerbating factor, Graham was not by nature a cautious general; requiring him to act against his instincts was probably bound to produce an overreaction.

It should also be added that whereas the ground proved totally unsuitable for a cavalry pursuit of the retreating French, it was ideal for a fighting withdrawal. And until the final panic set in, the French offered just that, a fighting withdrawal in which the troops behaved admirably. By the time retreat turned to rout, there was no real risk that either the Allied cavalry, struggling with the terrain, or the Allied infantry, most of which had been on the move since dawn, would overwhelm them.

When Vitoria is considered from the French perspective, it may well be surmised that it was a battle lost from the moment Joseph, in Jourdan's absence, oversaw the dispositions of his army. This was certainly the implicit opinion of Jean Sarramon as he listed the king's mistakes, from a front that was too wide for an outnumbered force to sustain to his failure to destroy the bridges, set defences at the fords and on the crest of the Puebla Heights, or even secure a line of retreat. As a result, the French were left in a position where they were forced into a general action without even the most basic provision having been made for their defence. Sarramon also wondered why no-one had taken the initiative and reconnoitred the terrain.

When it came to the actual battle, Sarramon instanced as crucial to the French defeat Gazan's errors in the placing and movement of his troops and Jourdan's failure to recognize the danger to his right, which (as noted above) led him to weaken his centre, a mistake made more comprehensive by the failure to protect Durana and the Great Road, where only an inadequate force of *Josefinos* was posted to guard this crucial escape route.[118]

Whatever the rights and wrongs of these various judgements, contemporary and modern, one thing is clear. 'Once again the war of independence in the Iberian Peninsula had played an undeniable role in the destiny of Napoleon I.'[119] He would later call the long campaign his Spanish ulcer. On 21 June 1813, the ulcer had finally burst.

Chapter 7

Consequences

As night fell on 21 June, the troops that had continued to press the French beyond Vitoria gave up their pursuit. Those that had never come near the town settled into their bivouacs, bone-weary by their own accounts. Even the plunderers retired to gloat over their rich pickings and enjoy the largesse of unlimited rations. It might be argued that men who had behaved admirably during a harassing advance, who had been on the move since daybreak and who had carried out their commander's orders in all respects until the French were driven from the field deserved the chance to enjoy their triumph in their own way. As we have seen, that was not Wellington's opinion, and he was justified in as far as those who caroused the longest (which included some officers, as Scherer made clear) were in no fit state to continue the pursuit until well into the following day.

It has to be conceded that, however much Wellington deserves to be admired for his military talents, he could not or would not understand the men who served under him. In his dispatch, produced for public consumption, he had written: 'I cannot extol too highly the good conduct of all the General Officers, Officers, and soldiers of the army in this action.'[1] Yet on 2 July he wrote to Bathurst:

> It is quite impossible for me or any other man to command a British army under the existing system. We have in the service *the scum of the earth* [my italics] as common soldiers; and of late years we have been doing everything in our power, both by law and by publications, to relax the discipline by which alone such men can be kept in order. The officers of the lower ranks will not perform the duty required from them for the purpose of keeping their soldiers in order; and it is next to impossible to punish any officer for neglects of this description. As for the non-commissioned officers, as I have repeatedly stated, they are as bad as the men, and too near them, in point of pay and

situation, by the regulations of late years, for us to expect them to do anything to keep the men in order. It really is a disgrace to have any thing to say to such men as some of our soldiers are.[2]

If anything redeems this outburst, reminiscent of similar comments after the retreat of 1812, it is the 'some' of that final sentence. An army as disreputable as Wellington suggests could never have performed as it did, not only on 21 June but also during the month that preceded it.

For the French the coming of darkness only compounded the disorder that existed in all but the Army of Portugal. The other troops struggled on in what they could only hope was the direction of Salvatierra. That first night, as panic eased and exhaustion took its toll, groups of men clustered round small fires until there were thousands of them illuminating the hillside, enough, according to Fée, to convince any pursuers that their enemy had rallied. As for Joseph, having ridden non-stop from Vitoria to Salvatierra, he now had the poor comfort of a meal definitely not fit for a king, with only d'Erlon and just two ministers for company. Eventually, Jourdan arrived. He made only one comment on the disaster that had overtaken them: 'Well, gentlemen, they *would* have their battle, and it is a lost battle.'[3]

By the following morning, most of the survivors were at or within reach of Salvatierra. They still had their arms but few other possessions. Nor were the officers in a much better state, having lost their baggage and in many cases their men. Some sort of order was restored, enough for the army to march on, but many of the soldiers would take several days to find their units. The 22nd was another of the grim days, wet and miserable, that had made Gomm think of November. And the effect of the gloomy weather was compounded by the need to continue the retreat. Yet there was just one glimmer of consolation. There was no sign of any Allied pursuit which meant they could hope to put some distance between themselves and their enemy as they set out on what many of them must have realized was a march back to France. As Joseph and Jourdan rode directly to Pamplona, the troops trudged along behind them.

The sole objective now was to bring the army to the safety of French soil. On the 23rd Joseph instructed Reille, whose corps was obviously in the best order, to march to Tolosa, where Foy was assumed to be. When Reille pointed out that the route might well bring him into contact with the enemy, the order was altered so that he was now to march his troops to San Estevan and then on to Irun, in order to guard the lower Bidassoa against an Allied invasion. Only when the two convoys had crossed the border and it became clear that Wellington was not planning any such invasion did Reille finally leave Spain.

The Armies of the Centre and the South continued their march to Pamplona, arriving there on the 24th. The governor would not allow the troops to enter the town which says much about the state they were in. They had been demoralized before the battle. Now they were demoralized, disordered and defeated. Joseph stayed in Pamplona long enough to strengthen the garrison with an extra 3,000 men and also to send parties in all directions to scour the country for supplies. The Allies were drawing closer, however. Even before the Army of the Centre had reached the town the Light Division and Alten's cavalry had caught up with Darmagnac's division. Darmagnac managed to extricate his troops with considerable skill, but the two guns that had been brought from the battlefield were lost. One was taken and the other was destroyed when it toppled 15ft down a hillside. Then, on the night of the 24th, Gazan and the Army of the South crossed into France by the Pass of Roncesvalles, and d'Erlon, by the Pass of Maya, having received an additional order to maintain contact with Reille.

With the main army either over the border or close enough to it to effect a quick crossing, that left Clausel and Foy dangerously exposed. On the 22nd June Clausel had been at Trevino, a day's march from Vitoria, with 14,000 men. He had sent scouts ahead towards Logroño and they returned with news of the defeat. Clausel now searched for the main French army, moving east towards Viana, then north. On the 23rd, although he now knew where to direct his march, he was warned that the Allies were near, whereupon he retraced his steps, reaching Logroño on the 24th. His purpose was to take up the garrison before marching on, and this required him to stay until the following day.

Clausel, however, was now Wellington's principal target. The Allied commander learnt from an intercepted letter that the French general had intended to make for Salvatierra from Trevino. Most of the Allied troops had marched out of Vitoria by midday on the 22nd, but Wellington had already called in the Sixth Division to the town, where he also left the Fifth Division, D'Urban's and the heavy cavalry, and a small detachment from each battalion to collect in the abandoned French guns. As a result of the information in the letter, he sent the Fifth Division to Salvatierra, while the other troops were ordered to advance on Logroño.

On the 25th, though, Clausel moved on, first following the course of the Ebro to Mendavia, and then heading north to Pamplona. News that Mina was in the vicinity caused him to change direction yet again, in the direction of Tudela. When Wellington learnt that Clausel had been at Mendavia, however, he immediately surmised that Tudela was his objective and ordered Mina to move there, while he set up his own pursuit. On the 26th he issued the relevant orders. Hill's column was to stay and invest Pamplona, except for Byng's brigade and Morillo's Spaniards, who were to advance towards Roncesvalles in order to put pressure on the Army of the South. He then marched towards Tudela with the Hussar Brigade and the Third, Fourth, Seventh and Light Divisions, making in the first instance for Tafella.

Clausel reached Tudela on the 27th. Warned of Wellington's advance, he destroyed the bridge and the stores held by the garrison, re-crossed the Ebro and made for Zaragoza. He was followed by Mina, although Clausel seems to have thought that the pursuing force was Wellington's. After a three-day march the French reached Zaragoza, from where Clausel wrote to Suchet that he intended his next position to be on the river Gallego. Then, if Wellington sent more troops to the east, he, Clausel, would be able to join the marshal. On the other hand, if Joseph brought his army back, Clausel would join him. This second possibility makes clear that he had not yet appreciated the true nature of the disaster that had befallen the French at Vitoria. The only force fit to fight from the main army was Reille's, which had been reinforced from Bayonne. As for Suchet, whatever threat the Anglo-Sicilian and Spanish forces offered, and Murray had just raised the siege of Tarragona, he was not about to become Wellington's target.

Wellington had now decided to leave dealing with Clausel to Mina, who assiduously spread rumours that the Allies were approaching. On 3 July, Clausel abandoned his baggage, left General Paris, the governor, and the garrison to defend the place against Mina, and also Sanchez, still intent on harrying the French, and marched up the Gallego to Jaca, which he reached on the 6th. Here he waited for news from either Suchet or Joseph, but when he learnt on the 11th that General Paris had been defeated by Mina, he took his troops back to France.

General Foy at Mondragon had been much closer to the action on 21 June than Clausel at Trevino, so that on the 22nd he was in a distinctly more dangerous position. Wellington had already detached Longa's and Girón's troops to overtake the convoys, which would bring them to Mondragon. Foy had been forewarned of the likelihood of an Allied incursion by panic-stricken fugitives and then by men who had left the posts they were supposed to be holding along the Great Road. He reacted quickly. At Vergera, which the second convoy had already reached, having departed from Mondragon early in the morning, he urged Maucune to send it on its way with all speed and then join him. He next marched back to Mondragon with two battalions in the hope of gaining time for the convoy to make enough progress to keep it clear of the Allies, only to encounter the Spanish troops as they advanced along the Great Road. Foy was outnumbered three to one, but he decided to make a stand, again to help the convoy on its way. Even though more troops came in, he eventually had no choice but to make a fighting withdrawal which cost him over 200 men and six guns.

On the 23rd, Wellington ordered Graham to take his troops, except the Fifth Division which was to remain at Salvatierra, towards Villafranca, on the Great Road via the San Adriano Pass. His task was to take up any French retreating in that direction and seize one or both the convoys if they had taken that route. Thanks to some confusion the order went astray, giving Wellington the chance to vent his spleen on Captain Norman Ramsey RA, whom he came upon in the wrong place according to the order.[4] Even when Graham finally departed on the 23rd, because of poor staff work he missed the pass. At the same time Foy had returned to Mondragon, having discovered that the Spanish troops had extended to the east, as if to link up with other Allied troops using the San Adriano Pass on their advance. He was waiting for the outlying garrisons to come in, and at the same time was sending orders to Maucune to direct the convoy to make straight for Tolosa while bringing his division to Villafranca. Then, late at night, news arrived that an Allied column (Graham's) was advancing to cut off his retreat. At 3 am on the 24th Foy was himself marching for Villafranca.

Graham did not approach Villafranca until late on the 24th. Although Foy's troops could be seen on the march, the Allies found their way blocked by Maucune's division and Foy's Italian brigade, which had just come into position at Béazain. A sharp fight followed. Maucune, attacked by Halkett's brigade of the First Division and Pack's Portuguese, resisted strongly, while the Italian brigade held out against Bradford's Portuguese. It finally took a flank attack to break down the French defence, only for Graham to discover that another two brigades from Foy's division were posted in front of Villafranca. As the Allies moved to attack these troops, Maucune was able to withdraw and follow Foy. By this time it was too late to continue the fight. Foy's troops also withdrew, leaving Graham in possession of Villafranca. He had lost over 90 men, but the French had lost more than 200.

The following day there was yet another encounter, at Tolosa, between Foy and Graham, who now had Longa's and Girón's leading troops with him. The town, which lies in a defile and was an essential post on the Great Road, had strong defences, and Foy felt sufficiently secure to make a stand. As events would prove, any frontal attack alone was likely to suffer heavily but Graham sent Longa to make an extended flanking movement on the right, while a lesser movement was made by Bradford to distract the enemy. Longa would then be able to attack the position from the rear, strengthened by some Spanish irregulars whom General Mendizabel was bringing up. Pack and some of Girón's light troops also made a flanking movement on the left to further distract the French. Longa and Mendizabel took far longer to come into action than Graham had expected and, with the day fading, he decided to send in Halkett's brigade. As already suggested, though, when Halkett launched an attack head on the KGL troops were repulsed with heavy casualties. The Spanish were now skirmishing with the defenders and threatening to overwhelm them, but it was only when the Allied guns blew in the gates of Tolosa that the position became impossible to hold. Under cover of darkness, however, Foy was able to withdraw his remaining troops, for he himself admitted to losing 400 men, the true number probably being higher, and a further 200 were taken prisoner. Allied losses, none of which were British, were similarly heavy in what had been a short, fierce and bloody contest.

Graham halted for the next two days while he tried to make contact with the main Allied force. This enabled Foy to advance towards Ernani and call in yet more of the garrisons. And then, when the second convoy finally crossed into France on the 27th, the first having already arrived, he was free to follow it. He put 3,000 troops into San Sebastian under the command of General Rey, who had safely delivered the first convoy. Then he continued his retreat, stopping only to put a garrison into Passages. On 1 July he crossed the Bidassoa into France, although not before he had driven off some of Girón's troops. The same day the men at Passages surrendered to Longa.

July 1st was also the day when Wellington decided to halt the pursuit. He needed to secure his supply lines and his army needed a pause to recuperate from their exertions. Furthermore, there were two strong fortresses in his rear that needed to be taken, for which purpose Hill continued to blockade Pamplona and Graham invested San Sebastian. There was some attempt at a counter-movement from the Army of the South, which Joseph sent into the Baztan Valley. It was short-lived, however, when Hill handed over command at Pamplona to the Spanish General, Enrique O'Donnell, and took two British and two Portuguese brigades to deal with this incursion. On 7 July the French were driven back across the Pyrenees.

This was not the end of the struggle. Soult would arrive to re-form the French army and the fight would continue. But this only delayed the now inevitable invasion of France.

* * *

As might be expected and as a near-contemporary work makes clear,

> The joy and congratulation with which the intelligence of the victory of Vittoria was received in England cannot be described. Every man was sensible that this victory bore, on its very front, more decisive marks of usefulness, as well as of glory, that any of the former victories which Lord Wellington had gained. Many of his former triumphs had been obtained at a great cost of blood, without any permanent advantage; but the victory of Vittoria presented a happy and glorious contrast to some of the barren victories of former campaigns: the rout of the enemy was complete, extensive, and signal; each successive day proved its magnitude and importance; the enemy had lost all his artillery, which, with a French army, is of a value inestimable; but above all, the moral effect of this achievement transcended all Lord Wellington's previous victories. The British government and

people displayed their sense of his high deserts in the most marked and gratifying manner; the marshal's staff captured on the occasion had been sent over to the prince regent, who in return created Lord Wellington a field-marshal, and the Spanish government, as a proof of their sense of obligation for his services, elevated him to the rank of Duke of Vittoria.[5]

For Joseph and Jourdan the story was very different. Joseph was forced by his brother to accept the restoration of the Bourbon ruling family in the person of Ferdinand VII, although he always maintained he had never actually abdicated. He would enjoy another brief period of nominal command as Lieutenant General of the Empire during the battle for Paris in 1814, but he would eventually live as an exile in the United States after his brother's fall from power the following year. Jourdan accepted the restoration of the Bourbons, supported Napoleon during the Hundred Days, being rewarded with a very limited command, and then accepted the Bourbons again after Waterloo. He would end his life as governor of Le Invalides.

While there were celebrations in Britain and dismay in France, it was in Central Europe that the Allied victory at Vitoria had the most immediate effect. The battle coincided with a truce between Napoleon and the combined powers of Austria, Prussia and Russia. Despite a setback against the Prussians at Bautzen on 20 May, Napoleon was very much on the offensive and the tide was running with him. He was concerned by the length of his supply lines, however, and also sensed some lack of commitment to the coalition in the Austrians, so he took a chance and agreed to a truce, which was to last until 15 August. Before that date, the news of Vitoria reached Vienna. The Austrians had been wavering, but, learning of the crushing nature of the French defeat and their virtual ejection from Spain, Emperor Francis II committed himself to the alliance. With Wellington now threatening France from the south and his Central European enemies once more unified, Napoleon's future suddenly looked very grim.

If there is any one thing that signifies the magnitude of the victory at Vitoria, it has to be Beethoven's Battle Symphony. Few battles have been celebrated in music and none, surely, closer to the event than Beethoven's composition. It is not one of his great works. It was written for a friend who wanted something to celebrate 'Wellington's Victory' that could be performed on his panharmonicon, a mechanical contraption that reproduced the sound of military instruments. Unfortunately, the resultant composition was beyond the capacity of any such machine, so Beethoven rewrote the piece for orchestra, dedicating it to the Prince Regent. It was first performed in December 1813, at a benefit concert for soldiers wounded at the Battle of Hanau. The irony of the composition lies in the fact that Beethoven was formerly one of Napoleon's most ardent admirers, seeing him as a bearer of liberty. And then Napoleon made himself emperor. By 1813 Wellington was the hero of the day.

Appendix 1

Wellington's Army in the Vitoria Campaign Marching Strength 25 May 1813

Cavalry

	Off.	Men	Total
R. Hill's Brigade: 1st & 2nd Life Guards, Horse Guards	42	828	870
Ponsonby's Brigade: 5th Dragoon Guards, 3rd & 4th Dragoons	61	1,177	1,238
G. Anson's Brigade: 12th & 16th Light Dragoons	39	780	819
Long's Brigade: 13th Light Dragoons	20	374	394
V. Alten's Brigade: 14th Light Dragoons, 1st Hussars KGL	49	956	1,005
Bock's Brigade: 1st & 2nd Dragoons KGL	38	594	632
Fane's Brigade: 3rd Dragoon Guards, 1st Dragoons	42	800	842
Grant's Brigade: 10th, 15th, 18th Hussars	63	1,561	1,624
D'Urban's Portuguese Brigade 1st, 11th, 12th Cavalry		685	685
Campbell: 6th Portuguese Cavalry		208	208

Wellington and the Vitoria Campaign 1813

Infantry

	Off.	Men	Total
1st Division (General Howard) Stopford's Brigade: 1st Coldstream Guards, 1st Scots Guards, 1 company 5/60th	56	1,672	1,728
Halkett's Brigade; 1st, 2nd, 5th Line KGL, 1st & 2nd Light KGL	133	2,993	<u>3,126</u>
			4,859
2nd Division (General Sir Rowland Hill) Cadogan's Brigade: 1/50th, 1/71st, 1/92nd, 1 company 5/60th	120	2,657	2,777
Byng's Brigade: 1/3rd, 1/57th, 1st Prov. Battn (2/31st & 2/66th), 1 company 5/60th	131	2,334	2,465
O'Callaghan's Brigade: 1/28th, 2/34th, 1/39th, 1 company 5/60th	122	2,408	2,530
Ashworth's Portuguese: 6th & 18th Line, 6th Caçadores		3,062	<u>3,062</u>
			10,834
3rd Division (General Sir Thomas Picton) Brisbane's Brigade: 1/45th, 74th, 1/88th, 3 companies 5/60th	125	2,598	2,723
Colville's Brigade: 1/5th, 2/83rd, 2/87th, 94th	120	2,156	2,276
Powers Portuguese Brigade: 9th & 21st Line, 11th Caçadores		2,460	<u>2,460</u>
			7,459
4th Division (General Sir G. Lowry Cole) W. Anson's Brigade: 3/27th, 1/40th, 1/48th, 2nd Prov. Battn (2nd & 2/53rd), 1 company 5/60th	139	2,796	2,935
Skerret's Brigade: 1/7th, 20th, 1/23rd, 1 company Brunswick Oels	123	1,926	2,049
Stubb's Portuguese Brigade: 11th & 23rd Line, 7th Caçadores		2,842	<u>2,842</u>
			7,826

Appendix 1 195

	Off.	Men	Total
5th Division (General Oswald) Hay's Brigade: 3/1st, 1/9th, 1/38th, 1 company Brunswick Oels	109	2,183	2,292
Robinson's Brigade: 1/4th, 2/47th, 2/59th, 1 company Brunswick Oels	100	1,961	2,061
Spry's Portuguese Brigade: 3rd & 15th Line, 8th Caçadores		2,372	2,372
			6,725
6th Division (General Pakenham) Stirling's Brigade: 1/42nd, 1/79th, 1/91st, 1 company 5/60th	127	2,327	2,454
Hinde's Brigade: 1/11th, 1/32nd, 1/36th, 1/61st	130	2,288	2,418
Madden's Portuguese Brigade: 8th & 12th Line, 9th Caçadores		2,475	2,475
			7,347
7th Division (General Lord Dalhousie) Barnes' Brigade: 1/6th, 3rd Prov. Battn, 9 companies Brunswick Oels	116	2,206	2,322
Grant's Brigade: 51st, 68th, 1/82nd, Chasseurs Britanniques	141	2,397	2,538
Lecor's Portuguese Brigade: 7th & 19th Line, 2nd Caçadores		2,437	2,437
			7,297
Light Division (General Charles Alten) Kempt's Brigade: 1/43rd, 1st & 3rd/95th	98	1,979	2,077
Vandeleur's Brigade: 1/52nd, 2/95th	63	1,399	1,462
Portuguese Brigade: 17th Line, 1st & 2nd Caçadores			1,945
			5,484
Silveira's Portuguese Division: Da Costa's Brigade: 2nd & 14th Line		2,492	2,492

	Off.	Men	Total
A. Campbell's Brigade: 4th & 10th Line, 10th Caçadores		2,795	2,795
			5,287
Pack's Portuguese Brigade: 1st & 16th Line, 10th Caçadores		2,297	2,297
Bradford's Portuguese Brigade: 13th & 24th Line, 5th Caçadores		2,392	2,392
Artillery: Royal Horse Artillery & drivers	23	780	803
Field Artillery, Train, Ammunition Column etc.	100	2,722	2,822
KGL Artillery	17	335	352
Portuguese Artillery			330
			4,307
Engineers & Sappers	41	302	343
Staff Corps	21	126	147
Wagon Train	37	165	202
Total strength			81,276

Appendix 2

Spanish Troops under Wellington's Command (as of 1 June)

Fourth Army (General Girón)

	Off	Men	Total
Morillo's Division	172	4,379	4,551
Losada's Galician Division	295	5,560	5,855
P. Barcena's Division	235	4,908	5,143
Porlier's Asturian Division	124	2,284	2,408
Longa's Division	130	3,000	3,130
Penne Villemur's Cavalry	194	2,434	2,628
Julian Sanchez's Cavalry	90	1,200	1,290
Artillery	20	400	420
	1,260	24,165	25,425

Appendix 3

The French Army under the Command of Joseph Bonaparte during the Vitoria Campaign
(based on 1 May returns)

The Army of Portugal (General Honoré Reille)

Infantry:	
4th Division (General Sarrut) Fririon's Brigade: 2eme léger, 36eme de la ligne	2,590
Menne's Brigade 4eme léger, 65eme de la ligne	<u>1,985</u>
	4,575
5th Division (General Maucune) Montfort's Brigade: 17eme léger, 15eme de la ligne	1,746
Pinoteau's Brigade: 66eme de la ligne, 82eme de la ligne, 86eme de la ligne	<u>2,248</u>
	3,994
6th Division (General Lamartinière) Gauthier's Brigade: 118eme de la ligne, 119eme de la ligne	1,692
Menne's Brigade: 120eme de la ligne, 122eme de la ligne	<u>2,217</u>
	3,909
Cavalry: Mermet's Division	
Curto's Brigade: 3eme hussars, 22eme chasseurs, 26eme chasseurs 13eme chasseurs, 14eme chasseurs	1,651
Boyer's Brigade: 6eme dragons, 11eme dragons, 15eme dragons, 25eme dragons	<u>1,428</u>
	3,079

Total Infantry	12,478
Total Cavalry	3,079
Total Artillery, Field Train, Engineers, Waggon Train, Gendarmes	4,157
	19,714

The Army of the South (General Gazan)

Infantry:	
1st Division (General Leval) Mocquery's Brigade: 9eme léger, 24eme de la ligne	2,430
Morgan's Brigade: 88eme de la ligne, 96eme de la ligne	1,930
	4,360
2nd Division (General Cassagne) Braun's Brigade: 16eme léger, 8eme de la ligne	2,018
Blondeau's Brigade: 51eme de la ligne, 54 de la ligne	2,343
	4,361
3rd Division (General Villatte) Rignoux's Brigade: 27eme léger, 63eme de la ligne	2,935
Lefoi's Brigade: 94eme de la ligne, 95eme de la ligne	2,890
	5,825
4th Division (General Conroux) Jean Rey's Brigade: 32eme de la ligne, 43eme de la ligne	3,649
Schwitter's Brigade: 55eme de la ligne, 58eme de la ligne	2,598
	6,247
5th Division Maransin's Brigade: 12eme léger, 45eme de la ligne	2,861
6th Division (Darricau) Baille de Saint-Pol's Brigade: 21eme léger, 100eme de la ligne	2,711

Remond's Brigade: 28eme léger, 103eme de la ligne	<u>1,984</u>
	4,695
Cavalry: Pierre Soult's Division: Vinot's Brigade: 2eme hussars, 21eme chasseurs	501
2nd Brigade: 5eme chasseurs, 10eme chasseurs	<u>896</u>
	1,397
Tilly's Division: Ismert's Brigade: 2eme dragons, 4eme dragons, 26eme dragons	1,222
Ormancey's Brigade: 14eme dragons, 17eme dragons, 27eme dragons	<u>1074</u>
	2,296
Digeon's Brigade: Sparre's Brigade: 5eme dragons, 12eme dragons	865
2nd Brigade: 16eme dragons, 21eme dragons	<u>827</u>
	1,692
Total Infantry	23,488
Total Cavalry	3,485
Artillery and Field Train	<u>2,712</u>
	31,685

Army of the Centre (General Drouet, Comte d'Erlon)

Infantry:	
1st Division (General Darmagnac): Chassé's Brigade: 28eme de la ligne, 75eme de la ligne	2,089
Neuenstein's Brigade: 2eme de Nassau, 4eme de Baden, Frankfurt	<u>2,678</u>
	4,767
Cavalry:	
Trelliard's Division: 13eme dragons, 18eme dragons, 19eme dragons, 22 dragons	1,046

Avy's Brigade: 27eme chasseurs, chasseurs de Nassau	<u>484</u>
	1,530
Spanish Division (Marquis de Casapalacios): Infantry Brigade: Castille, Toledo, Royal Etranger	2,234
Cavalry Brigade: 1eme, 2eme chasseurs, chasseurs d'Avila, hussards de Guadalajara	<u>200</u>
	2,434
Guarde Royale (Jamin, Marquis de Bermuy): Infantry: Grenadiers, voltigeurs, fusiliers	1,763
Cavalry:	
Chevau-légers, hussards	<u>450</u>
	2,213
Total infantry:	13,125
Total cavalry:	<u>2,182</u>

Based on returns as in Sarramon, pp. 671–7 and Oman VI, pp. 754–6. Units have been placed with whichever of the three armies they belonged to, although the text makes clear that some were transferred to a different army in the course of the campaign.

Appendix 4

Allied Losses at the Battle of Vitoria

	Killed		Wounded		Missing		Total
	Officers	Men	Officers	Men	Officers	Men	
INFANTRY							
1st Division (General Howard)							
Stopford's Brigade:							
1st Coldstream Guards	x	x	x	x	x	x	x
1/3rd Guards	x	x	x	x	x	x	x
Halkett's Brigade:							
1st, 2nd 5th Line K.G.L.	x	1	x	1	x	x	2
1st Light K.G.L.	x	1	1	7	1	7	9
2nd Light K.G.L.	x	4	x	39	x	x	43
Divisional total	x	6	1	47	x	x	54
2nd Division (General Sir William Stewart)							
Cadogan's Brigade:							
1/50th	x	27	7	70	x	x	104
1/71st	3	41	12	260	x	x	316
1/92nd	x	4	x	16	x	x	20
Byng's Brigade:							
1/3rd	x	3	7	96	x	x	110
1/37th	x	5	2	21	x	x	28
1st Prov.Battn (2/31st & 2/66th)	x	3	2	35	x	x	40
O'Callaghan's Brigade:							
1/28th	x	12	17	171	x	x	199
2/34th	x	10	3	63	x	x	76
1/39th	x	26	8	181	x	x	215

Appendix 4 203

	Killed		Wounded		Missing		Total
	Officers	Men	Officers	Men	Officers	Men	
Ashworth's Brigade:							
6th Line	x	1	x	10	x	1	12
18th Line	x	x	x	1	x	x	1
6th Caçadores	1	1	x	7	x	x	9
3rd Division (General Sir Thomas Picton)							
Brisbane's Brigade:							
1/45th	x	4	4	66	x	x	74
74th	x	13	4	66	x	x	83
1/88th	x	23	x	187	x	x	215
5/60th (3 companies)	x	2	2	47	x	x	51
Colville's Brigade:							
1/5th	2	22	6	133	x	x	163
2/83rd	2	18	4	50	x	x	74
2/87th	1	54	12	177	x	x	244
94th	x	5	6	56	x	x	67
Power's Portuguese Brigade:							
9th Line	3	43	9	157	x	x	212
21st Line	3	55	8	115	x	x	187
11th Caçadores	x	3	2	7	x	x	12
4th Division (General Sir Lowry Cole)							
W. Anson's Brigade:							
3/27th	x	7	3	32	x	x	42
1/40th	x	5	3	34	x	x	42
1/48th	x	1	x	18	x	x	19
2nd Prov. Battn. (2nd & 2/53rd)	x	4	x	6	x	x	10
Skerrett's Brigade:							
1/7th	x	2	x	2	x	x	4
20th	x	3	x	1	x	x	4
1/23rd	x	1	x	3	x	x	4
Stubb's Portuguese Brigade:							
11th Line	1	36	6	109	x	1	153
23rd Line	x	20	3	35	x	x	58
7th Caçadores	x	9	4	21	x	x	35

	Killed		Wounded		Missing		Total
	Officers	Men	Officers	Men	Officers	Men	
5th Division (General Oswald)							
Hay's Brigade:							
3/1st	x	8	7	96	x	x	111
1/9th	1	9	x	15	x	x	25
1/38th	x	x	1	7	x	x	8
Robinson's Brigade:							
1/4th	1	12	6	72	x	x	91
2/47th	2	18	4	88	x	x	112
2/59th	x	11	8	130	x	x	149
Spry's Portuguese Brigade:							
3rd Line	x	2	3	8	x	x	13
15th Line	x	6	3	19	x	x	28
8th Caçadores	x	13	2	25	x	x	40
7th Division (Lord Dalhousie)							
Barnes' Brigade:	No casualties taken						
Grant's Brigade:							
51st	1	10	x	21	x	x	32
68th	2	23	9	91	x	x	125
1/82nd	1	5	3	22	x	x	31
Chasseurs Britanniques	x	29	2	109	x	x	140
light company Brunswick Oels	1	x	x	5	x	x	6
Lecorr's Portuguese Brigade:							
7th Line	x	x	x	x	x	6	6
Light Division (General Charles Alten)							
Kempt's Brigade:							
1/43rd	x	2	2	27	x	x	31
1/95th	x	4	4	37	x	x	45
3/95th	x	7	x	16	x	x	24
Vandeleur's Brigade:							
1/52nd	1	3	1	18	x	x	23
2/95th	x	x	1	8	x	x	9

Appendix 4

	Killed		Wounded		Missing		Total
	Officers	Men	Officers	Men	Officers	Men	
Manley Power's Portuguese Brigade:								
1st Caçadores	x	2	x	2	x	x	4
3rd Caçadores	x	x	x	1	x	x	1
17th Line	x	7	1	20	x	x	28
Silveira's Portuguese Division								
Da Costa's Brigade:		No casualties taken					
A. Campbell's Brigade:	x	2	x	1	x	7	10
Pack's Independent Brigade								
1st Line	x	3	x	x	x	x	3
16th Line	1	10	3	24	x	x	37
4th Caçadores	x	16	1	18	x	x	35
Bradford's Independent Brigade								
13th Line	x	x	x	1	x	16	17
24th Line	x	x	x	3	x	3	6
5th Caçadores	x	4	x	5	x	2	11
Morillo's and Longa's Divisions	4	85	10	453	x	x	562

CAVALRY								
R. Hill's Brigade:								
Household Cavalry		No casualties taken						
Ponsonby's Brigade	x	x	x	2	x	x	2
G. Anson's Brigade:								
12th Light Dragoons	1	3	x	8	x	x	12
16th Light Dragoons	x	7	1	13	x	x	21
Long's Brigade:	x	x	x	1	x	x	1
V. Alten's Brigade:		No casualties taken						
Bock's Brigade:	x	1	x	x	x	x	1

	Killed		Wounded		Missing		Total
	Officers	Men	Officers	Men	Officers	Men	
Fane's Brigade:								
3rd Dragoon Guards	x	3	1	4	x	x	8
1st Royal Dragoons	x	x	x	1	x	x	1
Grant's Brigade:								
10th Hussars	x	6	x	10	x	x	16
15th Hussars	x	10	2	47	x	x	59
18th Hussars	1	10	2	21	x	x	34
Portuguese Cavalry	x	x	x	2	x	x	2
Royal Horse Artillery	x	4	1	35	x	x	40
Field Artillery	x	5	x	18	x	x	23
KGL Artillery	x	2	x	5	x	x	7
Portuguese Artillery	No casualties taken						
Royal Engineers	x	x	1	x	x	x	1
General Staff	x	x	8	x	x	x	8
Total British Losses	20	489	192	2.749	x	223*	3.675
Total Portuguese Losses	9	233	44	592	x	43	921
Total Spanish Losses	4	85	246	453	x	x	562
Total Allied Losses	33	807	246	3.794	x	266	5.158

* The missing were all stragglers, with the exception of 40 men of the 1/71st, who were taken prisoner.
Data from Oman VI, pp.757–60.

Appendix 5

French Losses at the Battle of Vitoria

	Killed Officers	Killed Men	Wounded Officers	Wounded Men	Missing Officers	Missing Men	Total
ARMEE DU PORTUGAL							
4eme division (Sarrut)							
2eme léger	2	22	3	178	x	44	249
36eme de la ligne	x	5	9	113	x	34	161
4eme léger	x	14	6	75	2	78	175
65eme de la ligne	x	10	5	139	2	68	224
6eme division (Lamartinière)							
118eme de la ligne	2	17	6	150	1	46	222
119eme de la ligne	3	27	9	92	x	42	173
120eme de la ligne	1	20	3	48	x	2	74
122eme de la ligne	1	6	2	72	x	26	107
Cavalerie léger (Curto)							
3eme hussards	x	6	4	18	x	12	40
26eme chasseurs	x	1	4	x	x	12	17
14eme chasseurs	x	9	2	7	x	4	22
22eme chasseurs	x	3	1	5	x	1	10
13eme chasseurs	x	x	x	8	x	x	8
Division de dragons (Mermet)							
6eme dragons	x	2	1	12	x	x	15
11eme dragons	x	5	2	8	x	x	15
15eme dragons	1	8	3	43	x	x	57
25eme dragons	x	1	2	15	x	x	18
Unite isolee (Armee du Nord)							
3eme de la ligne	x	7	2	20	x	75	104
Artillery & Engineers etc				No returns			

208   Wellington and the Vitoria Campaign 1813

	Killed Officers	Killed Men	Wounded Officers	Wounded Men	Missing Officers	Missing Men	Total
ARMEE DU MIDI							
1eme division (Leval)							
9eme léger	1	28	x	72	2	63	166
24eme de la ligne	x	14	1	68	2	106	191
88eme de la ligne	x	17	x	94	x	22	133
96eme de la ligne	1	39	5	161	x	50	256
3eme division (Villatte)							
27eme léger	x	3	x	8	x	x	11
63eme de la ligne	x	21	1	102	x	11	135
94eme de la ligne	x	9	x	35	x	5	49
95eme de la ligne	x	10	x	77	x	6	93
4eme division (Conroux)							
52eme léger	1	21	6	300	1	24	353
43eme de la ligne	x	36	9	216	1	80	342
55 de la ligne	1	2	1	61	1	61	127
58eme de la ligne	1	15	8	135	1	100	260
5eme division:avant garde (Maransin)							
12eme léger	2	21	4	310	4	25	366
45eme de la ligne	1	59	9	200	x	48	317
6eme division (Darricau)							
21eme léger	x	22	4	67	x	47	140
100eme de la ligne	x	14	5	70	x	98	187
28eme léger	x	7	2	104	1	62	176
103eme de la ligne	1	46	5	148	x	122	322
Cavalerie léger (P.Soult)							
2eme hussards	x	x	x	x	x	1	1
21eme chasseurs	x	x	x	x	x	x	x
5eme chasseurs	x	x	x	x	x	1	1
10eme chasseurs	x	x	x	x	x	1	1
1eme division de dragons (Tilly)							
2eme dragons	x	x	x	x	1	2	3
4eme dragons	x	x	x	x	x	1	1
14eme dragons	x	1	x	x	x	x	1
26eme dragons	x	1	x	19	x	x	20

Appendix 5   209

	Killed		Wounded		Missing		Total
	Officers	Men	Officers	Men	Officers	Men	
2eme division de dragons (Digeon)							
5eme dragons	x	2	4	33	x	3	42
12eme dragons	x	12	1	8	x	x	21
16eme dragons	x	x	x	6	x	x	6
21eme dragons	x	4	3	27	x	x	34
Artillery	1	20	x	366	x	100	100
Engineers etc	1	2	x	2	x	23	28
ARMEE DU CENTRE							
1eme division (Darmagnac)							
28eme de la ligne	3	15	6	152	1	296	473
75eme de la ligne	2	32	10	79	x	228	351
2eme Nassau	2	20	10	205	2	228	467
4eme Baden	1	16	3	56	x	39	115
Frankfurt	1	13	1	22	x	x	37
2eme division (Cassagne)							
16eme léger	x	2	x	3	x	21	26
8eme de la ligne	x	x	x	6	x	52	58
51eme de la ligne	x	4	3	31	x	52	90
34eme de la ligne	x	3	x	30	x	53	86
Cavalerie léger (Avy)							
27eme chasseurs	x	1	x	3	x	51	55
Chasseurs de Nassau	x	1	x	x	x	x	1
Division de Dragons (Trelliard)							
13eme dragons	x	3	1	2	x	11	17
22eme dragons	x	3	x	14	x	10	27
18eme dragons	x	x	x	x	x	31	31
19eme dragons	x	x	x	1	x	4	5
Division Espagnole (Casapalacio)							
Tolede	1	x	x	x	x	200	201
Castille	x	x	x	x	x	100	100
Cavalerie	3	9	x	21	x	x	35
Artillery	No returns						
Engineers etc	x	x	x	x	x	4	4

There are no returns for the King's Royal Guard, although 11 officers are known to have been killed or wounded.

	Killed		Wounded		Missing		Total
	Officers	Men	Officers	Men	Officers	Men	
Total General:							
Armee du Portugal	10	162	61	1,009	5	444	1,691
Armee du Midi	9	404	68	2,251	14	939	3,755
Armee du Centre	13	122	34	625	3	1,376	2,173
Total	32	688	163	3,955	22	2,795	7,619

The statistics for the Army of Portugal cover the period 27 May–1 July, for the Army of the South, 20–28 June, and for the Army of the Centre, 21 June.

Data from Sarramon, pp. 688–91 from the returns as noted above. Oman VI, p. 761, identifies 391 men in the Army of the South who were identified separately from prisoners, missing, being described as 'Disparus'.

Appendix 6

Wellington's Vitoria Dispatch

To Earl Bathurst
MY LORD, Salvatierra, 22nd June, 1813
The enemy, commanded by King Joseph, having Marshal Jourdan as the Major General of the army, took up a position, on the night of the 19th instant, in front of Vitoria: the left of which rested upon the heights that end at La Puebla de Arganzon, and extended from thence across the valley of the Zadorra, in front of the village of Ariñez. They occupied with the right of the centre a height which commanded the valley of the Zadorra. The right of their army was stationed near Vitoria, and was destined to defend the passages of the river Zadorra, in the neighbourhood of that city. They had a reserve in rear of their left, at the village of Gomecha. The nature of the country through which the army had passed since it had reached the Ebro, had necessarily extended our columns; and we halted on the 20th, in order to close them up, and moved the left to Murguia, where it was most likely it would be required. I reconnoitred the enemy's position on that day, with a view to the attack to be made on the following morning, if they should still remain in it.

We accordingly attacked the enemy yesterday, and I am happy to inform your Lordship, that the Allied army under my command gained a complete victory, having driven them from all their positions; having taken from them 151 pieces of cannon, waggons, of ammunition, all their baggage, provisions, cattle, treasure, &c, and a considerable number of prisoners.

The operations of the day commenced by Lieut. General Sir Rowland Hill obtaining possession of the heights of La Puebla, on which the enemy's left rested, which heights they had not occupied in great strength. He detached for the service one brigade of the Spanish division, under General Morillo; the other brigade being employed in keeping the communication between his main body on the high road from Miranda to Vitoria, and the troops detached to the heights. The enemy, however, soon discovered the importance of these heights, and reinforced their troops there to such an extent, that Lieut. General Sir Rowland Hill was obliged to detach, first, the 71st regiment and the light infantry battalions of General Walker's brigade, under the command of Lieut. Colonel the Hon. H. Cadogan, and successively other troops to the same point; and the Allies not only gained, but maintained possession of these important heights throughout their operations, notwithstanding all the efforts of the enemy to retake them.

The contest here was, however, very severe, and the loss sustained considerable. General Morillo was wounded, but remained in the field: and I am concerned to have to report, that Lieut. Colonel the Hon. H. Cadogan has died of a wound which he received. In him His Majesty has lost an officer of great merit and tried gallantry, who had already acquired the respect and regard of the whole profession, and of whom it might have been expected that, if he had lived, he would have rendered the most important services to his country.

Under cover of the possession of these heights, Sir Rowland Hill successively passed the Zadorra, at La Puebla, and the defile formed by the heights and the river Zadorra, and attacked and gained possession of the village of Subijana de Álava, in front of the enemy's line, which the enemy made repeated attempts to regain.

The difficult nature of the country prevented the communication between our different columns moving to the attack from their stations on the river Bayas at as early an hour as I had expected, and it was late before I knew that the column, composed of the 3rd and 7th divisions, under the command of the Earl of Dalhousie, had arrived at the station appointed for them. The 4th and Light divisions, however, passed the Zadorra immediately after Sir Rowland Hill had possession of Subijana de Álava; the former at the bridge of Nanclares, and the latter at the bridge of Tres-puentes; and almost as soon as these had crossed, the column, under the Earl of Dalhousie arrived at Mendoza; the 3rd division, under Lieut. General Sir Thomas Picton, crossed at the bridge higher up, followed by the 7th division, under the Earl of Dalhousie. These four divisions, forming the centre of the army, were destined to attack the height on which the right of the enemy's centre was placed, while Lieut. General Sir Rowland Hill should move forward from Subijana de Álava to attack the left. The enemy, however, having weakened his line to strengthen his detachment on the hills, abandoned his position in the valley as soon as he saw our disposition to attack it, and commenced his retreat in good order towards Vitoria.

Our troops continued to advance in admirable order, notwithstanding the difficulty of the ground. In the mean time, Lieut. General Sir Thomas Graham, who commanded the left of the army, consisting of the 1st and 5th divisions and General Pack's and Bradford's brigades of infantry, and General Bock's and Anson's of cavalry, and who had been moved on the 20th to Murguia, moved forward from thence on Vitoria, by the high road from that town to Bilbao. He had besides, with him the Spanish division under Colonel Longa; and General Girón, who had been detached to the left, under a different view of the state of affairs, and had afterwards been recalled, and had arrived on the 20th at Orduña, marched that morning from thence, so as to be in the field in readiness to support Lieut. General Sir Thomas Graham, if his support had been required.

The enemy had a division of infantry with some cavalry advanced on the great road from Vitoria to Bilbao, resting their right on some strong heights covering the village of Gamarra Mayor. Both Gamarra and Abucheco were strongly occupied as *têtes de pont* and the bridges over the Zadorra at these places. Brigadier General Pack and his Portuguese brigade, and Colonel Longa with his Spanish division, were directed to turn and gain the heights, supported by Major General Anson's brigade of light dragoons, and the 5th division of infantry under the command of General Oswald, who was desired to take command of all these troops.

Lieut. General Sir Thomas Graham reports, that in the execution of this service the Portuguese and Spanish troops behaved admirably. The 4th battalion of caçadores and the 8th caçadores, particularly distinguished themselves. Colonel Longa, being on the left, took possession of Gamarra Major.

As soon as the heights were in our possession, the village of Gamarra Major was most gallantly stormed and carried by Major General Robertson's brigade of the 5th division, which advanced in columns of battalions, under a very heavy fire of artillery and musketry, without firing a shot, assisted by two guns of Major Lawson's brigade of artillery. The enemy suffered severely, and lost three pieces of cannon.

The Lieut. General then proceeded to attack the village of Aburcheco with the first division, by forming a strong battery against it, consisting of Captain Dubourdieu's brigade, and Captain Ramsey's troop of horse artillery; and under cover of this fire, Colonel Halkett's brigade advanced to the attack of the village, which was carried; the light battalions having charged and taken three guns and a howitzer on the bridge. This attack was supported by General Bradford's brigade of Portuguese infantry.

During the operation at Abucheco the enemy made the greatest efforts to repossess themselves of the village of Gamarra Major, which were gallantly repulsed by the 5th division, under the command of Major General Oswald. The enemy had, however, on the heights on the left of the Zadorra, two divisions of infantry in reserve; and it was impossible to cross the bridge till the troops which moved upon the enemy's centre and left had driven them through Vitoria.

The whole then co-operated in the pursuit, which was continued by all till after it was dark.

The movement of the troops under Lieut. General Sir Thomas Graham, and their possession of Gamarra and Abechuco, intercepted the enemy's retreat by the high road to France. They were then obliged to turn to the road towards Pamplona; but they were unable to hold any position for a sufficient length of time to allow their baggage and artillery to be drawn off. The whole, therefore, of the latter which had not already been taken by the troops in their attack of the successive positions taken up by the enemy in their retreat from their first position at Ariñez and on the Zadorra, and all their ammunition and baggage, and every thing they had were taken close to Vitoria. I have reason to believe that the enemy carried off with them one gun and one howitzer only.

The army under King Joseph consisted of the whole of the armies of the South, and of the Centre, and of four divisions and all the cavalry of the army of Portugal, and some troops from the army of the North. General Foy's division of the army of Portugal was in the neighbourhood of Bilbao; and General Clausel, who commanded the army of the North, was near Logroño with one division of the army of Portugal commanded by General Taupin and General Van-der-Maesen's division of the army of the North. The 6th division of the allied army under Major-General the Hon. E. Pakenham was likewise absent, having been detained at Medina de Pomar for three days, to cover the march of our magazines and stores.

I cannot extol too highly the good conduct of all the General Officers, Officers, and soldiers of the army in this action. Lieut. General Sir R. Hill speaks highly of the conduct of General Morillo and the Spanish troops under his command, and of that of Lieut. General the Hon. W. Stewart, and the Conde de Amarante, who commanded divisions of infantry under his direction. He likewise mentions the conduct of the Hon. R.W. O'Callaghan, who maintained the village of Subijana de Álava against all the efforts of the enemy to regain possession of it, and that of Lieut. Colonel Rooke of the Adjutant General's department and Lieut. Colonel the Hon. A. Abercromby of the Quarter Master General's department. It was impossible for the movements of any troops to be conducted with more spirit and regularity than those of their respective divisions by Lieut. Generals the Earl of Dalhousie, Sir Thomas Picton, Sir Lowry Cole and Major General Baron Charles Alten. The troops advanced in *echelons* of regiments in two, and occasionally in three lines; and the Portuguese troops in the 3rd and 4th divisions, under the command of Brigadier Power and Colonel Stubbs, led the march with steadiness and gallantry never surpassed on any occasion.

Major General the Hon. C. Colville's brigade was seriously attacked in its advance by a very superior force well formed, which it drove in, supported by General Inglis's brigade of the 7th Division, commanded by Colonel Grant of the 82nd. These officers and the troops under their command distinguished themselves.

Major General Vandeleur's brigade of the Light division was, during the advance upon Vitoria, detached to the support of the 7th division; and Lieut. General the Earl of Dalhousie has reported most favourably of its conduct. Lieut. General Sir Thomas Graham particularly reports his sense of the assistance he received from Colonel De Lancy, the Deputy Quarter Master General, and from Lieut. Colonel Bouverie, of the Adjutant General's department, and from the officers of his personal staff; and from Lieut. Colonel the Hon. A. Upton, Assistant Quarter Master General, and Major Hope, Assistant Adjutant General, with the 1st division; and Major General Oswald reports the same of Lieut. Colonel Berkeley of the Adjutant General's department, and Lieut. Colonel Gomm of the Quarter Master General's department.

I am particularly indebted to Lieut. General Sir Thomas Graham, and to Lieut. General Sir Rowland Hill, for the manner in which they have respectively conducted the service entrusted to them since the commencement of the operations which have ended in the battle of the 21st; and for their conduct in that battle; as likewise to Marshal Sir W. Beresford for the friendly advice and assistance which I have received from him upon all occasions during the late operations.

I must not omit to mention likewise the conduct of General Girón, who commands the Galician army, who made a forced march from Orduña, and was actually on the ground in readiness to support Lieut. General Sir Thomas Graham.

I have frequently been indebted, and have occasion to call the attention of your Lordship to the conduct of the Quarter Master General Sir George Murray, who in the late operations, and in the battle of the 21st of June, has again given the greatest assistance. I am likewise much indebted to Lord Aylmer, the Deputy Adjutant General, and to the officers of the departments of the Adjutant and Quarter Master General respectively; and also to Lord Fitzroy Somerset, and Lieut. Colonel Campbell and those of my personal staff; and to Lieut. Colonel Sir Richard Fletcher, and the officers of the Royal Engineers.

Colonel his Serene Highness the Hereditary Prince of Orange was in the field as my aide-de-camp, and conducted himself with his usual gallantry and intelligence.

Mariscal de Campo, Don Luis Wimpffen, and the Inspector General Don Thomas O'Donoju, and the officers of the staff of the Spanish army have invariably rendered me every assistance in their power in the course of these operations; and I avail myself of this opportunity of expressing my satisfaction with their conduct; as likewise with that of Mariscal de Campo Don Miguel Álava; and of Brig. General Don Josef O'Lalor, who have been so long and usefully employed with me.

The artillery was most judiciously placed by Lieut. Colonel Dickson, and was well served; and the army is particularly indebted to that corps.

The natures of the ground did not allow of the cavalry being generally engaged; but the General Officers commanding the several brigades kept the troops under their command respectively close to the infantry to support them, and they were most active in the pursuit of the enemy after they had been driven through Vitoria.

I send this dispatch by my aide de camp Captain Fremantle, whom I beg leave to recommend to your Lordship's protection. He will have the honor of laying at the feet of His Royal Highness the colours of the 4th Batt. 100th regiment, and Marshal Jourdan's baton of a Marshal of France taken by the 87th regiment.

I enclose a return of the killed and wounded in the late operations, and a return of the ordnance, carriages, and ammunition taken from the enemy in the action of the 21st last.

I have the honor to be, &c.
WELLINGTON.

Notes

Chapter 1: Preparations
1. Aitchison, *An Ensign in the Peninsular War*, p. 222.
2. Girod de l'Ain, *Vie Militaire de Général Foy*, p. 193.
3. Hope, *The Iberian and Waterloo Campaigns*, p. 122.
4. Howell, in *Memorials of the Last War I*, p. 107.
5. McGrigor, unpublished papers.
6. Wood, *The Subaltern Officer*, p. 165.
7. Wheeler, *The Letters of Private Wheeler*, p. 104.
8. Brown, *The Autobiography, or Narrative of a Soldier*, pp. 201–02.
9. Aitchison, p. 234.
10. Wellington, *Dispatches* X, p. 67.
11. Ibid., pp. 239–40.
12. Jones, *Account of the War in Spain, Portugal and the South of France* II, p. 143.
13. Harding-Edgar, *Next to Wellington: General Sir George Murray*, p. 250.
14. John Cooke, pp. 178–9.
15. Bell, *Soldier's Glory* p. 64.
16. Leach, *Captain of the 95th Rifles*, p. 184.
17. Hartley, unpublished journal.
18. Schaumann, *On the Road with Wellington*, pp. 363–5.
19. Officer of Dragoons, *The British Cavalry on the Peninsula*, p. 79.
20. Bell, p. 64.
21. Wellington, *Dispatches* X, p. 310.
22. Dickson, *The Dickson Manuscripts* V, p. 831.
23. Ibid., p. 882.
24. Frazer, *Letters of Colonel Sir Augustus Simon Frazer, K. C. B.*, p. 78.
25. Larpent, *Private Journal of F.S. Larpent* I, p. 175.
26. Frazer, pp. 100–01.
27. Simmons, *A British Rifle Man*, pp. 277–8.
28. Kincaid, *Adventures in the Rifle Brigade*, p. 97.
29. Wellington, *Dispatches* X, pp. 104–05.
30. Jourdan, *Memoires militaire*, pp. 449–50.
31. Bell, p. 66.
32. Patterson, *Camp and Quarters* II, p. 210.
33. Bonaparte, *Confidential Correspondence with his Brother Joseph*, p. 248.
34. Jean-Claude Lorblanchès, *Les Soldats de Napoleon en Espagne et Portugal 1807–1814* (L'Harmttan, Paris, 2007), p. 440.

35. D'Espinchal, *Souvenirs Militaires* II, pp. 120–1.
36. Jourdan, p. 462.
37. Hope, *The Iberian and Waterloo Campaigns*, pp. 128–9.
38. Gomm, *Letters and Journals of Field Marshal Sir William Maynard Gomm G. C. B.* I, p. 298.
39. Wellington, *Dispatches* X, p. 336.
40. Ibid., p. 372.
41. Ibid.

Chapter 2: The Campaign Begins
1. Jones, *Account of the War in Spain, Portugal and the South of France 1808–1814* II, pp. 148–9.
2. Wellington, *Dispatches* X, pp. 386–7.
3. Gomm I, p. 209.
4. Dansey, *The Letters of 2nd Captain Charles Dansey RA*, p. 66.
5. Larpent I, p. 167.
6. Aitchison, pp. 236–7.
7. Wood, p. 278.
8. Vandeleur, *With Wellington's Outposts*, p. 78.
9. Daniell, *Journal of an Officer in the Commissariat Department*, pp. 196–7.
10. Swabey, *Diary of Campaigns in the Peninsula for the Years 1811, 12 and 13*, pp. 201–02.
11. Jourdan, pp. 462–3.
12. Ibid., p. 464.
13. Webber, *With the Guns in the Peninsular War*, p. 147.
14. John Cooke, *A True Soldier Gentleman*, p. 186.
15. Leach, p. 187.
16. Costello, *Costello; the True Story of a Peninsular Rifleman*, p. 212.
17. Rous, *A Guards Officer in the Peninsular War*, p. 59.
18. Glover, *Wellington's Peninsular Victories*, p. 86.
19. Frazer, pp. 120–4.
20. Jourdan, p. 464.
21. Blakiston, *Twelve Years Military Adventure* II, p. 94.
22. Browne, *The Napoleonic War Journal of Thomas Henry Browne*, pp. 206–07.
23. Webber, p. 148.
24. Blakiston II, p. 94.
25. James Archibald Hope, *Campaigns with Hill and Wellington*, p. 142.
26. Leith Hay, *A Narrative of the Peninsular War* II, p. 159.
27. Gomm I, p. 300.
28. Wheeler, p. 111.
29. Swabey, p. 188.
30. Ibid., p. 189.
31. Vandeleur, p. 85.
32. Wheeler, p. 112.

33. Officer of Dragoons, pp. 80–1.
34. Swabey, p. 192.
35. Larpent I, p. 204.
36. Officer of Dragoons. pp. 82–3.
37. Hope, *The Iberian and Waterloo Campaigns*, p. 139.
38. John Cooke, p. 182.
39. Dobbs, *Recollections of an Old 52nd Man*, p. 36.
40. Hope, *Campaigns with Hill and Wellington*, p. 143.
41. John Cooke, p. 183.
42. Leach, p. 188.
43. Jones II, p. 132.

Chapter 3: From the Esla to the Ebro
1. Quoted in Fortescue, *A History of the British Army* IX, pp. 146–7.
2. D'Espinchal II, pp. 140–1.
3. Wellington, *Supplementary Dispatches and Memoranda*, pp. 627–8.
4. Webber, p. 156.
5. Daniell, p. 199.
6. Frazer, p. 134.
7. Blakiston II, p. 101.
8. Green, *The Vicissitudes of a Soldier's Life*, p. 153.
9. Swabey, p. 193.
10. Vandeleur, p. 88.
11. John Cooke, p. 184.
12. Larpent I, p. 218.
13. Hartley, unpublished journal.
14. Hope, *The Iberian and Waterloo Campaigns*, p. 141.
15. Larpent I, p. 216.
16. Hope, *The Iberian and Waterloo Campaigns*, p. 141
17. Surtees, *Twenty-Five Years in the Rifle Brigade*, pp. 193–4.
18. Green, p. 154.
19. Tomkinson, *Diary of a Cavalry Officer*, p. 239.
20. Dickson V, p. 903.
21. Scherer, *Recollections of the Peninsula*, pp. 232–3.
22. Cadell, *The Slashers: the Campaigns of the 28th Regiment*, pp. 94–5.
23. Webber, pp. 163–4.
24. Jourdan, p. 469.
25. Ibid., p. 470.
26. D'Espinchal II, p. 144.
27. Scherer, pp. 233–4.
28. Kincaid, p. 99.
29. Simmons, p. 287.
30. Swabey, p. 196.
31. D'Espinchal II, pp. 144–5.

32. Wellington, *Dispatches* X, p. 453.
33. Ibid., p. 436.
34. Tomkinson, pp. 240–1.
35. Gomm I, p. 303.
36. Hope, *The Iberian and Waterloo Campaigns*, p. 143.
37. Frazer, pp. 144–5.
38. Blakiston II, p. 104.
39. Webber, pp. 106–07.
40. Tomkinson, p. 241.
41. Larpent I, pp. 228–9.
42. Dickson V, p. 991.
43. Surtees, p. 196.
44. Heneghan, *Campaigns with the Field Train*, p. 149.
45. Browne, p. 209.
46. John Cooke, pp. 186–7.
47. Simmons, p. 287.
48. Broughton, *Letters from Portugal, Spain and France 1812–1814*, p. 86.
49. Hartley, unpublished journal.
50. Swabey, p. 197.
51. Frazer, p. 148.
52. Scherer, pp. 235–6.
53. Webber, p. 171.
54. Kincaid, p. 100.
55. Costello, p. 215.
56. Brown, p. 205.
57. Wellington, *Dispatches* X, p. 442.
58. Frazer, pp. 150–1.

Chapter 4: The Road to Vitoria
1. D'Espinchal II, pp. 145–6.
2. Leith Hay II, p. 172.
3. Ibid., p. 175.
4. Ibid., p. 182.
5. Blakiston II, p. 106.
6. Douglas, *Douglas's Tale of the Peninsula and Waterloo 1808–1815*, p. 71.
7. Gomm I, p. 306.
8. Tomkinson, p. 242.
9. Wellington, *Supplementary Dispatches*, p. 641.
10. Vandeleur, pp. 92–3.
11. Douglas, p. 72.
12. Tomkinson, p. 242.
13. Hale, *The Journal of James Hale*, p. 106.
14. Hay, *Reminiscences 1808–1815 under Wellington*, p. 102.
15. Leach, pp. 191–2.

16. Blakiston II, p. 107.
17. John Cooke, p. 188.
18. Surtees, p. 199.
19. Blakiston II, pp. 107–08.
20. Leach, pp. 192–3.
21. Jourdan, p. 472.
22. Wellington, *Supplementary Dispatches*, p. 647.
23. Larpent I, pp. 239–40.
24. Swabey, p. 199.
25. Kincaid, p. 102.
26. Tomkinson, p. 243.
27. Aitchison, pp. 240–1.
28. Leith Hay II, pp. 183–4.

Chapter 5: The Eve of Battle
1. Leith Hay II, p. 184.
2. Oman, *A History of the Peninsular War* VI, pp. 389–90.
3. Leith Hay II, pp. 184–5.
4. Ibid., pp. 185–6.
5. Wellington, *Supplementary Dispatches*, p. 648.
6. Tomkinson, pp. 243–4.
7. Jourdan, p. 473.
8. Hay, pp. 106–08.
9. Rous, pp. 63–4.
10. Douglas, p. 72.
11. Bell, pp. 66–7.
12. Quoted in J. Hill, *Wellington's Right Hand*, p. 109.
13. Ibid.
14. Robertson, *The Journal of Sergeant D. Robertson*, p. 101.
15. Howell I, p. 112.
16. Officer of Dragoons, p. 92.
17. Blakiston II, pp. 109–10.
18. Lawrence, *The Autobiography of Sergeant William Lawrence*, p. 132.
19. Surtees, p. 201.
20. Green, p. 160.
21. Wheeler, pp. 116–17.
22. Browne, p. 211.
23. Leith Hay II, p. 186.
24. Ibid., pp. 187–90.
25. Oman VI, p. 409, suggests that Picton was out of favour because the intemperate letters of complaint he had been writing to headquarters as his division ran short of food.
26. Wellington, *Supplementary Dispatches*, pp. 652–3.

Chapter 6: 'The Waterloo of the Peninsula': the Battle of Vitoria
1. Hale, p. 107.
2. Douglas, p. 72.
3. Robertson, p. 101.
4. Cadell, p. 95.
5. Schaumann, pp. 373–4.
6. Officer of Dragoons, p. 94.
7. Browne, p. 212.
8. Scherer, pp. 236–7.
9. Jourdan, pp. 475–6.
10. D'Espinchal II, p. 148.
11. Oman VI, pp. 390–1.
12. Howell I, pp. 112–13.
13. Patterson, *Camp and Quarters*, p. 205.
14. Hope, *The Iberian and Waterloo Campaigns*, pp. 146–7.
15. Patterson, *Camp and Quarters*, p. 208.
16. Ibid., p. 206.
17. Hildyard, *Historical Record of the 71st*, p. 90.
18. Hope, *Campaigns with Hill and Wellington*, pp. 149–52.
19. Hope, *The Iberian and Waterloo Campaigns*, pp. 147–9.
20. Howell, pp. 113–14.
21. Hope, *The Iberian and Waterloo Campaigns*, p. 150.
22. Heneghan, p. 153.
23. Robertson, p. 104.
24. Patterson, *Camp and Quarters*, pp. 169–70.
25. Scherer, p. 128.
26. Bell, pp. 68–9.
27. Blakiston II, pp. 112–13.
28. Ibid., p. 113.
29. John Cooke, p. 190.
30. Surtees, pp. 203–04.
31. Kincaid, pp. 104–05.
32. John Cooke, pp. 191–2.
33. Jourdan, p. 478.
34. John Cooke, p. 192.
35. Brown, pp. 205–06.
36. Daniell, p. 214.
37. Robinson, *Memoirs of Lieutenant General Sir Thomas Picton* II, pp. 195–6.
38. Brown, pp. 206–07.
39. Green, p. 160.
40. Wheeler, p. 117.
41. Dickson V, p. 926.
42. Kincaid, p. 106.
43. Blakiston II, p. 114.

44. Leith Hay II, pp. 197–8.
45. John Cooke, pp. 192–3.
46. See Oman VI, pp. 414–15 for further discussion.
47. Kincaid, p. 106.
48. Colville, *The Portrait of a General*, pp. 119–20.
49. Ibid, pp. 121–3.
50. Jourdan, p. 478.
51. Ibid, pp. 478–9.
52. Tomkinson, p. 247.
53. Hale, p. 108.
54. Tomkinson, p. 245.
55. Hay, pp. 111–12.
56. Tomkinson, p. 249.
57. Douglas, pp. 72–3.
58. Hale, p. 109.
59. Jourdan, p. 479.
60. Dickson V, p. 916.
61. Green, pp. 162–3.
62. Quoted in Oman VI, p. 423.
63. Jourdan, pp. 277–80.
64. Dickson V, pp. 922–3.
65. Ibid., p. 925.
66. Ibid., p. 916.
67. Heneghan, p. 154.
68. Schaumann, p. 376.
69. Wood, p. 184.
70. Blakiston II, p. 115.
71. Hope, *The Iberian and Waterloo Campaigns*, p. 151.
72. Tomkinson, pp. 250–1.
73. Hay, p. 113.
74. John Cooke, pp. 196–7.
75. Hamilton, *Hamilton's Campaign with Moore and Wellington*, p. 144.
76. Brown, pp. 208–09.
77. Officer of Dragoons, pp. 97–8.
78. Ibid., pp. 99–100.
79. Hartley, unpublished journal.
80. Leith Hay II, pp. 202–03.
81. Blakiston II, p. 117.
82. Scherer, pp. 242–3.
83. Costello, pp. 225–6.
84. Brown, pp. 216–17.
85. Green, p. 167.
86. Scherer, p. 243.
87. Tomkinson, p. 254.

88. Wellington, *Dispatches* X, p. 473.
89. Schaumann, p. 378.
90. Browne, p. 219.
91. Larpent I, pp. 246–8.
92. Leith Hay II, pp. 211–13.
93. Browne, p. 219.
94. Costello, pp. 228–9.
95. Larpent I, p. 244.
96. Playford, *The Memoirs of Sergeant-Major Thomas Playford*, p. 24.
97. Henry, *Events of a Military Life*, p. 151.
98. Ibid., p. 153.
99. Ibid., p. 154.
100. Ibid, pp. 155–6.
101. Frazer, pp. 157 & 159.
102. Lawrence, pp. 134–5.
103. Browne, p. 218.
104. Gomm I, p. 370.
105. Dickson V, p. 917.
106. Surtees, p. 212.
107. Tomkinson, p. 256.
108. Jourdan, p. 477.
109. Dickson V, pp. 924–5.
110. D'Espinchal II, p. 154.
111. Ibid., p. 155.
112. Girod de l'Ain, pp. 208–09.
113. Marcel, *Campagnes en Espagne et au Portugal 1808–1814*, pp. 106–08.
114. Oman VI, p. 446.
115. Ibid., p. 449.
116. Fortescue IX, p. 189.
117. Wellington. *Supplementary Dispatches*, p. 653.
118. Sarramon, *La Bataille de Vitoria*, pp. 551–2.
119. Ibid., p. 552.

Chapter 7: Consequences
1. Wellington, *Dispatches* X, p. 450.
2. Ibid., p. 496.
3. Fée, *Souvenirs de la Guerre d'Espagne* pp. 249–50.
4. Fortescue IX, pp. 199–200.
5. Baines, *History of the Wars of the French Revolution* II, pp. 265–6.

Select Bibliography

Unpublished Material
Sir James McGrigor, Papers.
Hartley, Andrew, Journal.

Primary Sources
Aitchison, John (ed. W. F. K. Thompson), *An Ensign in the Peninsular War: the Letters of John Aitchison* (Michael Joseph, London, 1981).
Atkinson, C.T., 'A Peninsular Brigadier: Letters of Major General Sir F. P. Robinson K.C.B. Dealing with the Campaign of 1813', *Journal of the Society for Army Historical Research* Vol. 34, December 1956.
Bell, Major General Sir George, *Soldier's Glory* (Spellmount, Tunbridge Wells, 1991).
Belmas, Jacques Vital, *Précis des Campagnes et des Siéges d'Espagnes et de Portugal de 1807 à 1814* (A. Leneveu, Paris, 1839).
Blakiston, John, *Twelve Years' Military Adventure in Three Quarters of the Globe* (New York, 1829).
Blanco, Richard L., *Wellington's Surgeon General: Sir James McGrigor* (Dike University Press, Durham N.C., 1970).
Bonaparte, Napoleon, *The Confidential Correspondence of Napoleon Bonaparte with his Brother Joseph* (John Murray, London, 1855).
Broughton, Samuel, *Letters from Portugal, Spain and France 1812–1814* (Nonsuch Publishing Ltd, Stroud, 2005).
Brown, William, *The Autobiography, or Narrative of a Soldier* (J. Patterson, Kilmarnock, 1829).
Browne, Thomas Henry (ed. Roger Norman Buckley), *The Napoleonic War Journal of Thomas Henry Brown 1807–1816* (The Bodley Head for The Army Records Society, London, 1987).
Cadell, Charles, *The Slashers: the Campaigns of the 28th Regiment of Foot during the Napoleonic Wars by a Serving Officer* (Leonaur, 2008).
Cole, Sir Lowry, *Memoirs of Sir Lowry Cole* (Ken Trotman Ltd, Cambridge, 2003).
Cooke, John (ed. Eileen Hathaway), *A True Soldier Gentleman: the Memoirs of Lt. John Cooke 1791–1813* (Shinglepicker, Swanage, 2000).
Cooke, Robert Duffield (ed. Gareth Glover), *At Wellington's Head Quarters: the Letters of Robert Duffield Cooke, Army Pay Corps 1811–1814* (Ken Trotman Publishing, Huntingdon, 2009).

Cooper, John Spencer, *Rough Notes of Seven Campaigns 1809–1815* (Spellmount, Staplehurst, 1996).
Costello, Edward (ed. Eileen Hathaway), *Costello: the True Story of a Peninsular War Rifleman* (Shinglepicker, Swanage, 1997).
Daniell, John Edgecombe, *Journal of an Officer in the Commissariat Department of the Army* (London, 1820).
Dansey, Captain Charles, *The Letters of 2nd Captain Charles Dansey Royal Artillery 1806–1813* (Ken Trotman Publishing, Huntingdon, 2006).
Delavoye, Alex M., *Life of Thomas Graham, Lord Lynedoch* (Richardson & Co., London, 1880).
D'Espinchal, Hippolyte, *Souvenirs Militaires, 1792–1814* (Société d'éditions littéraires et artistique, Paris, 1901).
Dickson, Sir Alexander (ed. John H. Leslie), *The Dickson Manuscripts* (Ken Trotman, Cambridge, 1991).
Dobbs, Captain John, *Recollections of an Old 52nd Man* (Spellmount, Staplehurst, 2000).
Donaldson, John, *The Eventful Life of a Soldier during the Late War in Portugal, Spain and France* (William Tate, Edinburgh, 1827).
Douglas, John (ed. Stanley Monick), *Douglas's Tale of the Peninsula and Waterloo 1808–1815* (Lee Cooper, London, 1997).
D'Urban, Major General Sir Benjamin, *The Peninsular War Journal 1809–1817* (Greenhill Books, London, 1988).
Fée, Antoine L. A., *Souvenirs de la Guerre d'Espagne dite de l'indepéndance 1809–1813* (Berger-Lavreult, Paris, 1856).
Frazer, Sir Augustus Simon (ed. Edward Sabine), *Letters of Colonel Sir Augustus Simon Frazer, K. C. B. Commanding the Royal Horse Artillery* (Longman, Brown, Green, Longmans and Roberts, London, 1854).
Girod de l'Ain, Maurice, *Vie Militaire de Général Foy* (Plon, Paris, 1900).
Gomm, Sir William Maynard (ed. Francis Culling Carr-Gomm), *Letters and Journals of Field Marshal Sir William Maynard Gomm G. C. B.* (John Murray, London, 1881).
Green, John, *The Vicissitudes of a Soldier's Life or a Series of Occurrences from 1806–1815* (Ken Trotman Ltd, Cambridge, 1996).
Haggard, D. J. and Fitzgerald, E., 'With the Tenth Hussars in Spain: Letters of Edward Fox Fitzgerald', *Journal of the Society for Army Historical Research* Vol. 44, June 1966.
Hale, James, *The Journal of James Hale, Late Sergeant of the Ninth Regiment of Foot* (IX Regiment, 1998).
Hamilton, Sgt Anthony, *Hamilton's Campaigns with Moore and Wellington during the Peninsular War* (Spellmount, Staplehurst, 1998).
Hay, Captain William C. B. (ed. Mrs S. C. I. Wood), *Reminiscences 1808–1815 under Wellington* (Ken Trotman Ltd, Cambridge, 1992).
Heneghan, Richard D., *Campaigns with the Field Train: Experiences of a British Officer during the Peninsular War and Waterloo Campaigns of the Napoleonic Wars* (Leonaur, 2007).

Henry, Walter, *Events of a Military Life: being Recollections after Service in the Peninsula War, Invasion of France, the East Indies, St Helena, Canada and Elsewhere* Vol. I (William Pickering, London, 1843).

Hope, James (revised by S. Monick), *The Iberian and Waterloo Campaigns: the Letters of Lieutenant James Hope, 92nd (Highland) Regiment 1811–1815* (The Naval and Military Press Ltd, Heathfield, 2000).

Hope, James Archibald, *Campaigns with Hill and Wellington* (Leonaur, 2010).

Howell, Thomas, *Journal of a Soldier in the Seventy-First Regiment (Highland Light Infantry) from 1806–1815, in Memorials of the Late War in Two Volumes* (Constable and Co., Edinburgh, 1828).

Jones, John T., *Account of the War in Spain, Portugal and the South of France from 1808–1814 Inclusive*, 2 vols (London, 1821).

Jourdan, Maréchal (ed. Le Vicomte de Grouchy), *Mémoires militaires du maréchal Jourdan (guerre d'Espagne)* (Ernest Flammarion, Paris, 1899).

Kincaid, Captain J., *Adventures in the Rifle Brigade in the Peninsula, France and the Netherlands from 1809–1815* (Leo Cooper, London, 1997).

Knowles, Lieutenant Robert, *The War in the Peninsular: Some Letters of a Lancashire Officer* (Spellmount, Staplehurst, 2004).

Larpent, F. S. (ed. Sir George Larpent), *The Private Journal of F.S. Larpent Esq., Judge Advocate to the British Forces in the Peninsula* (London, 1853).

Lawrence, William (ed. George Nugent Bankes), *The Autobiography of Serjeant William Lawrence* (Simpson, Low, Marston, Searle & Rivington, London, 1886).

Leach, Jonathan, *Captain of the 95th Rifles: an Officer of Wellington's Sharpshooters during the Peninsular, South of France and Waterloo Campaigns of the Napoleonic Wars* (Leonaur, 2005).

Leith Hay, Andrew, *A Narrative of the Peninsular War* (Henry Washbourne, London, 1834).

Le Mesurier, Peter (ed. Adrian Greenwood), *Through Spain with Wellington: the Letters of Lieutenant Peter Le Mesurier of the 'Fighting Ninth'* (Amberley, Stroud, 2016).

Marcel, Capitaine Nicolas, *Campagnes en Espagne et Portugal 1808–1814* (Éditions du Grenadier, n.d.).

Officer of Dragoons, An, *The British Cavalry on the Peninsula* (London, 1832; Mark Thompson Publishing reprint).

Playford, Thomas (ed. Gareth Glover), *The Memoirs of Sergeant-Major Thomas Playford 1810–1830* (Ken Trotman Publishing, Huntingdon, 2006).

Patterson, John, *Adventures with the Dirty Half Hundred: the Peninsular Reminiscences of an Officer of H.M. 50th Regiment of Foot* (Leonaur, 2009).

Patterson, Major John, *Camp and Quarters: or Scenes and Impressions of Military Life*, 2 vols (Saunders and Otley, London, 1840).

Robertson, David, *The Journal of Sergeant D. Robertson, late 92nd Foot, comprising the different campaigns between the years 1797 and 1813* (Ken Trotman Publishing, Huntingdon, 2018).

Rous, John (ed. Ian Fletcher), *A Guards Officer in the Peninsular: the Peninsular Letters of John Rous, Coldstream Guards 1812–1814* (Spellmount Ltd, Tunbridge Wells, 1992).
Schaumann, August Ludolf Friedrich, *On the Road with Wellington: the Diary of a War Commissary* (Greenhill Books, London, 1999).
Scherer, Moyle, *Recollections of the Peninsula* (Spellmount Ltd, Staplehurst, 1996).
Simmons, Major George (ed. Lt Col. Willoughby Verner), *A British Rifle Man: Journals and Correspondence during the Peninsular War and the Campaign of Wellington* (Greenhill Books, London, 1982).
Surtees, William, *Twenty-Five Years in the Rifle Brigade* (Greenhill Books, London, 1973).
Swabey, Lieutenant William (ed. Colonel F. A. Whinyates), *Diary of Campaigns in the Peninsula for the Years 1811, 12 and 13* (Ken Trotman, London, 1984).
Tomkinson, The Late Lt Col. Tomkinson (ed. James Tomkinson), *The Diary of a Cavalry Officer in the Peninsular War and Waterloo Campaign 1809–1815* (Swan Sonnenschein & Co., London, 1895).
Vandeleur, John (ed. Andrew Bamford), *With Wellington's Outposts: the Peninsular and Waterloo Letters of John Vandeleur* (Frontline Books, Barnsley, 2015).
Webber, Captain William (ed. Richard Henry Wollocombe), *With the Guns: the Peninsular War Journal of Captain William Webber, Royal Artillery* (Greenhill Books, London, 1991).
Wellington, Duke of, *The Dispatches of Field Marshal the Duke of Wellington during his Various Campaigns from 1799 to 1818* Vol. X (John Murray, London, 1838).
Wellington, Duke of, *Supplementary Dispatches and Memoranda of Field Marshal Arthur, Duke of Wellington, K. G.: Peninsula, 1810–1813* (John Murray, London, 1855).
Wheeler, William (ed. B. H. Liddell Hart), *The Letters of Private Wheeler 1809–1815* (The Windrush Press, Gloucestershire, 1951).
Wood, Captain George, *The Subaltern Officer* (Ken Trotman, Cambridge, 1986).
Wray, Samuel (ed. Gareth Glover), *The Military Adventures of Private Samuel Wray 61st Foot 1796–1815* (Ken Trotman, Huntingdon, 2009).

Secondary Sources
Baines, Edward, *History of the Wars of the French Revolution Vol. II* (Longman, Hurst, Rees, Orme and Brown, London, 1817).
Beatson, F.C., *Wellington and the Pyrenees Campaign Vol. I From Vitoria to the Bidassoa* (Leonaur, 2007).
Blanco, Richard L., *Wellington's Surgeon General: Sir James McGrigor* (Duke University Press, Durham N.C., 1974).
Clarke-Kennedy, A. E., *Attack the Colours: The Royal Dragoons in the Peninsula and at Waterloo* (The Research Publishing Company, London, 1974).
Colville, John, *The Portrait of a General: a Chronicle of the Napoleonic Wars* (Michael Russell, Salisbury, 1980).

Esdaile, Charles, *Peninsular Eyewitnesses: the Experience of War in Spain and Portugal 1808–1813* (Pen & Sword, Barnsley, 2008).
Fletcher, Ian, *Vittoria 1813: Wellington Sweeps the French from Spain* (Osprey Publishing Ltd, Wellingborough, 1998).
Fortescue, the Hon. J. W., *A History of the British Army Vol. IX* (The Naval and Military Press Ltd., Uckfield, 2004).
Fortescue, the Hon. J. W., *A History of the British Army Vol. IX–X – Maps* (The Naval and Military Press Ltd., Uckfield, 2004).
Glover, Michael, *Wellington's Peninsular Victories* (The Windrush Press, Gloucestershire, 1996).
Harding-Edgar, John, *Next to Wellington: General Sir George Murray: the Story of a Scottish Soldier and Statesman, Wellington's Quartermaster General* (Helion & Co., Warwick, 2018).
Henriques, Mendo Castro, *Vitória e Pirenéus 1813* (Tribuna, Lisboa, 2009).
Hildyard, Henry J.T. (compiler), *Historical Records of the 71st Highland Regiment* (Harrison and Sons, London 1876).
Hill, Joanna, *Wellington's Right Hand Man: Rowland, Viscount Hill* (Spellmount, Staplehurst, 2013).
Lachouque, Henry, Tranie, Jean, and Carmigniani, J-C, *Napoleon's War in Spain: the French Peninsula Campaigns 1807–1814* (Arms and Armour, London, 1993).
Lawford, Lt. Col. J. P., *Vitoria 1813* (Charles Knight & Co. Ltd, Tonbridge, 1973).
Lipscombe, Nick, *Wellington's Eastern Front: the Campaigns on the East Coast of Spain 1810–1814* (Pen & Sword, Barnsley, 2016).
Lorblanches, Jean-Claude, *Les Soldats de Napoleon en Espagne et Portugal 1807–1814* (L'Harmttan, Paris, 2007).
McGuigan, Ron & Burnham, Robert, *Wellington's Brigade Commanders: Peninsula and Waterloo* (Pen & Sword, Barnsley, 2017).
Morewood, John, *Waterloo General: the Life, Letters and Mysterious Death of Major General Sir William Ponsonby 1772–1815* (Pen & Sword, Barnsley, 2016).
Myatt, Frederick, *Peninsular General: Sir Thomas Picton 1758–1815* (David & Charles, Newton Abbott, 1980).
Napier W. F. P., *History of the War in the Peninsula and the South of France from the Year 1807 to the Year 1814 Vol. V* (Constable and Co. Ltd, London, 1993).
Oman, Sir Charles, *A History of the Peninsular War Vol. VI* (Greenhill Books, London, 1996).
Robinson, H. B., *Memoirs of Lieutenant General Sir Thomas Picton* (Richard Bentley, London, 1836).
Robinson, Ian, *A Commanding Presence: Wellington in the Peninsula 1808–1814: Logistics, Strategy, Survival* (Spellmount, Stroud, 2008)
Sarramon, Docteur Jean, *La Bataille de Vitoria: La fin de l'aventure napoléonienne en Espagne* (J. C. Bailly Edit Histeur, Paris, 1985).
Saunders, Tim and Yuill, Rob, *The Light Division in the Peninsula 1811–1814* (Pen & Sword, Barnsley, 2020).
Weller, Jac, *Wellington in the Peninsula* (Greenhill Books, London, 1992).

Index

Aitchison, Lt John 1–2, 3–4, 27–8, 47, 88, 145
Alten, Maj Gen C. 80, 84, 215
Alten, Maj Gen Viktor 20, 25, 35, 53, 80, 86, 107, 186
ammunition 123, 163, 172
Anson, Brig Gen William 26, 43, 53, 151, 161, 213
artillery 10–11, 12, 16–17, 29, 33, 41, 216; French 77, 105, 116, 149, 152, 154–5, 160; positioning of 116, 149; transport difficulties 67–8, 71, 72, 134–5
Ashworth, Brig Charles 25, 151
Ávila 15, 17, 33, 39

Badajoz vii, 1
baggage trains 75, 83, 84, 91
Barnes, Maj Gen Edward 132
Bathurst, Lord 10–11, 14, 23, 64–5, 168, 184–5, 211–17
Beethoven, Ludwig van 191–2
Bejar 22
Bell, Lt George 10, 15–16, 100–1, 125, 177
Beresford, Marshal William 10–11, 71, 216
billhooks 7
Blakiston, Capt John 38, 54–5, 67, 83, 84, 102–3, 126, 135, 155, 156, 164–5
Bock, Maj Gen Eberhard von 26, 43, 53, 158, 163
Bonaparte, Joseph viii, 1, 2, 14–16, 19, 21, 25, 29, 49, 77; abdication 191; activities at Vitoria 113–15, 127, 129; at Burgos 61–3; communications from Napoleon 17–18, 30; dispatches from France 50–1, 53; escape of 169–70, 185; plans for controlled withdrawal 156–7; reputation 57, 183; responsibility for defective French position at Vitoria 115–17; strategy 30–2, 61–2, 85, 90–2, 94, 148; travelling to Vitoria 73–4
Bonaparte, Napoleon vii, 16; communications to Joseph Bonaparte 17–18, 30; truce with Austria, Prussia and Russia 191
Boticas 28
Boyer, Brig Gen Pierre 95, 141, 143, 158
Bradford, Lt Gen Thomas 20, 25–6, 43, 53, 144, 189
Braganza 24, 26, 28, 32
Brisbane, Thomas 133–4, 138, 151
British Army: advances 31–5, 43, 53–9, 67–72, 78–81, 85–6; campaign preparations 2–14, 19, 20–1, 23–4; camps 41–2, 57, 58, 72; Commissariat 1, 32, 55, 58, 68, 72, 101; condition of vii, viii, 2–4, 33–4; contact with civilians 45–6, 55–6, 70, 72–3, 134; deployment at Vitoria 95–7, 107–9, 151; discipline 6, 8–9, 10, 184–5; Graham's intervention at Vitoria 141–8; marching strength 25 May 1813 ; officers` 9–10, 54–5; praise for 178; quarter master general's efficiency 6–7; reinforcements 8–9; reviews by Wellington 38–9; skirmishes 22, 46–7, 55, 81–4, 86–7, 88; soldiers' accounts viii–ix; supplies 6, 7–8, 14, 65, 67–8; uniforms 2
British Army units 120; First Div 20, 26, 27–8, 29, 53, 65, 69, 80, 81, 144,

145, 168, 213; Second Div 20, 22, 25, 26, 31, 33, 53, 60, 86, 102, 112–13, 151; Third Div 20, 26, 29, 43, 53, 54, 69, 96, 107–8, 127, 131–2, 134–6, 138, 148, 151, 156, 161, 167, 212; Fourth Div 20, 26, 28, 43, 53, 56, 69, 73, 80, 81, 82, 86, 102, 107, 125–6, 128, 130, 136, 148, 151; Fifth Div 20, 22, 26, 29, 43, 53, 65, 69, 72, 82, 144, 146, 158, 168, 186–7, 213; Sixth Div 20, 26, 28, 43, 53, 71, 214; Seventh Div 20, 26, 28, 43, 73, 96, 108, 127, 132, 134–5, 136, 139–40, 212; 1st Dragoons 10; 1st Foot Guards 3, 8; 1st German Hussars 82; 2nd Life Guards 34, 56–7; 3rd Dragoon Guards 10; 9th Dragoons 9; 9th Rgt 82; 10th Hussars 166; 12th Light Dragoons 28, 82, 97–8, 144, 146, 158, 159–60, 161; 14th Light Dragoons 169; 15th Hussars 130, 158, 162; 16th Light Dragoons 59, 158, 161; 18th Hussars 9–10; 23rd Rgt 38; 28th Rgt 60, 110, 125; 34th Rgt 60, 124–5; 40th Rgt 103; 43rd Rgt 7–8, 161; 45th Rgt 3, 73, 161; 50th Rgt 22, 117–18, 120, 121–3; 51st Rgt 3, 44, 73, 104; 52nd Rgt 83, 150; 58th Rgt 55; 68th Rgt 103–4, 149–50; 71st Rgt 2, 117, 118, 119, 120, 122–3, 136, 212; 82nd Rgt 3; 87th Rgt 169–70; 92nd Rgt 2, 101, 118, 120, 121–3; 95th Rgt 13, 33, 57, 70, 72, 82, 84, 138; Brunswick Light Infantry 44; Coldstream Guards 34;; Greenjackets 138, 150; Household Brigade 9–10, 34, 53, 71, 107; Hussar Brigade 8, 9–10, 26, 46–7, 53, 60, 107, 128; Light Div 20, 25, 33, 53, 60, 69, 70, 72, 78, 80, 82, 84, 86, 87, 88, 102, 103, 107, 125–6, 128, 136, 151, 156, 164–5; Oxford Blues (Horse Guards) 8, 34, 56–7; Royal Horse Artillery (RHA) 12; Royal Scots 146
Broughton, Ass Surg Samuel 70–1
Brown, Pte William 3, 73, 131, 161, 166–7

Browne, Capt Thomas 38, 70, 104, 112, 170, 171, 177
Bull, Capt Robert 12
Bulletin, The 16–17
bullocks 11, 58
Burgos vii, 1–2, 14, 15, 49, 52–3, 59, 61–5
Byng, Brig John 124, 125, 151

Cadell, Capt Charles 60–1, 110–11, 117, 125
Cadogan, Lt Col the Honourable Henry 102, 118, 120, 148, 174, 212,
Caffarelli, Gen Louis-Marie-Joseph 15, 16, 17
Cairnes, Capt Michael 11, 59, 134–5
Cameron, Col John 117, 120, 148, 151, 155
campaign preparations: army supplies 6, 7–8, 14; British preparations 2–14, 19, 21–2, 23–4; encounters between Allies and the French 22, 46–7, 55; financial problems 4–5; French preparations 14–19, 21–2; objectives 14; pontoons 11, 26, 43–4, 45
Casapalacios, Marquis de 95, 141, 145, 157–8
Cassagne, Gen Louis 30, 39, 95, 121, 129, 130, 136, 139, 151
Castaños, Gen Francisco Javier 5, 54
casualties 189; Allied 47, 138, 146, 163, 172; French 37, 47, 155, 171–2; wounded 172–4
cavalry 25, 45, 56, 61, 86, 158–60; inaction at Vitoria 161–3
Chassé, Gen David 140–1, 141
Ciudad Rodrigo vii, viii, 1, 16–17, 34
Clarke, Gen Henri 14, 15, 30, 50, 179
Clausel, Gen Bertrand 17, 18, 19, 30, 31, 50, 51, 53, 62, 75, 85, 89, 90, 126–7; in retreat 186–7
Cole, Gen Sir Lowry 73, 106, 125–6, 148, 149, 151, 215
Colvile, Gen John 131, 137, 138, 139–40, 141, 151, 155, 156, 157, 215
Conroux, Gen Nicolas 30, 39, 149

Index 233

Cooke, Lt John 7–8, 33, 48, 56, 83, 127, 128, 129, 130, 136, 160
Costello, Pte Edward 34, 72–3, 165–6, 172
Crispiana 151, 152, 155
Curto, Brig Gen Jean-Baptiste 99, 141, 142, 158

Dalhousie, Lt Gen 96, 97, 103, 107–8, 128, 130, 132–3, 134, 135, 145, 149, 150, 181–2, 212, 215
Daniell, Capt John Edgecumbe 29, 54, 131–2
Dansey, RA, Capt Charles 27
Darmagnac, Gen Jean-Baptiste 30, 31, 52, 62, 63, 95, 130, 136, 137, 139, 186
Darricau, Gen Augustin 30, 31, 32, 35, 45, 94, 148, 149, 151
D'Erlon, Count see Drouet, Gen Jean-Baptiste, Count d'Erlon
Dickson, Lt Col Alexander 11, 12–13, 68–9, 149, 154, 177, 216
Digeon, Gen Alexandre 30, 46, 142, 143, 158, 162
diseases and illness 2–4, 8
Douglas, Cpl John 79, 81, 100, 110, 143, 146–7
Douro, River 19, 23, 25, 26; crossing of 28–9, 48
Downman, Col Thomas 12
Drouet, Gen Jean-Baptiste, Count d'Erlon , 30, 39, 50, 95, 140–1, 148, 152, 156, 161
drunkenness 28, 38, 169
D'Urban, Brig Gen Benjamin 10, 20, 26, 43, 53, 86, 107

Ebro, River 59, 62, 65–6, 77; crossing of 67–72
Esla, River 43–5
España, Gen Carlos d' 5, 25, 49
Espinchal, Capt Hippolyte d' 20, 40, 51–2, 55, 61, 63–4, 75, 77, 85, 115, 180
Espoz y Mina, Francisco 22, 30, 66

Fane, Maj Gen Sir Henry 10, 25, 35, 36, 53
Fischer, Col 12
Fletcher, Lt Col Sir Richard 66–7, 216

food rations/supplies 57–8, 65, 70, 72–3, 78, 79, 100, 101–2, 103–4, 110, 134
forced marches 47, 54–5, 100, 102
Foy, Gen Maximillian 2, 18, 22, 62, 90, 180, 186; in retreat 188–90
Frazer, Col Augustus 11, 12, 33–4, 35–7, 54, 71, 73–4, 175, 177
French Army 1, 14–15, 35, 214; Burgos, retreat from 61–5, 66–7; campaign preparations 14–19, 21–2; condition of vii–viii, 1; criticism of 177–8; defeat at Vitoria 148–63; discipline 77; evacuation of Madrid 40–1; observation of British movements 78, 79; positions at Vitoria 94–5, 99, 103, 111–14, 114, 115–17, 118, 126–7, 141–2, 143, 148–9; in retreat 75–8, 82–4; at Salamanca 35–8; supplies 52; survivors 185–6; travelling to Vitoria 75–89; Wellington's pursuit of 186–90
French Army units: Army of Portugal 1, 15, 16, 17–18, 19, 21–2, 29–30, 31, 49, 50, 51, 59–60, 61–2, 63, 75, 80, 82, 91, 95, 137, 157, 160, 181; Army of the Centre 18, 30, 49, 52, 55, 63, 77, 85, 88, 114, 121, 136, 155, 156–7, 186; Army of the North 16, 17, 18, 19, 22, 31, 53, 62, 75; Army of the South 1, 17, 18, 29–30, 49, 52, 63, 77, 85, 88, 94, 114, 118, 121, 122, 124, 125, 136, 148, 152–3, 156–7, 160, 179, 186, 190; 2eme Hussars 20; 55eme de la ligne 125; 58eme de la ligne 125; 103eme de la ligne 139; 118eme de la ligne 146; 119eme de la ligne 146
Fririon, François Nicholas 143, 145, 158

Gamarra Mayor 93, 141, 142, 143–4, 145–8, 157, 213
Gardiner, Maj 46, 60, 107
Gazan, Countess 170–1
Gazan, Gen Honoré, Count 17, 25, 29–30, 31, 32, 33, 39, 50, 75–6, 76, 78, 94–5, 105; activities at Vitoria 114, 120, 126, 148, 152, 156, 161; defence of Army of the South 152–3; held responsible for French defeat 179, 183; letters to Wellington 51–2, 55, 106

Girón, Gen Pedro Augustín 5, 18, 21, 26, 42, 43, 49, 52, 53, 55, 78, 86, 96, 108, 213, 216
Glover, Michael 35
Gomm, Lt Col William 22–3, 26–7, 41, 65–6, 79, 177, 215
Gordon, Col James Willoughby 6
Gough, Lt Col Hugh 140
Graham, Lt Gen Sir Thomas 4, 8, 25, 27, 42, 43, 53, 55, 60, 68, 80, 85–6, 141; activities at Vitoria 96–7, 108, 141–8, 213–14, 215–16; criticism of 88, 182; pursuit of French Army 188–90
Grant, Col Sir Colquoun 9, 26, 43, 46–7, 139, 149, 151, 156, 157, 161, 162
Great Road 21, 49, 59, 86, 89, 90, 93–4, 141, 142–3, 151, 183
Green, John 55–6, 58, 103–4, 134, 149–50, 167
grog 57
guerillas vii, 5, 14–15, 19, 20, 21–2, 30, 66, 116, 177

Hale, Sgt James 82, 110, 143, 147
Halkett, Lt Col Colin 145, 189
Hamilton, Sgt Anthony 161
Hartley, Cpl Andrew 8–9, 57, 163
Hay, Capt William 82, 97–9, 144
Heneghan, Assistant Commissary (Field Train) Richard 69–70, 123, 154, 157, 172
Henry, Ass Surg Walter 173–5
Hill, Lt Col Robert 25
Hill, Maj Gen Sir Rowland 1, 18, 19, 25, 31, 32–3, 36, 47–8, 55, 60, 86; activities at Vitoria 96, 101, 107, 108–9, 117–25, 128, 129, 132, 149, 156, 211–13, 215–16; horse 111, 117; opinion of senor officers' conduct 215; Wellington reviews troops 38–9
Hope, Lt James 2, 22, 47, 48, 57, 66, 118, 121–3, 155–6
horses 10, 11, 48, 111, 117
Howell, Pte Thomas 2, 117, 122

intelligence 21, 32, 40

Jourdan, Marshal Jean-Baptiste 19, 21, 29, 32–3, 50, 75, 78, 84, 90, 97, 179, 185; activities at Vitoria 113–15, 121, 122, 129, 140–1, 148, 151, 152; at Burgos 62–3; criticism of 177–8, 180; escape of 169–70; and Joseph Bonaparte 15, 16, 17, 30–1, 61, 94; later career 191; obstinacy 115; on Salamaca 37–8

Kempt, Gen Sir James 128, 130, 136, 151
kettles 7–8
Kincaid, Capt John 13, 64, 72, 87, 128, 138, 171

La Hermandad 137, 140–1, 148, 151
La Mancha 14, 15
Lamartinière, Gen Thomas 62, 114, 141, 157–8
landscape and scenery 68–70, 71–2
Larpent, Francis Seymour 6, 11, 12, 20, 27, 45–6, 56–7, 68, 86–7, 170; on battle aftermath 172–3
Lawrence, Sgt William 103, 175–6
Leach, Capt Jonathan 33, 82–3, 84
Lecor, Charles 132
Leith Hay, Capt Andrew 40–1, 88–9, 91, 116, 135–6, 159–60, 164; and Countess Gazan 170–1; description of valley at Vitoria 92; prisoner exchange 51, 75–7, 105–10
Leon 14, 18
Leval, Gen Jean François 30, 31–2, 32, 39–40, 76, 94, 114, 136–7, 137–8, 139, 148, 151, 153, 156
lice 2, 3
Liverpool, Lord 13–14
Longa, Francisco de 5, 22, 66, 97–9, 116, 143, 144–5, 156, 158, 177, 189, 213; Wellington's opinion of 145

McGrigor, Surgeon General James 2–3, 174, 175
McLeod, Maj Gen 68–9
Madrid 15, 40–1
Maransin, Gen Jean-Pierre 30, 120, 179
Marcel, Capt Nicolas 180–1

Index

Margarita 108, 137, 138, 139, 140–1
Maucune, Gen Antoine 18, 21, 30, 31, 32, 50, 52, 78, 82–3, 84, 180, 188–9
Medina del Rio Seco 21, 30, 49, 53, 55
Menne, Brig Gen Jean-Baptiste 143, 158
Mermet, Gen Julien 40, 85, 95, 141, 143, 145
Mina, Francisco 187
mines 63–4
Miranda del Ebro 68, 74, 77
Morales de Toro 46–7
Morgan, Gen Jacques 138–9
Morillo, Gen Pedro 5, 25, 54, 60, 107, 112, 118, 119–20, 122, 136, 148, 151, 155, 177, 179, 211–12, 215
Murray, Maj Gen George 6–7, 8, 24, 26, 216
Murray, Lt Gen John 85

Napoleon *see* Bonaparte, Napoleon

O'Callaghan, Lt Col Richard 60, 124, 125, 151, 174, 215
Old Castile 15, 16, 25
Oman, Charles 71, 115–16, 134, 137, 163, 181–2
Orsay, Baron d' 75–6
Ortiz de Zarate, Jose 128–9
Osma 78, 79, 80, 81, 82, 88
Oswald, Maj Gen 144, 213

Pack, Maj Gen Dennis 20, 25, 26, 43, 53, 143–4, 158, 213
Packenham, Maj Gen Edward 71
Palencia 18, 50, 56–7
Pamplona 14, 73, 90, 96, 113, 185, 186, 187, 190
Patterson, Capt John 16, 117–19, 123–4, 177
Picton, Maj Gen Thomas 8, 107–8, 130, 132–3, 135, 136, 137, 139, 149, 212, 215
Pisuerga 50, 52
Playford, Sgt Thomas 34, 173
plundering 72–3, 78, 84, 165–8
Ponsonby, Maj Gen the Honourable William 26, 43, 53, 60, 161

pontoons 11, 26, 43–4, 45
Popham, Capt Sir Home Riggs 14
Portuguese troops 10, 16, 17, 20, 26, 34, 57, 60, 143–4, 151, 154, 177
Power, Maj Gen Manley 137, 138, 151, 154
press reports 1–2
prisoners of war 47, 48, 171; exchange of 51, 75–6, 105–6; wounded 175–6
Puebla Heights 118–24, 127, 148, 179, 211–12

Ramsey, Capt Norman 80, 188
reconnaissance 22–3, 31, 42–3, 51, 94, 97, 99, 104–5, 106–7, 113–15
Reille, Gen Honoré, Count 16, 18, 21, 25, 30, 31, 32, 50, 52, 60, 61, 62, 77–8, 82; activities at Vitoria 95, 99, 114, 116–17, 137, 141–3, 152; decision to retreat 157–8, 160; at a meeting of generals 85; positions on eve of Vitoria 96, 99; praise for 180; in retreat 185–6
Rey, Gen Emmanuel 91, 190
Rey, Brig Gen Jean-Pierre 121, 125, 136
river crossings 28–9, 43–5, 48, 67–72
Robertson, Sgt David 101, 110, 123, 213
Robinson, Maj Gen Frederick 146, 147
Rous, Lt John 34, 100, 145

Salamanca vii, 1, 15, 17, 20, 24, 25, 28, 31, 33, 35–9
San Martin 68, 69
San Millan 82–4
San Sebastian 14, 190
Sanchez, Julian 5, 25, 40, 47, 49, 53, 55, 76, 187
Sarramon, Jean 183
Sarrut, Gen Jacques 18, 21, 30, 62, 77, 78, 114, 141, 142, 143, 157, 158, 175
Schaumann, Assistant Commissary August 9, 111–12, 168–9
Scherer, Capt Moyle 60, 64, 71–2, 112–13, 124, 165, 167
Segovia 18, 30, 41, 49
Silveira, Lt Gen Francisco da 25, 60, 101, 112, 125, 151
Simmons, Lt George 13, 64, 70, 87, 168

Smith, Capt Harry 150
Smith, Capt Webber 162
Soult, Marshal Nicholas-Jean de Dieu 1, 16, 17, 75, 152, 190
Soult, Gen Pierre 30
Spanish troops 26, 34, 54, 60, 97–8, 118–20, 122, 136, 142, 143, 144–5, 155, 177, 213
Stewart, Lt Gen the Honourable William 48, 57, 72, 111, 215
Stubbs, Col 148, 151, 154
Suchet, Marshal Louis-Gabriel, Duke of Albufera 1, 2, 24, 85
surgeons 2–3, 173–6
Surtees, Quartermaster William 57–8, 69, 82, 84, 103, 127, 177–8
Swabey, Lt William 29, 42, 45, 56, 57, 64, 71, 87, 175

Tarragona 24, 85, 187
Tilly, Gen Jacques 30, 39, 121
Tirlet, Gen Louis 148, 151, 152
Toledo 15, 18, 30, 40, 76
Tolosa 144, 185, 188, 189
Tomkinson, Capt William 59, 65, 68, 79, 81, 88, 97, 98–9, 142, 144, 146, 158–9, 168, 177, 178, 180
Toro 17, 18, 19, 27, 48–9, 54
Tres Puentes, bridge 93, 128–9, 181, 212

Valladolid 15, 16, 18, 19, 55
Vandeleur, Gen John 28, 42–3, 56, 80–1, 130, 139, 150, 151, 156, 157, 215
Villafranca 188–9
Villatte, Gen Eugène-Casimir 30, 31, 32, 35, 37–8, 39, 94, 120, 122, 123, 137, 148, 151
Villemur, Luis Count Penne 40, 97–8
Vitoria, Battle of vii; actions on Puebla Heights 118–24, 127, 148, 179, 211–12; aftermath 164–76; anticipation of the battle 100–1, 102–4; assessments of 176–83, 190–1; Battle Symphony (Beethoven) 191–2; British Army deployment 95–7, 107–9, 151; centre columns, arrival of 125–41; consequences 184–92; description of valley at Vitoria 92–4; early events on 21 June 110–17; eve of the battle 90–109; French Army positions 94–5, 99, 103, 111–14, 114, 115–17, 118, 126–7, 141–2, 143, 148–9; French defeat on all fronts 148–63; Gamarra Mayor 93, 141, 143–4, 145–8, 157, 213; Graham's intervention 141–8; opening stages of the battle 117–25; plundering and looting 165–8; remembrance of the fallen 172; Wellington's despatch describing the battle 211–17
Vitoria (town) 88–9, 91; retreat of civilians 157, 164, 170–1

Walcheren 4
Waller, Col. 12
water supplies 87
weather 1, 8, 33, 56, 57, 78–9, 88, 100
Webber, Capt William 12, 33, 38, 53–4, 61, 67–8, 72
Wellington, Marquis of vii, 1, 130; and the army's condition 3, 4; campaign objectives 14; commander of Spanish forces 5; communications with Bathurst 10–11, 14, 23, 64–5, 168, 184–5, 211–17; confidence about the campaign 73; decision to attack Army of Portugal 59–61; failure to understand his men 184–5; under fire 127–8; French military chest, loss of 168; instructions to commanders 24; and lack of money for the campaign 4–5; leaves Portugal 34–5; opinion of Longa 145; pursuit of French Army 186–90; reconnaissance 104–5, 106–7, 112; review's Hill's troops 38–9; strategy viii, 21, 23, 25, 71, 85–6, 89, 91–2, 95–7, 107–9, 127, 128, 151; troops' confidence in 113; visits Burgos 66–7; Vitoria Dispatch 211–17
Wheeler, Pte William 3, 41–2, 44–5, 73, 104, 134, 157
Wood, Capt George 3, 27, 154
wounds 48, 172–4

York, Duke of 3, 8

Zamora 17, 45–6